NEW POSSIBILITIES, NEW PARADIGMS?

American Academy
of Physical Education Papers
No. 24

NEW POSSIBILITIES, NEW PARADIGMS?

American Academy
of Physical Education Papers
No. 24

Sixty-Second Annual Meeting
New Orleans, Louisiana
March 27-28, 1990

Published by Human Kinetics Publishers
for the American Academy of Physical Education

Editors
Roberta J. Park
Helen M. Eckert

Academy Seal designed by
R. Tait McKenzie

Managing Editor: Julia Anderson
Typesetter: Angela K. Snyder

ISBN 0-87322-313-6
ISSN 0741-4633

Library of Congress Cataloging-in-Publication Data

American Academy of Physical Education. Meeting (62nd : 1990 : New Orleans, La.)
New possibilities, new paradigms? : Sixty-second Annual Meeting, New Orleans, Louisiana, March 27-28, 1990.
p. cm. -- (American Academy of Physical Education papers, ISSN 0741-4633 ; no. 24)
Includes bibliographical references.
ISBN 0-87322-313-6 (soft cover)
1. Physical education and training--Study and teaching (Higher)--United States--Congresses. I. Title. II. Series: American Academy of Physical Education. Meeting. Academy papers ; no. 24.
GV365.A47 1990
769.071'173--dc20 90-23215
CIP

Printed in the United States of America
3 2 1

Human Kinetics Books
A Division of Human Kinetics Publishers, Inc.
Box 5076, Champaign, IL 61825-5076
1-800-747-4457

UK Office:
Human Kinetics Publishers (UK) Ltd.
PO Box 18
Rawdon, Leeds LS19 6TG
England
(0532) 504211

CONTENTS

The Past Before Us, Transitions Toward the Future

Roberta J. Park
University of California

In the late 19th century, the newly formed Association for the Advancement of Physical Education faced numerous challenges as it searched for professional focus and identity. American medicine, too, was confronted by serious dilemmas, two major ones being that

1. the field decidedly needed to be elevated and its clinical and scientific sides brought into balance, and
2. room had to be made in the expanding medical curriculum for an increasing number of scientific specialties.

Addressing the Society of American Naturalists, Henry Pickering Bowditch, for 27 years professor of physiology (10 as dean of the medical school) at Harvard University, observed that it was now imperative to distinguish "between those subjects which it is *essential* that every [medical] student know and those subjects which it is *desirable* that certain students *should* know" (Bowditch, 1898, p. 646).

Bowditch was not advocating the type of balkanization that would occur in 20th-century medicine, however. Quite the contrary! He defined medicine as a profession that involved the study of "the whole environment of man as far as it affects the production of a healthy mind in a healthy body" (Bowditch, 1898, p. 645), and he believed it was vital that doctors understand their specialties in relation to this wider environment. Similar concerns have arisen again in the 1980s—and in many fields besides medicine. John Remington (1988), for example, contends that some academic areas are in danger of losing their vitality as they become ever more narrowly defined. The task, then, is to balance depth and specialized preparation with the broader matrix of which that specialization is a part.

Within the last decade, medical education has again been the subject of considerable discussion. Addressing the annual meeting of the Association of American Medical Colleges, Steven Muller (1984), president of Johns Hopkins University, declared his support of the report *The General Professional Education of the Physician*. This affirmed the need for a common foundation of knowledge, skills, values, and attitudes and a sound general liberal arts and science (baccalaureate) education as the foundation upon which the professional preparation of physicians was to be built.

Last year, the American Academy of Physical Education program "The Evolving Body of Knowledge" raised many stimulating and thought-provoking issues. Although agreement on many important points was not attained, valuable steps were made toward the possibility of reconceptualizing the field and, in particular, the scientific and scholarly matrix from which it draws.

It seemed worthwhile to pursue these matters further. Therefore, the 1990 Academy meeting endeavored to extend last year's discussions. Particular attention was given to exploring potential strengths that may reside in a multidisciplinary field like "physical education." Does the field possess as-yet-unacknowledged possibilities for intellectual strengths that would enable us (working singly or with colleagues) to ask and answer questions that might not be posed in other fields? If so, in what combinations and at what interstices might such strengths lie? How might these be tapped? Are there individuals who are currently engaged in creative multidisciplinary studies? What are these studies? Are new organizational structures needed? What kinds of programs and units might ultimately ensue? The 1990 Academy meetings explored such questions by means of both data-based and theoretical papers.

Physical educators are not the only ones in higher education who have been attempting to reconceptualize their fields and disciplinary matrices. This tendency has been especially prominent in medicine and the biological sciences; it has also been occurring in sociology, history, and other fields.

Two models that have recently appeared in the literature might serve as stimuli for further discussions among Academy members. George Engel (1982) has proposed a "biopsychosocial model" for medical education that attempts to transcend false dichotomies that were created when biomedical studies were divorced from psychosocial investigations. According to Engel's proposed "hierarchy of natural systems" model, the subjects that should comprise a physician's education would range from molecules and cells to culture, society, and nation. The individual human being is placed at the highest of the organ/nervous system levels and the lowest of the social system levels. The individual human is, however, the *central* focus. Gary Nabel (1985) has suggested a model for medical education that integrates molecular, cellular, organ/system, individual, and social/historical/cultural approaches to studying human beings. It is important to note that Engel and Nabel are very concerned with *interactions* between and among levels, and that both models embrace clinical as well as disciplinary training. Similarly, departments of biological science are currently attempting to restructure themselves to facilitate research that focuses upon *interactions* between levels. Are we talking here of partial *paradigmatic* shifts? And can the evolving field of physical education learn from efforts under way in other fields?

The publication of Thomas Kuhn's *The Structure of Scientific Revolutions* (1962) engendered numerous debates over the formation of and change within professional fields and disciplines. In spite of what critics have found wrong with Kuhn's theories, these debates have had beneficial consequences. As Garry Gutting (1980) points out in *Paradigms & Revolutions: Applications and Appraisals of Thomas Kuhn's Philosophy of Science*, for Kuhn the fundamental unit (the paradigm) involved "not only empirical laws, but also models, methodological rules, values . . . [and] a distinctive way of 'seeing' all the phenomena of its domain'' (p. 12). The need to revisualize its domain currently confronts the field of physical education. The 1990 Academy meetings examined these matters around the theme ''New Possibilities/New Paradigms?''

As many of my predecessors have stated, these annual Academy meetings offer valuable opportunities for discussions of matters of import to the field. Reporting upon the founding of a new American Society for Research in Physical Education, George Fitz declared its members' intention to study problems related to physical education and ''report the results of their work in the form of papers to the Society at least once in every three years'' (Fitz, 1904, p. 60). Competing demands upon members' time, and the exigencies of World War I, resulted in the demise of this early group. The present American Academy of Physical Education was organized in 1930. Reflecting upon its founding, President R. Tait McKenzie (1932) declared the time propitious for an organization that might contribute to the ''philosophical and scientific progress'' of the field. Over the years, the Academy has been the forum for much lively and productive debate. With this same spirit, contributors to the 1990 meetings tackled their charge.

A few observations drawn from the American Association for the Advancement of Science's *Nineteen 89/90 Handbook* may be a fitting way to conclude these comments. Founded in 1848, the AAAS overcame early limitations and deficiencies of a ''gentleman amateur scientist'' orientation, as anatomists, physiologists, psychologists, and others intensified their commitments to experimental science and founded professional organizations of their own in the late 1800s and early 1900s. What the AAAS has described as ''this general drift into specialization'' has now come under scrutiny. To take a quote directly from the AAAS *Nineteen 89/90 Handbook*:

> [Of late, a new phase has been showing:] the move away from excessive fragmentation toward an involvement with the world around, with its emphasis on interdisciplinary research endeavors and interest in problems involving the mutual impact of science and society . . . a shift has taken place toward framing questions that deal with larger issues . . . . increasing emphasis is being placed on truly interdisciplinary symposia in which science is advanced through the illumination of key topics that will not bend to the attack of a single discipline. Individuals from widely diverse fields—including architecture, law, religion, art and the humanities—are often essential participants in this difficult and demanding task. (American Association for the Advancement of Science, *Nineteen 89/90 Handbook*, p. 93).

We should be reminded, also, that the AAAS is actively engaged in improving education from the primary grades to the college level, and in interpreting science to the general public. Now if interdisciplinarity, education, and the dissemination of knowledge are deemed major goals for the AAAS, they must surely be worthy goals for the field of physical education. If the AAAS is encouraged about possibilities that may accrue from a move away from the excessive and sometimes single-minded emphasis on ever-increasing fragmentation that was so pervasive in the 1970s and 1980s, is it not significant that physical education has already addressed this matter and is, hopefully, about to move forward with meaningful curricula and research that capitalizes on our multidisciplinary nature?

Except for anthropology, with its physical, cultural, and linguistic areas of study (to which are typically added such things as medical anthropology, area studies, and archaeology), I cannot think of a degree-granting department that is more inherently interdisciplinary than physical education. Neither can I think of many with the potential for a better blending of basic research and applied or clinical programs.

The 1990s could be very propitious, but only if we seize the opportunity and match words with deeds. Some things we already do very well. However, if we are ever to become a first-class profession, a greater dedication to science and scholarship *in our own right* is absolutely essential! Those institutions where graduate teaching and research is a major institutional goal will bear a particular, but by no means exclusive, responsibility in this regard. Additionally, new means must be found to reorient activities of the AAHPERD, the largest professional organization physical educators belong to along the lines that characterize respected professional organizations. (It is, for example, ludicrous that the AAHPERD devotes such a small portion of its efforts and resources to fostering research and disseminating the results of first-class science and scholarship.) If this is not possible, other agencies must fill this void and become articulate and authoritative voices for our field. Whether one of these could or should be the American Academy of Physical Education, I am not certain. What I am certain of is that the time for intelligent action is now!

References

AMERICAN Association for the Advancement of Science (1989/90). *Nineteen 89/90 Handbook*. Washington, DC: Author.

BOWDITCH, H.P. (1898). Reform in medical education. *Boston Medical and Surgical Journal*, **139**, 643-646.

ENGEL, G. (1982). The biopsychosocial model and medical education. *New England Journal of Medicine*, **306**(13), 802-805.

FITZ, G.W. (1904). American society for research in physical education. *American Physical Education Review*, **9**(1), 60-62.

GUTTING, G. (1980). *Paradigms and revolutions: Applications and appraisals of Thomas Kuhn's philosophy of science*. Notre Dame, IN: University of Notre Dame Press.

KUHN, T. (1962). *The structure of scientific revolutions*. Chicago: University of Chicago Press.

McKENZIE, R.T. (1932). The American Academy of Physical Education. *Journal of Health and Physical Education*, **3**(6), 14-16, 62.

MULLER, S. (1984). Medicine: A learned profession? *Journal of Medical Education*, **60**(2), 85-91.

NABEL, G. (1985). Order and human biology. *American Journal of Medicine*, **78**, 545-548.

REMINGTON, J.A. (1988). Beyond big science in America: The binding of inquiry. *Social Studies of Science: An International Review of Research in the Social Dimension of Science and Technology*, **18**(1), 45-72.

Biomechanics: An Interdisciplinary Science

Anne E. Atwater
University of Arizona

One of the objectives of this 62nd Academy Program is to look at familiar topics from a fresh perspective. An advantage of this process is that it may foster new concepts and approaches in our interactions with colleagues and in our pursuit of future professional activities.

Biomechanics is an ideal topic in which to launch an examination of interdisciplinary perspectives. Most physical educators and exercise scientists who are *not* biomechanists have obtained their understanding of this science by reading professional literature or by observing the teaching and research activities of their departmental colleagues who specialize in biomechanics. Based upon these studies and observations, they would correctly conclude that most biomechanists in physical education or exercise science departments tend to focus on the analysis of mechanical aspects of skilled human motion and the mechanics of equipment or protective gear used by sport and exercise participants.

The purpose of this paper is to provide an overview of the breadth and diversity of the field of biomechanics and to point out that sport biomechanics is but one of many subspecialties included within this broad field. For example, the topics listed in Table 1 illustrate the wide range of research interests pursued by individual biomechanists, as reflected by papers presented at professional meetings and by published articles, monographs, and books.

To encourage you to expand the way you view the *scope* of this field of biomechanics, I will concentrate my comments on four main topics.

1. The definition of biomechanics
2. Ways in which biomechanists from diverse disciplines communicate with each other
3. Some organizing themes around which biomechanics investigations are conducted
4. A brief view of future directions in which this science may advance

Definition of Biomechanics

The term *biomechanics* combines the words *biology* and *mechanics*; biomechanics involves the study of the structure and function of biological systems using

Table 1

Examples of Diverse Biomechanics Research Interests

Kinematics of the parachute landing fall
Torsion in ostrich knees
Red blood cell mechanics and blood flow in narrow capillaries
Gait patterns after toe-to-thumb transplantation
Mechanical stimulation of wound healing in trees
Bedsore biomechanics
Effect of prolonged walking on concrete on the knees of sheep
Postural kinematics of trumpet playing
Biomechanics of fruits and vegetables
Model experiments to study the stress distributions in a seated buttock
Mechanical properties of fish backbones in lateral bending and in tension
Force and impact determinations of certain karate kicks

the methods of mechanics. It is not surprising that debates persist regarding the best definition for *biomechanics*, given the diversity of the disciplines in which biomechanists conduct their work. Hatze (1974) has stated that this term appears to have almost as many definitions as there are researchers working in this field. Despite some differences of opinion, there is common agreement that the interdisciplinary science of biomechanics is based on, and draws substance from, a number of fundamental disciplines included in the biological and physical sciences (see Figure 1).

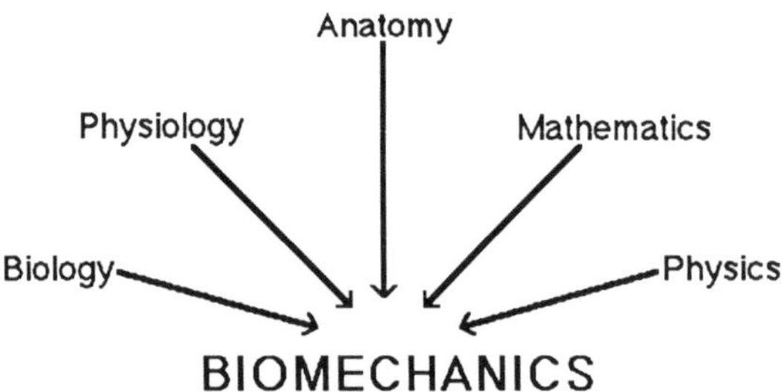

Figure 1 — Fundamental disciplines of biomechanics.

The fields in which the science of biomechanics is applied are quite numerous and far more wide-ranging than just sport and exercise science. From a historical perspective, one can trace the first attempts to integrate the study of biology and mechanics to Aristotle, who recorded his observations on the parts and movements of animals in the 3rd century B.C. (Fung, 1968). Modern biomechanics has a 300-year history in which the dominant theme has been the application of mechanical principles to the study of normal and pathological locomotion (Atwater, 1980). However, most of the significant contributions have occurred in the past 25 years as a vigorous and effective research community of biomechanists has emerged, having in common a more uniform background in fundamental sciences as well as familiarity with the latest analytical methods and technology (Zernicke, 1981).

Communication Among Biomechanists

In the 1960s, scholars active in biomechanics research faced a growing problem of deciding which journal to use as the primary source for disseminating research information. This dissatisfaction led to the creation, in 1968, of the *Journal of Biomechanics* as the focal point for original publications across the entire spectrum of biomechanics (Roberts & Evans, 1968). Although the *Journal of Biomechanics* is the premiere interdisciplinary publication in the field, many other journals also have provided a means for biomechanists to communicate their ideas and research results to colleagues within their home disciplines. Among these are *American Journal of Physical Medicine, Ergonomics, Human Factors, Journal of Biomedical Engineering, Journal of Bone and Joint Surgery, Journal of Experimental Biology, Journal of Zoology*, and *International Journal of Sport Biomechanics*.

In 1967, the first International Seminar on Biomechanics was held in Zurich, Switzerland. The initiative for this first of 12 biennial meetings was taken by the International Council of Sport and Physical Education under UNESCO. At the 4th International Seminar, held at Pennsylvania State University in 1973, the International Society of Biomechanics was founded to promote communication among researchers representing various fields concerned with the biomechanics of human movement (Bates, 1974). The major activity of this society has been the organization and conduct of the biennial International Congress on Biomechanics. Several different countries have hosted this congress, including the Netherlands, Canada, Japan, Poland, Sweden, and most recently, the United States—where the 12th biennial congress was held in Los Angeles in 1989. Membership in the International Society of Biomechanics now numbers 659, with representation from more than 35 countries and a variety of disciplines (see Figure 2).

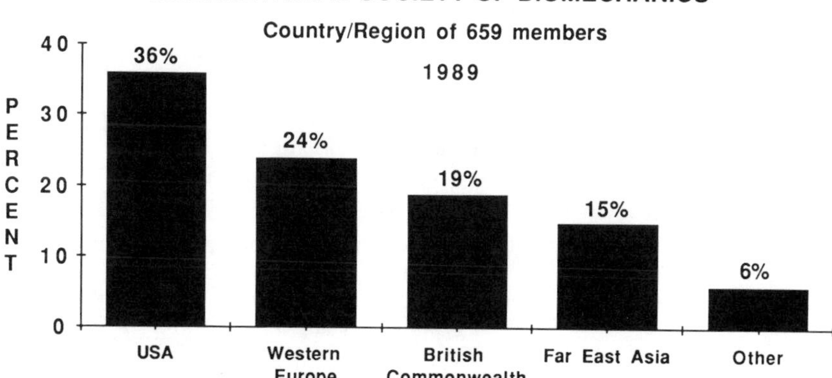

Figure 2 — International Society of Biomechanics membership.

To stimulate research and encourage communication and interaction among biomechanists from a variety of disciplines in the United States, the American Society of Biomechanics was founded in 1977. All members select one of five disciplinary categories when applying for membership. These categories are biological sciences, ergonomics and human factors, engineering and applied physics, health sciences, and exercise and sport sciences. To ensure representation from multiple disciplines on the organization's executive board, the president, past president, and president-elect must be from three different disciplinary categories.

Currently, membership in the American Society of Biomechanics numbers about 440. The largest percentage of members has identified with the category of engineering and applied physics; exercise and sport sciences is the second largest disciplinary category (see Figure 3). Although the representations from ergonomics and biology are considerably smaller, the biomechanists from these disciplines often receive acclaim at the annual meetings for their unique contributions to the diversity of the collegial interactions.

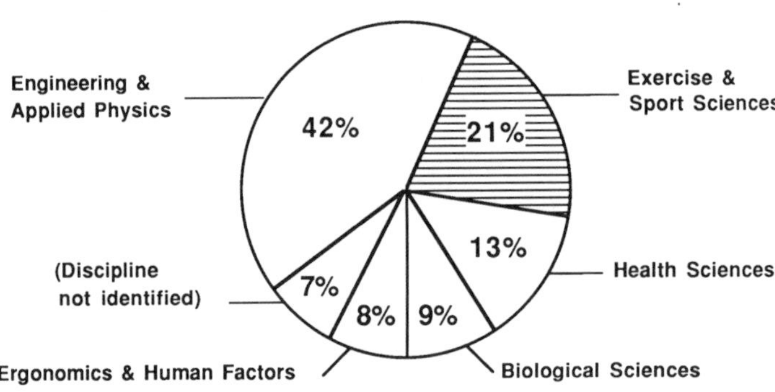

Figure 3 — Disciplines identified by members of the American Society of Biomechanics.

Communication among biomechanists also is facilitated by several other professional organizations that have stronger ties with specific disciplines. Some of these organizations are the American Society of Mechanical Engineers, the American College of Sports Medicine, the International Ergonomics Association, and the Human Factors Society. Biomechanics research information is disseminated at the regular meetings of these organizations and in their affiliated journals.

Perhaps the best sources of printed information reflecting the diversity of ideas and research on biomechanics are the various volumes of conference proceedings and program abstracts from the meetings organized by professional societies and by special interest groups. From these published materials and from biomechanics journals I will select examples of studies to illustrate the organizing themes around which biomechanics investigations are typically conducted.

Organizing Themes for Biomechanics Investigations

I have chosen the five disciplinary categories specified by the American Society of Biomechanics as themes that exemplify most biomechanics research. With respect to each category, I will identify the professional fields or disciplines that exhibit greatest interest in that theme and describe examples of topics that have been investigated.

Biological Sciences

Biomechanists who focus their research in the biological sciences often are located in Departments of Biology, Zoology, Anthropology, or Veterinary Sciences. One major focus of their research involves analysis of the mechanics of animal locomotion (in fact, of animal motion in general), including overland gaits such as the walk, pace, trot, hop, gallop, and jump of land mammals; snaking and burrowing motions of ground creatures; climbing, hanging, and brachiating motions of arboreal mammals such as monkeys; gliding and beating motions of birds and insects; and paddling, jetting, fanning, and undulating motions of fish and other aquatic life.

However, biomechanists in the biological sciences usually have broader goals than analyzing animal motion per se. Their goals involve addressing fundamental issues of comparative biomechanics, functional morphology, and the analysis of material properties of body tissues in living systems. For example, the backbones of fish representing two of four known swimming styles have been studied to determine whether differences in the mechanical behavior of their backbones reflect the observed differences in swimming styles. Isolated intervertebral joints in different regions of the fish backbones were tested in tension loading as well as lateral bending. It was concluded that the properties of the backbone, particularly its regional stiffness and elasticity, were well tuned to the particular swimming style used (Hebrank, 1982).

This type of search for relationships between form and function, as mediated by tissue mechanical properties, has guided many investigators in the biological sciences (Alexander & Goldspink, 1977). They ask, "Are there global design principles in nature, as there are in engineering?" More specifically, as body size and locomotor loads increase, either within or across species, what differences are observed in the shape of bones, their mechanical properties, and the resulting form of the locomotion? How do stride frequency and type of gait scale in relation to animal size, from mice to horses and even to dinosaurs?

Physical anthropologists have applied the principles of biomechanics in the form–function analysis of ancient fossils (Morbeck, 1984). Study of fossils of our ape and human ancestors permits a focus on such topics as

1. the size and shape of joint surfaces and how these would permit motion between body segments;
2. the size, shape, and cross-sectional areas of limb bone shafts that reflect loading conditions throughout a lifetime; and
3. fossil teeth, jaws, and limb bones that provide information on chewing and movement capabilities from which one can infer diet, posture, and locomotor patterns.

These findings on fossils are compared with what is known about living mammals and their musculoskeletal systems and movement capabilities and the material properties of bone. The ultimate goal of gathering biomechanical data on fossils and on living groups is to explain human origins and evolution.

The structural design and behavior of plants, as influenced by mechanical factors, also belongs in this category of biomechanical investigations. Some fascinating research by Tom McMahon and his students at Harvard University has identified elastic similarity as the principle underlying the mechanical design of most, if not all, trees (McMahon, 1975). His work has involved analysis of the branching patterns of trees, the relative sizes of tree limbs from trunk to twigs, and the bending of tree limbs in relation to their length. He concluded that a tree limb automatically begins to increase its diameter when the curvature induced by its weight exceeds a specific threshold. Interestingly, tree growth caused by this mechanical stimulus has an analogy to the remodeling in animal long bones induced by bending loads.

Ergonomics and Human Factors

The term *ergonomics* was created following World War II, when the areas of work physiology and industrial psychology were consolidated into this discipline dedicated to the study of humans at work (Tichauer, 1975). *Ergonomics* also is used as a synonym for *human engineering*. The field of *human factors* more broadly considers the effects of humans interacting in a system, or how humans respond to series of stimuli.

Biomechanists involved in ergonomics research can be found in a variety of disciplines including occupational safety and health, public health, and industrial engineering. They are basically concerned with conducting investigations on such topics as work measurement and prediction, material handling and load carrying stresses, machine control layout, protective equipment evaluation, and the analysis and improvement of design parameters for hand tools, machines, seats, floors, and vehicles. Their objective is to increase the productivity, efficiency, and safety of the work environment in general, and of humans interacting with hardware systems in particular.

For example, in the work environment of an operator who is seated, whether at a desk, at the wheel of a vehicle, or at an assembly-line station, several biomechanical factors must be analyzed and optimized to prevent occupational injury or inefficient performance. Among these are factors related to the seat, such as cushioning, support, and appropriate constraint (or lack of restraint), and factors related to the placement of the operator's instrument panel, work tools, or items to be manipulated. Are objects within easy reach of the operator, or must the operator's posture or movements be modified significantly to accomplish the desired task?

The analysis of load carrying and of pushing and pulling tasks is an important area of study in occupational biomechanics, especially when the enormity of worker injuries and their resultant financial cost is considered. Another aspect of ergonomics even more closely associated with injury prevention is the area of impact tolerance and protection. Biomechanical studies of impact forces and accelerations resulting in injury to various regions of the human body have been conducted using cadavers as well as instrumented dummies. These studies have led to improvements in numerous types of protective equipment ranging from better auto bumpers to safer air bags, airplane test-pilot ejection seats, football helmets, gymnastic landing mats, and techniques for landing from a parachute fall.

A unique application of the biomechanics of impact protection can be found in the area of agricultural engineering (Peleg, 1985). Apparently there is a 30% to 40% loss of fruits and vegetables due to mechanical damage caused by the highly mechanized procedures used today in harvesting, processing, packaging, and distribution. Each of these stages in the tree-to-market system has been analyzed to identify the nature and causes of the damage and subsequently improve the system to reduce the bruising and resultant spoilage of this produce.

Engineering and Applied Physics

Among the most active participants in biomechanics research during the past half-century have been engineers from various fields of specialization. Whereas most engineering professionals deal with inanimate linkages and materials, those working in bioengineering have applied their particular expertise to the analysis of living systems and materials.

Tissue biomechanics is a rapidly growing area of investigation in which the same techniques used to analyze the strength and deformation of metals, concrete, and synthetic materials found in bridges and buildings are employed in the study of biological tissues such as bones, ligaments, tendons, and cartilage. For example, the knee anterior cruciate ligament's response to different rates of imposed tension and shearing loads has been documented, as well as its strength and elongation at failure. The mechanical characteristics of other human tendons or ligaments or even artificial materials used to repair or replace this damaged ligament have been analyzed. The results of these investigations permit a surgeon to choose the best repair material based upon objective criteria rather than subjective opinion. Tissue biomechanics also includes the study of how human tissues respond to various chronic loading conditions ranging from immobilization and weightlessness to selective overloading produced by exercise or work demands.

During the 20th century, one of the earliest applications of engineering principles in a biological area was the design and construction of prosthetic limbs following World War I (Contini & Drillis, 1966). Major recent improvements have occurred in the techniques used to evaluate the effectiveness of a prosthesis or a rigid implant. In particular, the finite element analysis method, developed in engineering mechanics, is an advanced computer technique of structural stress analysis (Huiskes & Chao, 1983). It has been used with increasing frequency to analyze and optimize designs of prosthetic devices, of implants in bone that anchor artificial joints, and of fracture fixation devices.

Circulatory biomechanics is an area of investigation in which the principles of fluid dynamics are applied to the flow of blood through vessels and through heart valves and heart prostheses. Some of the topics studied in this area include wave propagation in blood flow, stress–strain relationships in arterial walls, and the deformation of red cells in capillaries.

Lastly, interest in dynamic systems and the interactions among the components of these systems has led some engineers to analyze motion control strategies and motion optimization. One interesting example in this area is the investigation of human control of a skateboard (Hubbard, 1980). The rider was modeled as a single, rigid body pinned to the board along the roll axis. Human input was taken to be a torque applied at the ankles. Various control schemes and differing amounts of feedback of rider tilt angle were studied, and a performance index for this tracking task was used to evaluate the experimental results.

Health Sciences

Biomechanists whose research focuses on topics in the health sciences may be located in Departments of Orthopedic Surgery, Restorative Medicine, Rehabilitation Sciences, or Orthodontics. An overlap is not uncommon between this category and the previous category of engineering and applied physics. Engineers and medical professionals often work together quite closely on many projects. Early phases of their collaborative research may involve development of a computer model or even an animal model for a new surgical technique or method of tissue reconstruction. Subsequent phases of the research may take place in the operating room or rehabilitation clinic to evaluate and to validate the models created in the laboratory.

Biomechanical research during the past few decades has contributed to the clarification of the mechanisms involved in many health problems such as scoliosis, bedsores, ulceration in diabetic feet, patellar chondromalacia, and head and cervical spine injuries resulting from auto accidents. Once the biomechanical basis of most injuries and pathologies is better understood, their prevention or correction can be facilitated (Viano, King, Melvin, & Weber, 1989).

Human locomotion analysis laboratories, often called *gait labs*, have been established in several major hospitals and clinics around the country. Biomechanists working in these labs often serve as one member of a team that helps patients adapt to a new prosthesis, such as a hip implant, or helps patients regain functional movement following surgical intervention for an injury or a pathological condition.

In recent years, biomechanists have become involved in helping the handicapped participate more fully in sports. Wheelchair design and propulsion techniques for sprinting and distance races have been studied (Sanderson & Sommer, 1985), and new knee and ankle joints in prosthetic limbs have been developed for individuals who want to run or ski more effectively (Enoka, Miller, & Burgess, 1982).

Exercise and Sport Sciences

Biomechanists with interests in topics related to exercise and sport sciences can be located in numerous disciplines, but most frequently they are associated with Departments of Sports Medicine, Kinesiology, Exercise Science, Physical Education, or Athletics. Of the five themes or categories of biomechanics research I have described thus far, examples of investigations in this category are undoubtedly the most familiar to this audience. Therefore, I will not elaborate on such studies and instead refer those who are interested in greater detail to biomechanics research articles published in the following journals: *International Journal of Sport Biomechanics*, *Medicine and Science in Sports and Exercise*, and *Research Quarterly for Exercise and Sport*.

Biomechanical studies of sport and exercise skills have expanded beyond the descriptive level and are reflecting an increased focus on the forces causing or modifying the movement, and on factors related to the mechanisms controlling force, work, and power output. Also, the biomechanics of fundamental motor skills such as running, jumping, and throwing are being systematically analyzed over the entire age span—from infants to the elderly. Highly coordinated and proficient sport performance still remains a challenge for the biomechanist, sometimes working in collaboration with other sport scientists, to analyze, explain, and improve.

Future Directions in Biomechanics

Given the significant growth and maturation of this interdisciplinary science of biomechanics during the past quarter century, I would anticipate a bright future. Biomechanists emerging from graduate programs in the related and supporting disciplines are now more uniformly knowledgeable in the biological, physical, and mathematical sciences and in the analytical techniques of engineering. This permits more effective interactions among biomechanists from various disciplines and should promote greater interdisciplinary collaboration and communication in the future.

Three specific areas that I believe will receive increased research focus by biomechanists in the future are

1. biomechanical mechanisms that generate and control movement,
2. adaptive mechanisms of biological tissues to various stimuli, and
3. biomechanics of injury prevention.

If progress in biomechanics during the next 25 years continues at the pace seen in the past 25 years, we should see significant advances made on these topics as well as in the many other areas of research included in the interdisciplinary science of biomechanics.

References

ALEXANDER, R. McN., & Goldspink, G. (Eds.) (1977). *Mechanics and energetics of animal locomotion*. London: Chapman & Hall.

ATWATER, A.E. (1980). Kinesiology/biomechanics: Perspectives and trends. *Research Quarterly for Exercise and Sport*, **51**(1), 193-218.

BATES, B.T. (1974). The fourth international seminar on biomechanics. *Journal of Health, Physical Education and Recreation*, **45**(2), 60-70.

CONTINI, R., & Drillis, R. (1966). Biomechanics. In H.N. Abramson, H. Liebowitz, J.M. Crowley, & S. Juhasz (Eds.), *Applied mechanics surveys* (pp. 161-172). Washington, DC: Spartan Books.

ENOKA, R.M., Miller, D.I., & Burgess, E.M. (1982). Below-knee amputee running gait. *American Journal of Physical Medicine*, **61**, 66-84.

FUNG, Y.C. (1968). Biomechanics—its scope, history, and some problems of continuum mechanics in physiology. *Applied Mechanics Reviews*, **21**(1), 1-20.

HATZE, H. (1974). The meaning of the term 'biomechanics.' *Journal of Biomechanics*, **7**, 189-190.

HEBRANK, M.R. (1982). Mechanical properties of fish backbones in lateral bending and in tension. *Journal of Biomechanics*, **15**, 85-89.

HUBBARD, M. (1980). Human control of the skateboard. *Journal of Biomechanics*, **13**, 745-754.

HUISKES, R., & Chao, E.Y.S. (1983). A survey of finite element analysis in orthopedic biomechanics: The first decade. *Journal of Biomechanics*, **16**, 385-409.

McMAHON, T.A. (1975, July). The mechanical design of trees. *Scientific American* (pp. 92-102).

MORBECK, M.E. (1984). Biomechanics and human evolution. *Proceedings of the 8th Annual Meeting of the American Society of Biomechanics*, **8**, 49-50.

PELEG, K. (1985). Biomechanics of fruits and vegetables. *Journal of Biomechanics*, **18**, 843-962.

ROBERTS, V.L., & Evans, F.G. (1968). Editorial. *Journal of Biomechanics*, **1**, 1.

SANDERSON, D.J., & Sommer, H.J. (1985). Kinematic features of wheelchair propulsion. *Journal of Biomechanics*, **18**, 423-429.

TICHAUER, E.R. (1975). Occupational biomechanics and the development of work tolerance. In P.V. Komi (Ed.), *Biomechanics V-A* (pp. 493-505). Baltimore: University Park Press.

VIANO, D.C., King, A.I., Melvin, J.W., & Weber, K. (1989). Injury biomechanics research: An essential element in the prevention of trauma. *Journal of Biomechanics*, **22**, 403-417.

ZERNICKE, R.F. (1981). The emergence of human biomechanics. In G.A. Brooks (Ed.), *Perspectives on the academic discipline of physical education* (pp. 124-136). Champaign, IL: Human Kinetics.

An Ecological Approach to Training

Christine L. Wells
Arizona State University

Muriel Gilman
Bemidji State University

Exercise physiology, as it currently exists in most departments of physical education, kinesiology, or exercise science, is the study of biological responses and adaptations to acute and chronic exercise. Exercise physiology laboratories are typically equipped with means to assess exercise capacity and cardiovascular, respiratory, and metabolic responses of intact organisms or tissue preparations. Numerous national and international journals publish hundreds of manuscripts per year dealing with exercise physiology. It is obvious that the field has grown considerably in its relatively short history.

Most research in exercise physiology can be categorized as either *performance based* or *health related*. Performance-based research has contributed significantly to the body of knowledge in sport, fitness, training, and human engineering. Health-related research deals with the role of exercise in wellness, the prevention of disease, or rehabilitation from illness or injury. This research has been more interdisciplinary in nature than has performance-based research. In fact, most health-related research in exercise physiology has been conducted under the aegis of the medical school, and there is a distinct trend today to avoid association with departments of physical education. Many young exercise physiologists are seeking appointments in medical schools because more funding opportunities exist in this arena than in physical education. Consequently, many serious investigators are orienting their careers in this direction.

If performance-based research in exercise physiology is to survive, a new approach is necessary. Piecemeal efforts to study human performance no longer attract major funding. Innovative, conceptual approaches that integrate other disciplines and that have wide relevance to various areas of human endeavor are required.

As an example of such an approach, we have chosen an area in which exercise physiology has already made a significant contribution—training to improve sport performance. Our example is particularly relevant because we believe that there are some major problems in sport today that a more innovative and broad-based approach to training might solve. Therefore, our paper should be considered a call for a wholistic approach to training for the purposes of improving performance and enhancing health. In our opinion, current training methods often result in the opposite—less than optimal performance, endangered health, and premature demise of promising athletic careers. By providing such a model we hope to demonstrate how performance-based research might survive in the multidisciplinary research arena.

The Human Ecosystem

Ecology deals with the interactions between organisms and their environments. An ecosystem is everything that influences an organism. The primary tenets of ecology are that nothing exists in isolation, nearly everything affects everything else, and nothing remains static. Stability (homeostasis) is a matter of balance among all sources of energy between an organism and its ecosystem. Instability or change in an ecosystem occurs when the kinetics of one or more factors are no longer balanced relative to the kinetics of another. If an organism is capable of compensatory responses to changes in its ecosystem, it will prosper. If the organism is not, it will decline and eventually perish.

The proposed model is human-centered and ecological in nature because it emphasizes the wholistic interrelationships between an individual and the biological-psychological-sociological variables that make up that individual's ecosystem. Figure 1 illustrates the scope of the human ecosystem as viewed from a biopsychosocial perspective.

In our opinion, the common notion of a physical training program is limited in scope of understanding and term of application. For most coaches and athletes, a training program consists of a well-planned series of activities specifically designed to enhance strength, endurance, flexibility, or speed. Other aspects of the human ecosystem are viewed as extraneous, and in fact are to be diminished

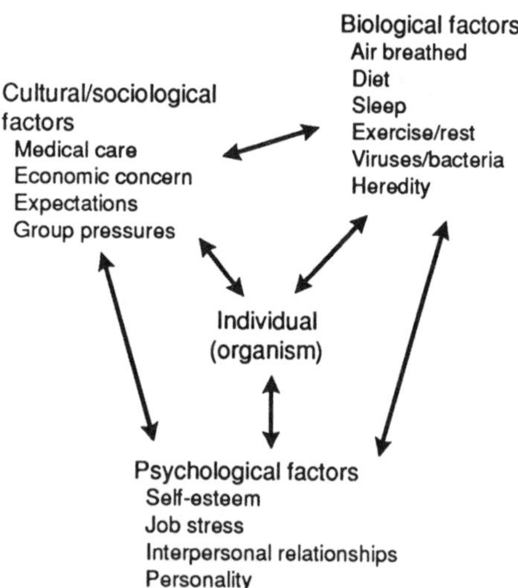

Figure 1 — The human ecosystem: a biopsychosocial model.

so that one may concentrate fully on the benefits to be derived from physical training. Although the importance of obvious biological correlates such as good nutritional habits and adequate rest are acknowledged and encouraged, they are seldom integrated into the training program. The same can be said for psychological techniques such as mental practice and anxiety-reduction exercises. Whereas most coaches and athletes would acknowledge the helpfulness of these techniques, if they are used at all they are considered extra activities rather than *essential* elements fully integrated into the training program. The failure to incorporate these and many other very important variables making up the human ecosystem suggests that the current concept of training is very limited in scope.

In addition, most envision a training program as a short-term period prior to a single competitive season. It is the exceptional or visionary coach or athlete who conceptualizes training for a more protracted goal such as winning an Olympic medal or attending two or three Olympiads. With the current surge of interest in Masters competition and the continuing interest in age-group competition and Olympic development, there is considerable opportunity for highly competitive experiences throughout the entire life span. Viewing physical training as something done only in one's youth is shortsighted.

The usual view of training must be expanded to account for, rather than exclude, all aspects of the human ecosystem. A conceptual model of training must recognize the *integration of body and mind* and the impact of sociocultural factors. Further, it must encompass a *lifelong perspective* for optimizing health as well as performance.

The Physical Activity, Lifestyle, and Health Continuum

Physical activity can be considered a continuum. At one extreme is the complete lack of movement that occurs with paralysis, unconsciousness, or coma. At the other extreme is the exhaustive physical effort that may characterize an extreme competitive effort or a life-and-death struggle. This is depicted in the far-left column of Figure 2, "continuum of physical activity." The column consists of a list of verbal descriptors. At intermediate levels along this scale are thresholds for particular effects.

Threshold for healthful benefits refers to a level of physical activity providing sufficient stimulus to promote general health but insufficient stimulus to improve physical fitness. *Threshold for cardiorespiratory benefits* represents that level of regular physical activity providing sufficient stimulus to not only promote general health but also improve cardiovascular-respiratory efficiency. Near the top of the column is *threshold of exhaustion*, which represents a level of activity from which one does not rapidly recover. If there is insufficient recovery between bouts of activity, the end result is not a healthful response but one that leads to a general state of exhaustion.

The middle column of Figure 2, "lifestyle classifications," provides verbal descriptors of persons whose regular physical activity patterns are characterized by the terms in the left column. The least active here are the physically disabled. Sedentary persons do not exercise sufficiently to achieve healthful benefits. Moderately active and highly active persons regularly exercise above the threshold for cardiorespiratory benefits and consequently display increasing levels of physical

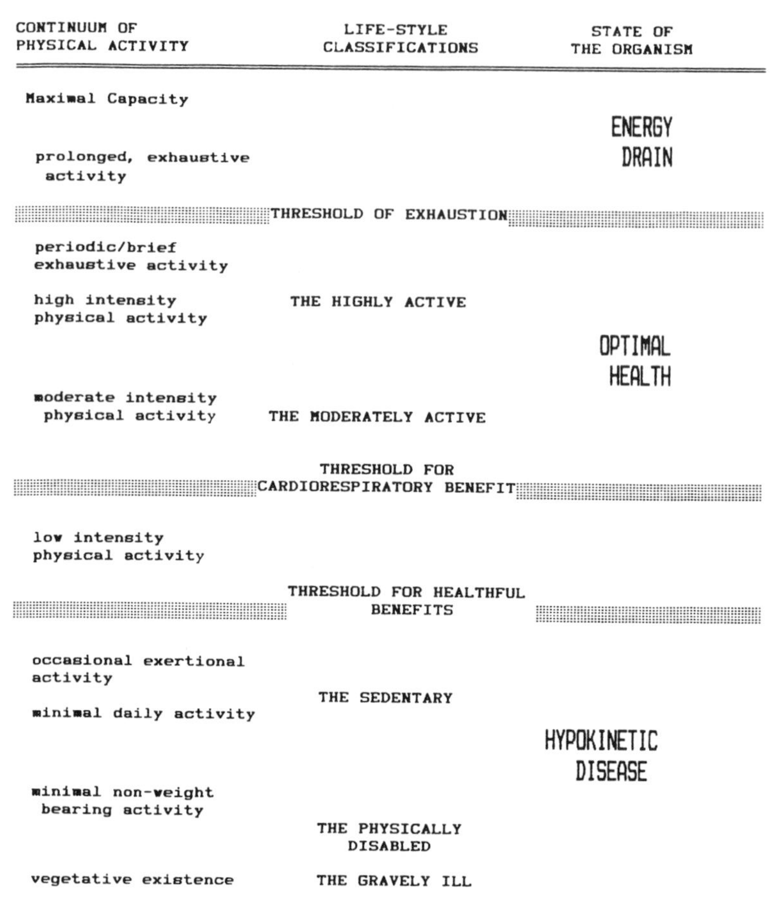

Figure 2 — The physical activity, lifestyle, and health continuum.

fitness. The healthy highly competitive athlete would be placed just below the threshold of exhaustion.

The right-hand column of Figure 2, "state of the organism," is intended to correspond to the descriptors for lifestyle classification and physical activity. These descriptors refer to one's current state of health and risk for developing future health problems. Obviously there are sedentary persons who display no evidence of hypokinetic disease. Nevertheless, there is considerable documentation in the medical literature that sedentary persons are at increased risk for *future* hypokinetic diseases.

The term *optimal health* is not intended to imply that all persons whose lifestyles are characterized by regular moderate to high-level physical activity are in optimal health. Rather, the descriptor indicates that these persons display relatively few risk factors known to be associated with hypokinetic diseases. Persons who can be classified as moderately active to highly competitive athletes usually have less fat, more lean body mass, better cardiorespiratory efficiency, greater insulin sensitivity, and higher bone density than sedentary persons. This places them at less risk for hypokinetic diseases as they grow older.

The descriptor *energy drain* refers to the state in which the individual is experiencing excessive energy output relative to energy input, resulting in an ecological imbalance. In this state maladaptive responses occur, such as a decrement in performance, overuse injuries, reproductive failure, increased incidence of respiratory illnesses, depression, "burnout," and possibly physical or mental collapse. This is comparable to, but more inclusive than, the current concept of overtraining. Energy drain has been previously referred to as the "stage of exhaustion" (Selye, 1956).

These continua should not be viewed as absolute or static, but rather as relative to the status of the individual. For example, high-intensity activity may be quite different for a genetically well-endowed 20-year-old compared to a less genetically endowed 60-year-old with modest athletic background. The healthy highly competitive athlete is likely to be training and competing at a level just below the threshold of exhaustion. This may be as true for the middle-of-the-pack marathoner who is very serious about training as for the world-class competitor. The obsessive/compulsive athlete is likely to be training at a level above the threshold of exhaustion or vacillating back and forth across the threshold of exhaustion. This may equally apply to a middle-of-the-pack marathoner, a world-class athlete, an aerobic-dance teacher, a ballerina, or a college-level athlete. The factor that determines a person's place on the continua is the relative effort put forth, not level of performance or competence.

Stress, Response, and Adaptation: A Matter of Balance

Figure 3 provides a schematic view of training. Figure 3a illustrates the beginning, or starting point, of a training program. The numbers are intended to serve merely as a simple illustration of the concepts we wish to emphasize; they do *not* represent real numbers or existing data. In Figure 3a, the individual has a beginning maximum capacity (Max Cap_1) of 100 for any given parameter, and a basal or resting level of 5 (which we will assume does not change with either time or training). Functional reserve capacity is the difference between maximum capacity and basal level (i.e., $100 - 5 = 95$). For the sake of simplicity, the training load will be held constant at 85% of the maximum capacity in the remaining two parts of the figure (in reality, the training load may not be constant, or may vary from 85%). The training load serves as a stressor to which the body responds in numerous ways, such as with increased oxygen uptake, elevated heart rate, and generation of metabolic heat. There are also psychological responses to the increasing stress. Eventually, with repeated applications of the training load, changes in the original responses are brought about by various morphological and biochemical adaptations. The tissues and organs stressed by the training load adapt to that level of stress and are consequently capable of responding to a higher maximal load. In other words, a training effect occurs.

Figure 3b is intended to illustrate adaptation to training early in a training program. Maximum capacity has now increased to 105. This means that the individual's functional reserve has also increased ($105 - 5 = 100$). For further adaptations to occur, the training load must now be adjusted. The relative training

STRESS, RESPONSE, and ADAPTATION

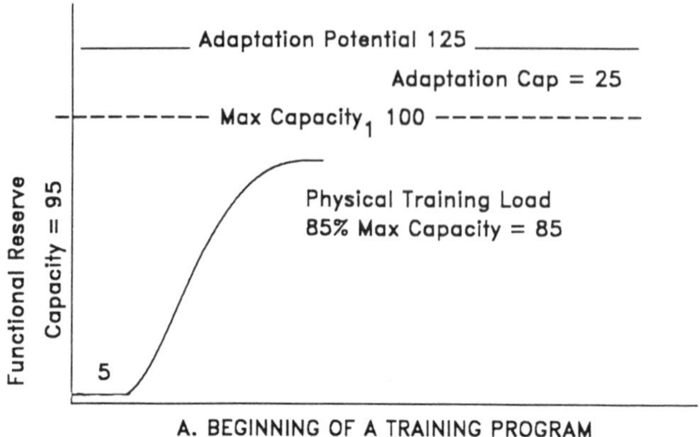

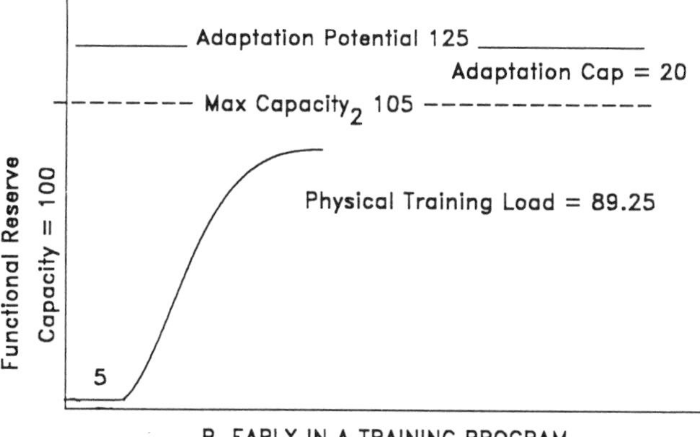

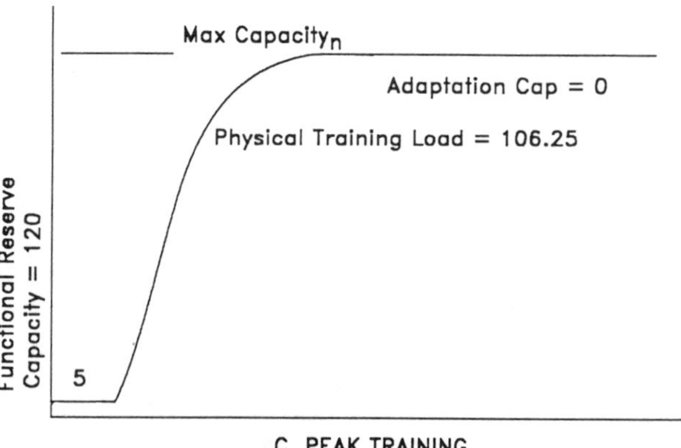

Figure 3 — Stress, response, and adaptation as shown (a) at the beginning of a training program, (b) early after starting the program, and (c) at the peak of training.

load remains at 85% of maximum capacity, but there has been a change in maximum capacity, and the new training load is 89.25 (85% of 105). Most likely, maximum capacity will again increase, as will functional reserve capacity.

Figure 3c is intended to show the result of a well-planned training program in which the individual experiences a peak condition for an important competition. Here, the maximum capacity (Max Cap_n) is now 125 (a 25% increase from that at the beginning of training shown in Figure 3a), functional reserve capacity is 120 (125 − 5), and the relative training load (85% of maximum capacity) is met at 106.25.

Adaptation potential, a purely theoretical concept proposed by Selye (1956), is a limit in the capacity of an organism to experience positive change, a latent excellence or ability that may or may not be developed. In Figure 3c, the individual has achieved his or her adaptation potential, a peak condition whereby a further increase in training will not result in further increases in maximum capacity. In fact, a further increase in training may reverse the process and result in a state of exhaustion and subsequent loss in performance.

In Figure 3a, the individual's adaptation capacity is 25 (adaptation potential minus Max Cap_1), in Figure 3b, adaptation capacity is 20 (adaptation potential minus Max Cap_2) and in Figure 3c, in which the individual has achieved his or her adaptation potential, adaptation capacity is zero. With response to training, more and more of one's adaptation potential is achieved, and further capacity for adaptation declines.

We maintain that adaptation potential is a function of the interrelationships among all factors affecting the organism and is *not* constant throughout the life span. The many factors affecting adaptation potential can perhaps be classified as intrinsic (inherent) and extrinsic (environmental). Two intrinsic factors are genetic endowment (e.g., inherited body type and muscle fiber distribution) and age (e.g., state of growth, development, and decline). Extrinsic factors would include biological, psychological, and sociocultural factors in one's ecosystem. The interrelationships among these intrinsic and extrinsic factors determine one's capacity for adaptation or change.

Figure 4 demonstrates the relationship between adaptation potential and functional reserve capacity throughout the life span for persons of different life-style classifications. Figure 4a represents those with sedentary lifestyles throughout life, and Figure 4b represents those with highly active lifestyles. It is assumed that the genetic potential of persons within these classifications is equal. It is obvious that there are considerable differences between the two groups in maximum capacity and functional reserve capacity throughout the life span, and in adaptation potential after the young adult years. The higher maximum capacity of persons with a highly active lifestyle is the result of organic adaptations to higher levels of imposed stress. Maximum capacity in sedentary persons usually rises until the young adult years and declines somewhat rapidly thereafter. By middle age, sedentary persons have a low physical working capacity and limited functional reserve capacity. In contrast, a highly active lifestyle results not only in a higher maximum capacity in the young adult years, but also in maintenance of that higher maximum capacity through the middle and later years of life. However, even individuals who continue a highly active lifestyle experience a general decline in physical working capacity sometime after age 50. It follows that the functional reserve capacity of the highly active is not only much higher than that of the sedentary but is also maintained for a much longer period of life.

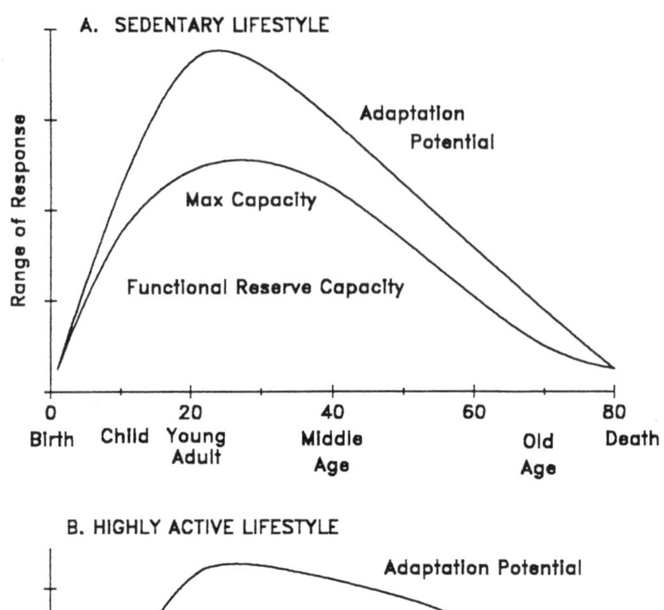

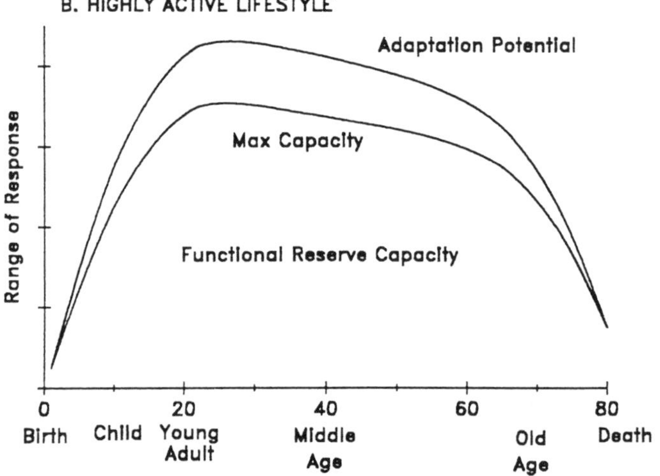

Figure 4 — Adaptation potential and functional reserve capacity throughout the human life span in (a) sedentary and (b) highly active lifestyles.

Adaptation potential is also very different between the sedentary and the highly active. It is assumed here that adaptation potential in one's early years is largely determined by genetic endowment. Therefore, the shape of the curves for adaptation potential in Figures 4a and 4b is identical until after the young adult years. Sometime following that age, the effects of a sedentary lifestyle may well have altered the organic potential for adaptation. A long-term period of relatively low stress characterized by a sedentary lifestyle will affect one's organic potential for response and attenuate that originally endowed genetically.

The Athlete's Ecosystem

The basic tenet of the proposed model is that the athlete's responsiveness to training is influenced by the relative balance of all the factors that make up that athlete's ecosystem. Therefore, it is appropriate to describe an athlete's ecosystem. Figure 5 presents the same general classifications of factors shown in Figure 1, with added details that may be specific to an athlete. The athlete's ecosystem encompasses many factors that are not usually given thoughtful consideration when planning a training program. We believe that failure to consider all factors that are of ecological importance to an athlete is a major mistake that may have serious consequences in terms of performance and health.

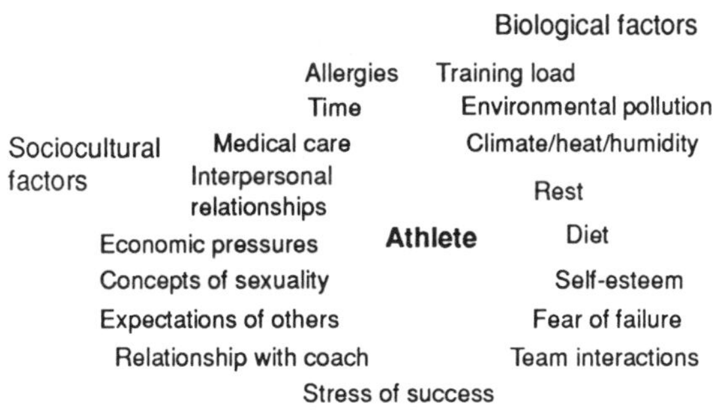

Figure 5 — The athlete's ecosystem.

Ecological Balance

The proposed model is based on the premise that the state of the athlete (organism), and hence her or his ability to adapt to a training load, is dependent upon the net effect of all forces that have an impact on that athlete. When there is a net balance of energy input and energy output, then the athlete is in a state of equilibrium. Stress (or energy output) is balanced by sufficient energy input to allow full recovery and results in no net energy loss. This is schematically illustrated in Figure 6. In such a state, the individual has considerable functional reserve capacity to meet the extraordinary demands of heavy physical training. In actuality, of course, the scenario is more complicated than this.

During periods of intense stress (for example, during a heavy training bout), the relative relationship between energy input and energy output is unbalanced, as in Figure 6b. Here, there is a momentary loss of energy from the system. This period of energy loss must be balanced by a period of recovery in which there is a momentary period of energy gain. This is shown in Figure 6c.

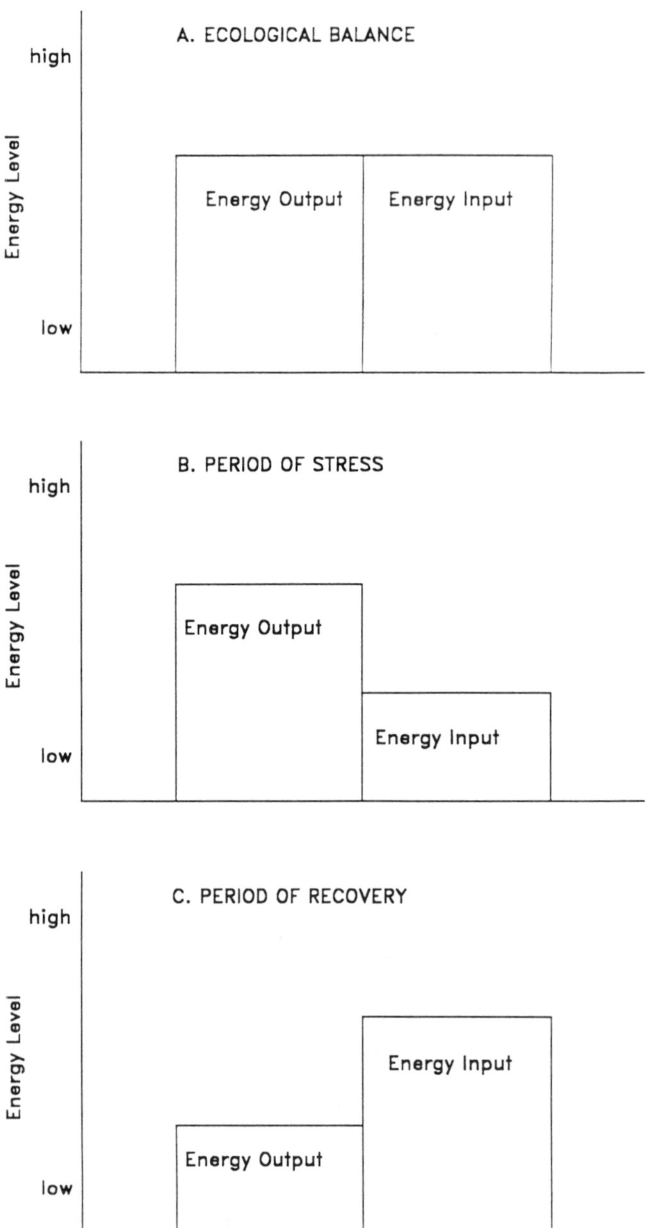

Figure 6 — Ecological balance in terms of energy levels during (a) period of balance, (b) period of stress, and (c) period of recovery.

There is nothing new or revolutionary in this description of stress and recovery, but we maintain that this simple concept is ignored by many athletes and coaches. If there is insufficient recovery, the athlete is eventually unable to maintain a net energy balance. This occurs very frequently in sport today, and unfortunately it is often an accepted sequence.

Athletes must train harder than ever before to remain truly competitive. Consequently, training loads are very heavy. Rather than following a stressful training period with a period of sufficient recovery, the athlete is often forced by time and economic constraints to turn to other aspects of his or her ecosystem that may be equally stressful (e.g., a job, a relationship, school). There are also extreme pressures to use illegal drugs or to use extreme dietary procedures to "make weight" or lose more body fat. In short, many athletes have little opportunity to balance energy input with energy output and seldom achieve a state of ecological balance.

Energy Drain

We refer to the general state in which energy input is insufficient to balance energy output as *energy drain*. Figure 7 provides the general schema (but is not limited to the factors shown here) for the energy drain concept. We propose that insufficient kilocalorie intake or a poor-quality diet, coupled with heavy physical training, extreme psychological stress, and too little rest and recovery yields net energy drain. Very simply, low energy input and high energy output results in a state of disorder (entropy) rather than balance within the athlete's ecosystem.

There are numerous signs and symptoms of net energy drain in athletes today. Reproductive failure is evidenced by amenorrhea and luteal-phase inadequacy in highly trained women, and by lowered basal testosterone and sperm counts in men. Overuse injuries are so frequent among highly trained athletes that they are considered a matter of course. Physicians today are concerned about recurring overuse injuries that lead to irreversible degenerative changes. There is considerable anecdotal evidence that heavy training adversely affects immunity, putting the athlete at increased risk for common colds, sore throats, Epstein-Barr virus, mononucleosis, and chronic fatigue syndrome. Burnout is a frequent cause of athlete dropout. Whether burnout is primarily psychological or biological in nature is undetermined. It is obvious, however, that burnout ends the careers of many athletes at a young age.

Another symptom of energy drain is a decline in performance (sometimes attributed to overtraining). Energy drain devastates an athlete's ability to adapt to training. With insufficient energy input, psychological and biological reserves are depleted and the individual is unable to achieve former levels of performance. Along with a decline in maximum capacity there is a decline in functional reserve capacity and the ability to achieve one's adaptation potential. Unless there is a rebalancing of the athlete's ecosystem, the athlete will eventually retire due to competitive failure, illness, or injury.

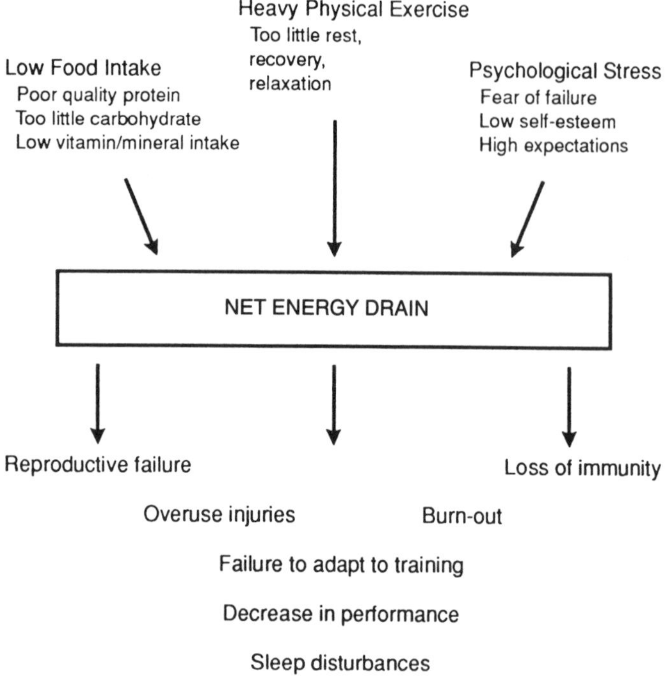

Figure 7 — Energy drain.

Most athletes experience energy drain at some point in their athletic careers. In some cases they withdraw from competition for a time and recover. Others may experience a serious illness or injury that forces them to rest. We contend that energy drain is completely avoidable. An ecological view of training illuminates the importance of maintaining balance between energy input and energy output. It is unfortunate that the more common view is "no pain, no gain" ("no guts, no glory"), in which the typical approach to a poor performance is to increase training with little or no consideration for the need for additional rest and recovery (or any of the other variables shown in Figure 4). Such factors as rest, recovery, nutrition, social support, and general human welfare are given little consideration. For example, if queried, most athletes and coaches would agree that rest and recovery are important features of a training program. If asked how they include rest and recovery in their training programs, they would most likely reply that there are occasional "easy days" incorporated into their training programs. Few could describe a comprehensive plan alternating periods of hard training with periods of recovery. Rather, most are locked into the view that hard training is everything and that an occasional easy day or day of rest is sufficient. Obviously, a parallel case can be made for such factors as diet, social support, and self-expectations. We maintain that new training paradigms that fully incorporate ecological factors are needed.

New Training Paradigms

Figure 8a gives a simple example of a typical training paradigm. Each training module (a, b, c) represents 1 week of training (including 1 day of rest that is not shown) in which the total training load is increased by 10% per week. Three modules of training are shown, representing a total of 21 days (18 days of training, 3 days of rest) and a net increase in training load of 30%. Competition follows shortly after achieving the final training module in this model.

Figure 8b shows an alternative model that integrates physical stress with rest and recovery. Each training module is divided into two parts. The first part is 6 days, including 1 rest day (not shown). The second part of each module (a_2, b_2, etc.) represents 2 days of training at a reduced training load (approximately one half to two thirds of the initial increment). This model requires 24 days (15 days of training at the same training loads as in Figure 8a, 3 days of rest, and 6 days of training at a reduced load) to increase the total training load 30%. The intent of the training days at reduced load is to allow more time for training adaptations to take place and to lower the average daily energy demand on the organism. Peak performance will most likely occur during periods d or e, after the body has recovered from the high stress level of module c and achieved a new level of net energy balance. Therefore, such a training plan must be implemented at least 30 days prior to competition. Further performance improvement would require a second training cycle. Future research should be directed to differing ways of incorporating rest days and days of lowered training intensity to achieve best results.

To achieve peak levels of performance at various times throughout a year or at various stages of one's competitive career requires a model in which training load is applied in sine-wave fashion. This allows the organism to gradually achieve new levels of net energy balance by alternatively applying high levels of stress with periods of recovery and adaptation. Training modules of any length (weeks, months, etc.) may be utilized. This is schematically shown in Figure 8c. Here, additional training cycles (shown here as modules a′, b′, c′, etc.) will result in further performance gains. The final level of each cycle serves as the base for each new training cycle.

We maintain that such a model is seldom envisioned in terms of life-span physical performance. Rather, cultural expectations seem caught in a time warp in which peak performance is thought to occur before age 25 and to deteriorate rapidly after that. Athletes often seem in a hurry to reach fame (and fortune) so they can move on to other aspects of life, retiring after breaking the world record or winning the championship. In many sports (e.g., distance running, triathlon, cross-country skiing), however, best performances are achieved between the ages 25 and 35 and are not followed by a sharp decline.

There is no physiological basis for a sharp decline in performance after one reaches her or his early 20s. The primary explanation for age at peak performance and age at retirement from sport appears to relate more to cultural expectations than to scientific principles. Variations of the model shown in Figure 7c can be used not only to capture world records and outstanding performances, but also to prepare for lifelong participation in sport.

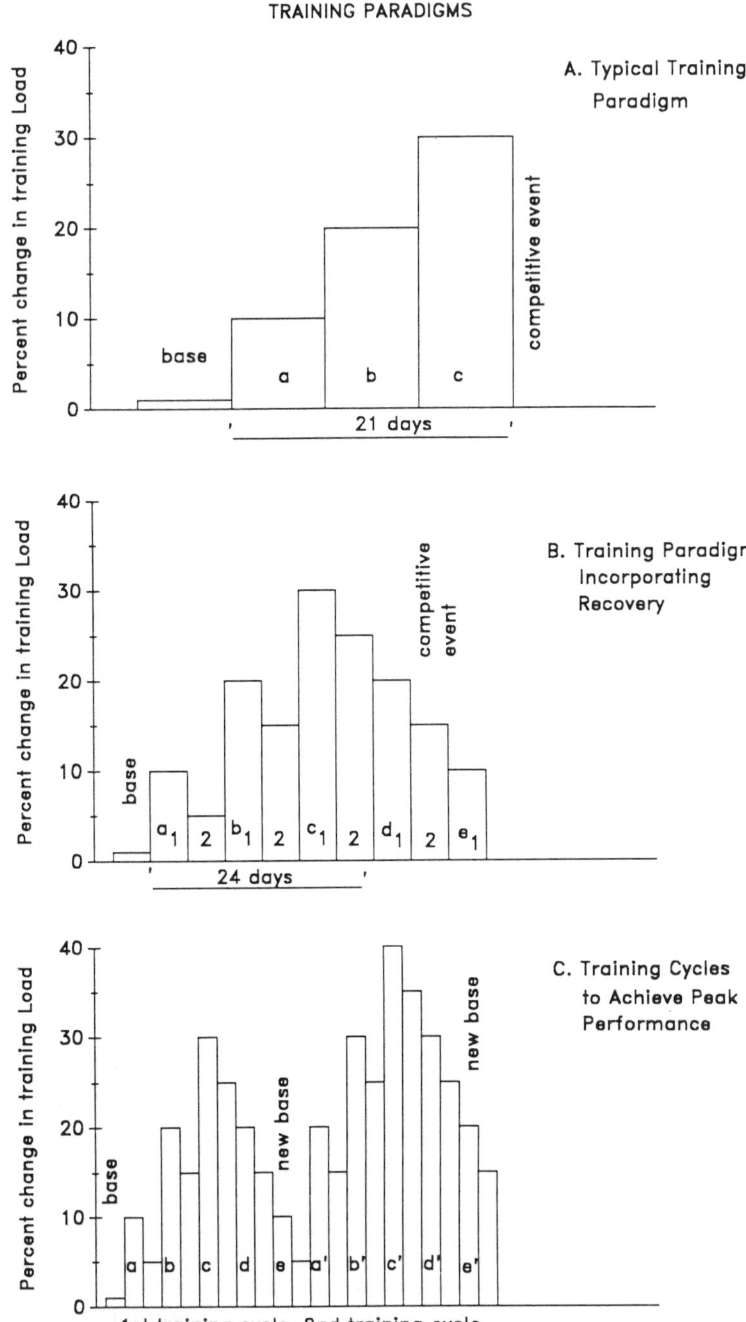

Figure 8 — Training paradigms: (a) typical training paradigm, (b) training paradigm incorporating recovery, and (c) training cycles to achieve peak performance.

By conceiving of training as occurring in cycles that fully incorporate rest and recovery, plus accounting for such other variables as nutrition, social support, and economic and family demands that are important aspects of an athlete's ecosystem, one can maintain a healthy, balanced life that includes sport participation throughout a lifetime. We maintain that one's competitive life span can and should be viewed in terms of decades, and not as a brief, highly intensive period of time that often leads to athletic self-destruction.

Performance-Based Research: Where Do We Go From Here?

In earlier years, people known as physical educators were generalists with a broad base of knowledge in physiology, kinesiology, learning theory, and psychology, plus good organizational skills. Specialization occurred with the knowledge explosion. With specialization has come increased depth of knowledge and mechanistic insights but loss of the broad perspective. In terms of training for high-level competition, the athlete is seen as a system of levers, muscles, nerves, organs, substrates, and enzymes, but not in a psychosociocultural context with many intervening energy demands. The big picture has been lost.

The usual remedy is a call for interdisciplinary research. However, interdisciplinary research has largely come to mean that a principal investigator engages the assistance of a few specialists to assist her or him with a major project. It does not necessarily mean that the research is broad-based, or comprehensive, or even that the specialists work together and mutually learn from each other. Therefore, the typical interdisciplinary approach is not what is needed here.

The proposed model calls for a new perspective, one that is comprehensive and broad-based, one in which sport scientists must call on other disciplines for truly integrated studies. The model considers the athlete a complex but unified organism with many intrinsic and extrinsic sources of energy exchange that vary throughout life. From such a wholistic point of view, interdisciplinary research can be directed to investigate interrelationships among such ecological factors as physical stress, dietary intake, immune responses, mental processes, and cultural forces. There is considerable need for such major undertakings, with ramifications for many fields of human endeavor. An ecological approach to training offers a challenging perspective from which physical educators can study a wide array of environmental factors and the human organism for the purposes of enhancing health and performance.

Reference

SELYE, H. (1956). *The stress of life*. New York: McGraw-Hill.

Fitness and Performance: Adult Health and the Culture of Youth

Robert M. Malina
University of Texas at Austin

The study of physical fitness and performance is a primary concern of the disciplines comprised by physical education, or more recently, the exercise and sport sciences, or *kinesiology*. Fitness and performance are related, in that performance on a variety of tests is often used to assess levels of fitness. The focus of studies of physical fitness and performance is largely on levels of fitness and outcomes of performance rather than on determinants. Further, there is quite often a lack of dialogue between those concerned with the biological or biomedical aspects and those concerned with the behavioral or social aspects of fitness and performance. Nevertheless, neither an exclusively biological nor an exclusively social or cultural approach to fitness and performance is sufficient to understand the complexities of these domains. A biocultural approach is essential and provides a broader perspective.

The central theme of this presentation is that current concepts regarding the fitness and performance of children and youth are outcomes of the interface of biology and culture. The interface varies with cultural perceptions of physical fitness and with different phases of the life cycle; what is relevant to one stage of the life cycle might not be equally applicable to another.

Although concepts of fitness may vary across time, the basic concept of physical fitness in the United States has been, with several slight modifications, reasonably consistent over the past 50 years or so. Cureton (1947, p. 18), for example, defined physical fitness in the 1940s as the "ability to handle the body well and the capacity to work hard over a long period of time without diminished efficiency." Components of fitness included physique, organic efficiency, and motor fitness. Subsequent definitions generally followed a similar theme. The definition of fitness presented by Clarke (1971) and slightly modified by the American Academy of Physical Education in 1979 is accepted by many in physical education and the exercise and sport sciences: "Physical fitness is the ability to carry out daily tasks with vigor and alertness, without undue fatigue and with ample energy to engage in leisure time pursuits and to meet the above average physical stresses encountered in emergency situations" (Definition of Physical Fitness, 1979, p. 28). This definition of fitness emphasized three basic components—muscular strength, muscular endurance, and cardiorespiratory endurance—but it also included components of motor fitness: power, agility, speed, and flexibility (Clarke, 1971).

Concern for the state of fitness or unfitness of American children and youth has also been consistent across time. Initially this concern focused largely on motor fitness, but more recently it has been directed toward problems of adult health. Cureton (1943), for example, described a lack of motor fitness in significant percentages of young adult males and discussed their unfitness in the context of the relatively large number of young men who were found physically deficient on registration for selective service (i.e., fitness for military preparedness). Shortly after World War II, in the context of the cold war and a high selective-service rejection rate in the Korean War, results of a survey with the Kraus-Weber test of "minimum muscular fitness" emphasized the general unfitness of American compared to European children (Kraus & Hirschland, 1954). The opening paragraph of a popular account of the results in *U.S. News and World Report* (What's Wrong with American Youths, 1954, p. 35) described the fitness of American youth as follows: "In terms of muscle and ability to do jobs requiring physical strength, the average American youth appears to be growing soft. His counterpart in some nations of Europe, enjoying fewer of the advantages of modern civilization, is stronger." Subsequently, a high prevalence of failure on the Kraus-Weber test was reported in several areas of the United States (Fox & Atwood, 1955; Kirchner & Glines, 1957; Phillips et al., 1955). It should be noted, however, that the Kraus-Weber test was developed as a clinical tool to evaluate the effects of treatment on adult patients with functional low back pain. It was applied to children in the context of predicting the prevalence of low back problems in the next generation of adults.

On the heels of the high prevalence of failures on the Kraus-Weber test among American children and criticisms of the test, several conferences on the fitness of American youth were convened, including the President's Conference on the Physical Fitness of American Youth in June, an AAHPER Conference on Youth Fitness in September of 1956 (The President's Conference, 1956), and the West Point Fitness Conference in September 1957 (West Point Conference, 1957). One result of the concern for the unfitness of American children and youth was the AAHPER youth fitness test that was administered to a national sample of schoolchildren during the 1957-1958 academic year (Hunsicker, 1957, 1958). Subsequently, comparison of the AAHPER youth fitness test results for American children in 1958 with those of British children in 1959 showed that the only test item on which British children did not equal or excel American children was the ball throw for distance in boys (Campbell & Pohndorf, 1961). In fact, performances of British girls, on the average, equaled or excelled those of American boys in five of the seven test items between 10 and 13 years of age.

In light of the publicity given to the preceding (in addition to a new president in the White House), greater emphasis was placed on fitness, essentially performance-based motor fitness, in physical education programs. Soviet success with Sputnik in 1957 was also a contributory factor. As activities of the United States space program accelerated, astronauts-in-training, being highly visible public figures, were often used to promote physical fitness among children and youth. American children responded to this emphasis and encouragement with markedly improved performances on the AAHPER youth fitness test in 1965 (Hunsicker & Reiff, 1966). Concern for being the best—"number one"—is, of course, a major theme in the American culture complex.

Along with concern for the unfitness of children and youth, mortality from coronary heart disease in the United States increased rather dramatically in the years following World War II (Stern, 1979), although the trend toward increasing mortality rates from coronary heart disease was already apparent early in the 20th century (Smil, 1989). Coronary heart disease mortality reached a peak in the late 1960s and has been declining since (Stern, 1979; Tyroler, 1988). Physical inactivity and low levels of physical fitness were implicated, among other factors, as significant contributors to the elevated mortality rates (Clarke, 1972; Fox & Skinner, 1964; Taylor, 1960). Reasons for the decline in heart disease mortality are many, but it is generally believed that changes in lifestyle, including reduction in smoking, dietary changes, decline in serum cholesterol levels, and increased leisure-time physical activity, in addition to improved medical services (e.g., coronary care units and related technology), have made important contributions.

Given the potential role of physical activity as a preventive factor in heart disease and, by extension, in obesity and musculoskeletal disorders (specifically of the lower back), the concept of health-related fitness emerged in the late 1970s (Falls, 1980; Plowman & Falls, 1978). It is at present the dominant focus in current discussions of the fitness of the American population in general and specifically of the unfitness of children and youth. The lack of fitness among children and youth is now related to a lack of aerobic power, a deficiency of strength and endurance, limited flexibility, and excessive fatness, and not to motor unfitness as in the 1950s and 1960s.

The concept of physical fitness of children and youth has thus evolved from a primary motor-performance focus to a health-related focus in the context of largely adult health concerns (initially, lower back problems and strength deficiency, as assessed by the Kraus-Weber test, and subsequently cardiovascular fitness relative to mortality from ischemic heart disease). These adult health concerns have resulted in a definition of the construct *health-related fitness* that is culturally based in a biomedical framework that holds a prominent position in the American culture complex. It is thus a culture-bound concept rooted in the biomedical community (see, for example, American Academy of Pediatrics, 1987; American College of Sports Medicine, 1988; Rowland, 1985). Being aerobically fit, strong, lean, and flexible is equated with being healthy and presumably reduces the risk of cardiovascular and perhaps other degenerative diseases. Images of health-related fitness, usually in the context of "perpetual young adulthood," are largely those portrayed by the megabillion-dollar "fitness industry" and the electronic and print media. Further, the suggested approach often has the appearance of applying adult exercise prescriptions to children and youth; for example: "Based on current information . . . it may be recommended that exercise programs with goals of improving aerobic fitness in prepubescent children should comply with standards recommended for training programs in adults" (Rowland, 1985, p. 496).

Children and youth, of course, are not miniature adults. Components of physical fitness, both motor and health-related, change as a function of growth and maturation. As applied to growing and maturing individuals, health-related physical fitness is based on one or both of these premises.

1. Regular physical activity during childhood and youth may function to prevent or impede the development of several adult diseases that include physical inactivity in a complex, multifactorial etiology—that is, degenerative diseases of the heart and blood vessels, obesity, and musculoskeletal disorders, specifically the low back syndrome, and perhaps others.
2. Habits of regular physical activity during childhood and youth may directly and favorably influence physical activity habits in adulthood and, in turn, favorably influence the health-related fitness of adults.

At present, however, the role of physical activity and physical fitness during childhood and adolescence as favorable influences on the health status of adults, as preventive factors in several diseases of adulthood, or as favorable influences on habitual physical activity in adulthood is not yet established (Malina, 1990). An important question that needs to be resolved is: When, if at all, during childhood and youth does regular physical activity exert its beneficial influence on subsequent adult health status? Or is regular physical activity during adulthood the key factor in the health-related fitness and health status of adults? In their comprehensive review of physical activity and cardiovascular health through the early 1960s, Fox and Skinner (1964, p. 744) noted that "there is a suggestion that recent activity is more important than activity earlier in life." Indeed, recent observations of Paffenbarger, Hyde, Wing, and Hsieh (1986, p. 609) echo those of Fox and Skinner 22 years earlier: "The rate of death from any cause was reduced with increased physical activity by alumni (at present), but . . . the sports-activity level in their student days did not have a similar effect on subsequent mortality." Given the apparent relationship between present activity and health status in adulthood, an important question then becomes: Is a physically active childhood and youth a precursor of a physically active lifestyle in adulthood?

Health-related physical fitness is also described as a "narrower concept focusing on the aspects of fitness that are related to day-to-day function and health maintenance" (Pate & Shephard, 1989, p. 3). It is reasonable to assume, however, that motor fitness is more relevant to the vast majority of the day-to-day activities of children and youth. Motor fitness (i.e., speed, agility, power, coordination, strength, and so on) expressed in skillful performance in a variety of fundamental movement patterns comprises the physical activities in which developing individuals engage.

There is most likely considerable interdependence between health- and motor performance–related physical fitness during childhood and youth. Nevertheless, many physical education programs are being encouraged to emphasize health-related activities, specifically aerobics, to the neglect and perhaps elimination of instruction and practice of fundamental motor skills. It has even been suggested by some (e.g., Parcel et al., 1987) that cardiovascular fitness should be the primary focus of the physical education curriculum. At times, aerobic activities are substituted for motor skill instruction and practice in the primary elementary grades, when many children have neither the attention span nor the fundamental movement skills required for prolonged and often specific exercise regimens. Thus, emphasis on health-related physical activities at young ages may conflict with one of the important developmental tasks of childhood—the development of a reasonable degree of proficiency in movement skills. Note, however, that the objectives of developing proficiency in motor skills and cardiovascular fitness are not mutually exclusive. It is possible to have a curriculum with a balance of both kinds of activities, and it is important that school physical education programs emphasize both the motor and health aspects of physical fitness. Reasonable proficiency in motor skills is necessary for activity participation, which leads to the development of aerobic power and muscular strength and endurance in a variety of contexts.

Initial exposure to the motor and health aspects of fitness should begin in primary grades, if not during preschool. However, the relative emphasis on each component of fitness should vary with age, as schematically illustrated in Figure 1. In preschool and primary grades, emphasis should be largely on the development of fundamental movement skills that contribute in large part to the components of motor fitness. As basic movement patterns are established and skill improves during middle childhood, relatively more emphasis should be placed upon the components of health-related fitness, with a corresponding reduction in emphasis on components of motor fitness. Thus, by about 10 years of age, there should be an equal emphasis on both motor and health-related fitness. As children enter the transition from childhood to adolescence, relatively more emphasis should be placed on components of health-related fitness, and this should continue through adolescence into young adulthood. Note, however, that the relative emphasis on motor fitness does not decrease to zero in late adolescence and young adulthood. There are in fact new motor skills that can be learned at these ages and later in adulthood that can contribute to both motor and health-related fitness (e.g., different dance skills, racket sports skills, and so on).

This view of relative emphasis on motor and health-related fitness during childhood and youth is consistent with available data on stability or tracking of indicators of fitness, motor performance, and risk factors. Stability is generally moderate to low during childhood and adolescence. Many correlations over intervals of 5 or more years do not reach 0.5, Bloom's (1964) suggested criterion for a stable trait, and thus have limited predictive utility. Stability from late adolescence into adulthood is somewhat better for blood pressure and lipids, though not for fatness. However, fatness, blood pressure, and lipids track better at the upper extremes of their distributions. Corresponding data for tracking of performance at the extremes (i.e., the low ends of the distributions) are lacking (Malina, 1990, in press).

Health-related physical fitness as it has developed is thus an adult-based concept applied to children and youth. Note, however, that it is primarily in adults that outcomes or end stages of chronic degenerative diseases are manifest, and the processes underlying the outcomes probably have their origins during childhood and youth. Hence, it is reasonable to apply the concept of health-related fitness to children and youth, particularly in a preventive role. It is intuitively correct to assume that physical activity enhances the health status of children and youth and in turn may influence the health status of individuals as

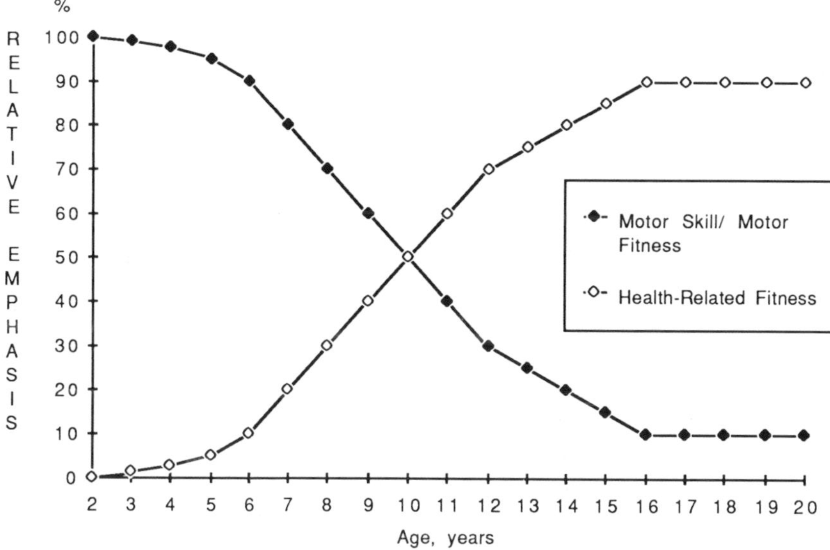

Figure 1 — Schematic illustration of changing relative emphasis on motor skill/ motor fitness and health-related fitness during childhood and youth.

adults. It is also intuitively correct to assume that habits of physical activity developed during childhood and youth may persist into a physically active lifestyle in adulthood and in turn impede the development of a variety of diseases. However, the evidence is not yet established, so caution may be warranted in blindly applying the adult-based concept of health-related physical fitness to children and youth.

Because stability of risk factors for cardiovascular disease tracks better from adolescence into adulthood, it appears that the transition from adolescence into adulthood is an important age period relative to health status. This is, of course, a period of transition from high school to an occupation or to college, each with its own demands. This period includes independence from the family and most likely changes in lifestyle that may influence many of the risk factors for cardiovascular disease and physical fitness (e.g., diet, habits of physical activity, alcohol consumption, smoking, and use of oral contraceptives). Time spent in physical activities also declines between adolescence and young adulthood (Malina, 1986), whereas smoking, alcohol consumption, and oral contraceptives are independently related to serum lipids and lipoproetins and blood pressure in 17- to 24-year-old individuals (Croft et al., 1987). Thus, changes in lifestyle during the transition from adolescence into adulthood that either directly or indirectly influence health-related physical fitness merit closer consideration.

Some evidence, though limited, does suggest an association between motor fitness during childhood and adolescence, and physical activity in young adulthood (Dennison, Straus, Mellits, & Charney, 1988). Physically active young adult males, 23 to 25 years of age, had better motor fitness scores as children

(10 to 11 years) and adolescents (15 to 18 years) than inactive young adult males. The active young adults performed, on the average, significantly better than inactive adults in the 600-yard run, sit-ups, the 50-yard dash, and the shuttle run during late childhood and adolescence. Further, boys whose performances on the 600-yard run were below the 20th percentile were at a significantly greater risk for physical inactivity as adults, which emphasizes the need to follow children and youth at the low extremes of the performance distribution and which is consistent with evidence suggesting that such risk factors as fatness, total serum and LDL-cholesterol, and hypertension track better at the upper extremes of the distributions.

Summary

The thesis that health-related physical fitness is a culture-bound concept developed in the context of adult health concerns has been described. The application of this concept to children and youth requires closer examination, and perhaps reexamination, specifically in the context of the developmental tasks and health concerns of childhood and youth. Developmental tasks are many, and one in particular, the development of reasonable proficiency in motor skills, may be influenced by too early an emphasis on health-related fitness. The application of an adult-based concept of health-related fitness thus may not be entirely consistent with the biocultural needs of childhood and youth. Health-related fitness should be integrated first into the health needs of children and youth and then into the health concerns of adults. The continuity between health status during childhood and adolescence and health status in adulthood, of course, needs systematic evaluation.

References

AMERICAN Academy of Pediatrics. (1987). Physical fitness and the schools. *Pediatrics*, **80**, 449-450.

AMERICAN College of Sports Medicine. (1988). Opinion statement on physical fitness in children and youth. *Medicine and Science in Sports and Exercise*, **20**, 422-423.

BLOOM, B.S. (1964). *Stability and change in human characteristics*. New York: Wiley.

CAMPBELL, W.R., & Pohndorf, R.H. (1961). Physical fitness of British and United States children. In L.A. Larson (Ed.), *Health and fitness in the modern world* (pp. 8-16). Chicago: Athletic Institute.

CLARKE, H.H. (1971). Basic understanding of physical fitness. *Physical Fitness Research Digest*, Series 1, No. 1.

CLARKE, H.H. (1972). Physical activity and coronary heart disease. *Physical Fitness Research Digest*, Series 2, No. 2.

CROFT, J.B., Freedman, D.S., Cresanta, J.L., Srinivasan, S.R., Burke, G.L., Hunter, S.M., Webber, L.S., Smoak, C.G., & Berenson, G.S. (1987). Adverse influences of alcohol, tobacco, and oral contraceptive use on cardiovascular risk factors during transition to adulthood. *American Journal of Epidemiology*, **126**, 202-213.

CURETON, T.K., Jr. (1943). The unfitness of young men in motor fitness. *Journal of the American Medical Association*, **123**, 69-74.

CURETON, T.K., Jr. (1947). *Physical fitness appraisal and guidance*. St. Louis: Mosby.

DEFINITION of physical fitness. (1979). *Journal of Physical Education and Recreation*, **50**(8), 28.

DENNISON, B.A., Straus, A.H., Mellits, E.D., & Charney, E. (1988). Childhood physical fitness tests: Predictor of adult physical activity levels? *Pediatrics*, **82**, 324-330.

FALLS, H.B. (1980). Modern concepts of physical fitness. *Journal of Physical Education and Recreation*, **51**(4), 25-27.

FOX, M., & Atwood, J. (1955). Results of testing Iowa school children for health and fitness. *Journal of Health, Physical Education and Recreation*, **26**(6), 20-21, 76.

FOX, S.M., & Skinner, J.M. (1964). Physical activity and cardiovascular health. *American Journal of Cardiology*, **14**, 731-746.

HUNSICKER, P.A. (1957). AAHPER's youth fitness project. *Journal of Health, Physical Education and Recreation*, **28**(November), 17.

HUNSICKER, P.A. (1958). *AAHPER youth fitness test manual*. Washington, DC: American Association for Health, Physical Education, and Recreation.

HUNSICKER, P.A., & Reiff, G.G. (1966). A survey and comparison of youth fitness 1958-1965. *Journal of Health, Physical Education and Recreation*, **37**(1), 23-25.

KIRCHNER, G., & Glines, D. (1957). Comparative analysis of Eugene, Oregon, elementary school children using the Kraus-Weber test of minimum muscular fitness. *Research Quarterly*, **28**, 16-25.

KRAUS, H., & Hirschland, R.P. (1954). Minimum muscular fitness tests in school children. *Research Quarterly*, **25**, 178-188.

MALINA, R.M. (1986). Energy expenditure and physical activity during childhood and youth. In A. Demirjian (Ed.), *Human growth: A multidisciplinary review* (pp. 215-225). London: Taylor & Francis.

MALINA, R.M. (1990). Growth, exercise, fitness, and later outcomes. In C. Bouchard, R.J. Shephard, T. Stephens, J.R. Sutton, & B.D. McPherson (Eds.), *Exercise, fitness, and health: A consensus of current knowledge* (pp. 637-653). Champaign, IL: Human Kinetics.

MALINA, R.M. (1990). Tracking of physical fitness and performance during growth. In G. Beunen, J. Ghesquiere, T. Reybrouck, & A.L. Claessens (Eds.), *Children and exercise* (Band 4, Schriftenreihe der Hamburg-Mannheimer-Stiftung fur Informationsmedizin) (pp. 1-10). Stuttgart: Ferdinand-Enke-Verlag.

PAFFENBARGER, R.S., Jr., Hyde, R.T., Wing, A.L., & Hsieh, C-C. (1986). Physical activity, all-cause mortality, and longevity of college alumni. *New England Journal of Medicine*, **314**, 605-613.

PARCEL, G.S., Simons-Morton, B.G., O'Hara, N.M., Baranowski, T., Kolbe, L.J., & Bee, D.E. (1987). School promotion of healthful diet and exercise behavior: An integration of organizational change and social learning theory interventions. *Journal of School Health*, **57**, 150-156.

PATE, R.R., & Shephard, R.J. (1989). Characteristics of physical fitness in youth. In C.V. Gisolfi & D.R. Lamb (Eds.), *Perspectives in exercise and sports medicine. Volume 2. Youth, exercise, and sport* (pp. 1-43). Indianapolis: Benchmark Press.

PHILLIPS, M., Bookwalter, C., Denman, C., McAuley, J., Sherwin, H., Summers, D., & Yeakel, H. (1955). Analysis of results from the Kraus-Weber test of minimum muscular fitness in children. *Research Quarterly*, **26**, 314-323.

PLOWMAN, S.A., & Falls, H.B. (1978). AAHPER youth fitness test revision. *Journal of Physical Education and Recreation*, **49**(9), 22-24.

THE President's Conference on Fitness of American Youth. (1956). *Journal of Health, Physical Education and Recreation*, **27**(6), 8-10, 30.

ROWLAND, T.W. (1985). Aerobic response to endurance training in prepubescent children: A critical analysis. *Medicine and Science in Sports and Exercise*, **17**, 493-497.

SMIL, V. (1989). Coronary heart disease, diet, and Western mortality. *Population and Development Review*, **15**, 399-424.

STERN, M.P. (1979). The recent decline in ischemic heart disease mortality. *Annals of Internal Medicine*, **91**, 630-640.

TAYLOR, H.L. (1960). The mortality and morbidity of coronary heart disease of men in sedentary and physically active occupations. In S.C. Staley, T.K. Cureton, L.J. Huelster, & A.J. Barry (Eds.), *Exercise and fitness* (pp. 20-39). Chicago: Athletic Institute.

TYROLER, A. (1988). Introduction. In M.W. Higgins & R.W. Luepker (Eds.), *Trends in coronary heart disease: The influence of medical care* (pp. 3-15). New York: Oxford University Press.

THE West Point Conference—fitness for youth. (1957). *Journal of Health, Physical Education and Recreation*, **28**(8), 40-42.

WHAT'S wrong with American youths: They're not as strong as Europeans. (1954, March 19). *U.S. News & World Report*, pp. 35-36.

The Failure of Sport Psychology in the Exercise and Sport Sciences

Rod K. Dishman
The University of Georgia

After 25 years in its modern era, the field of sport psychology has partly succeeded as a profession and has failed as an exercise and sport science (Dishman, 1989; Morgan, 1972). My goal in this paper is to provide examples to support this conclusion and offer plausible directions to correct it. I will describe research questions where the prevailing approaches in sport psychology have neither considered the uniqueness of exercise and sport settings nor capitalized on the advantages offered by integrating other disciplinary approaches from the exercise and sport sciences. Were sport psychology contributing to psychological science, its isolation from exercise and sport science might be defensible. However, I will argue that sport psychology has also failed as a psychological science. My central argument calls for an interdisciplinary or cross-disciplinary rebirth of sport psychology within the exercise and sport sciences.

A decade ago Harrison & Feltz (1979) outlined five steps for the successful professionalization of sport psychology:

1. Agreement upon a systematic, theoretical knowledge base
2. Establishment and promotion of a professional culture through professional organizations and journals
3. Publication of a code of ethics to which members adhere
4. A certification or accrediting body that regulates and standardizes training of sport psychologists and publicly recognizes achievement
5. Lobbying efforts until standards of training and certification are adopted as statutory law

In my view only step 2, the promotion of a culture, has fully received the attention of mainstream sport psychology. Step 3 has occurred only for the North American Society for the Psychology of Sport and Physical Activity (NASPSPA), and under some controversy. A consensus code for the many subfactions of sport psychology has not evolved, and although the NASPSPA code is closely patterned after the code of ethics of the American Psychological Association (APA), the APA code is only enforced for those sport psychologists who are APA members. Prior estimates show that only a small proportion of NASPSPA members are also members of the APA, and it is not clear how NASPSPA has enforced its code.

Steps 4 and 5 have clearly not evolved. The Association for the Advancement of Applied Sport Psychology (AAASP) will soon implement certification for its members, but only the U.S. Olympic Committee (USOC) and the Canadian Association of Sport Sciences (CASS) have implemented registries for sport psychologists who wish to work under their auspices. The progress of these two registries toward professional certification is murky. The USOC guidelines have been rejected by a number of constituencies in the field of sport psychology, and the conspicuous absence of the terms *psychologist* and *sport psychologist* in the Canadian Registry for Sport Behavioral Professionals reveals that the CASS has not resolved the earlier USOC dilemma of an umbrella registry for clinical, educational, and research applications by a diverse membership including psychiatrists, licensed psychologists, nonlicensed psychologists, and noncertified, nonlicensed specialists in motor learning, motor development, and sport psychology. It is instructive to note in the Canadian registry that sport psychology is listed as only one of many areas of training and that the registry review board has no legal power to control or restrict practice.

Perhaps meetings such as the International Seminar on Ethical Standards in Sport Psychology, organized by the European Federation of Sport Psychology (FEPSAC) and the Hellenic Society of Sport Psychology for May 1990 in Athens, Greece, will offer directions for resolving pressing issues of codification. A scientist-practitioner model of education and training for psychologists was sponsored in January 1990 by the Assembly of Scientist-Practitioner Psychologists and the Department of Clinical and Health Psychology at the University of Florida. Sessions such as this may offer important policy guidance for sport psychology, or a similar meeting for sport psychology sponsored by appropriate psychological associations may be useful.

The Professional Culture

Most energies in the field of sport psychology have been directed to step 2, the promotion of a professional culture (Dishman, 1983). Here considerable success has been achieved. During preparation for the 1984 winter and summer Olympic Games, at least 10 sport psychologists had on-site contact in training United States Olympic athletes (Suinn, 1985). The recent appointment of a resident sport psychologist and the establishment of the Department of Sport Psychology at the U.S. Olympic Training Center, and the on-site presence of the head of this department at the 1988 summer Olympic Games, are clear signs of an emerging sport psychology culture. Moreover, during its existence from 1986 to 1988 and in 1990, the Scientific Advisory Committee of the Sports Medicine Council of the U.S. Olympic Committee included sport psychologists, and the USOC initiated a sport psychology advisory panel as part of its Elite Athlete Program in 1982.

At least three widely circulated U.S. journals and one international journal are devoted exclusively to research and practice in sport psychology, and in North America four professional organizations have sport or exercise psychology as their principal interest. Another five have sport psychology interest groups within a broader based membership. However, this proliferation of a professional culture in sport psychology belies the unification of the field. Revealed is greater diversity and segregation of approaches and interests than would be predicted for a budding profession. Indeed, no tangible progress toward unification has been made since a special symposium convened to discuss the "fractionization of sport psychology" at the 1987 NASPSPA meeting in Vancouver, British Columbia. Representatives from NASPSPA, the Sport Psychology Academy of AAHPERD, the American College of Sports Medicine (ACSM), the Division of Exercise and Sport Psychology of the APA, the Canadian Association for Psychomotor Learning and Sport Psychology (SCAPPS), the International Society for Sport Psychology (ISSP), and AAASP participated.

Fractionation Impedes the Growth of Knowledge

In my view, this fractionation within the *fields* of sport psychology can ultimately be traced to a poorly developed theoretical knowledge base (Dishman, 1983). I wish to focus my comments on this.

The *International Handbook of Research in Sport Psychology* (Singer, Murphy, & Tennant, in press) recently commissioned by the ISSP and coordinated by Bob Singer, is a meritorious endeavor to provide a consensus of what is now known in the field. However, I believe it will reveal that there is indeed a lack of consensus over what constitutes the knowledge base among the various constituencies within sport psychology. I will provide examples where the knowledge base cannot develop without concerted efforts employing the traditions, methods, and knowledge of the exercise and sport sciences (Skinner, Corbin, Landers, Martin, & Wells, 1989). It is abundantly clear that the fields of exercise physiology, motor learning, biomechanics, and exercise epidemiology are not considered by most sport psychologists and that therefore most of their questions go unanswered.

The dissociation of sport psychology from the exercise and sport sciences is illustrated by the fact that of the 11,000 members of the American College of Sports Medicine, the world's largest and arguably most influential scientific organization in sport and exercise, less than 1% (74) claim psychiatry or psychology/sociology as the area of specialization. Important for the future is that this low rate extends to the student membership as well. In 1989, about 2,600 of the 37,000 AAHPERD members were members of the Sport Psychology Academy of NASPE, and only 97 were also among the 3,900 members of the Exercise Physiology Academy. Although the psychology and physiology academies account for about one third of AAHPERD members who identify research as their principal interest, this one third represents only 672 of 1,665 research-oriented members; it is unknown how many of the 97 individuals with dual memberships are researchers. Just 30% of the exercise physiology academy are researchers.

There has also been dissociation of sport psychology from the field of psychology. Of the 900 members of Division 47, Exercise and Sport Psychology of the APA, about one fourth are licensed clinicians who do little or no research. A small room would hold the researchers who have backgrounds in the exercise and sport sciences; only a handful of these individuals are members of the newly formed 3,000-member American Psychological Society, which has scientific, not professional, goals. Most sport psychologists from physical education departments appear to have strong allegiance to the newly formed splinter group from NASPSPA, AAASP. This organization promotes applied research and the sport psychology culture. It has many psychologists among its 500 members, but it does not appear to have as its mission an impact on psychological science or on exercise and sport science.

Much of this dissociation from the exercise and sport sciences can be traced to the formation of the North American Society for the Psychology of Sport and Physical Activity in 1967 and the Canadian Society for Psychomotor Learning and Sport Psychology in 1969. To my knowledge NASPSPA has met with other sport sciences only once, at the 1984 Olympic Scientific Congress in Eugene, Oregon, and typically holds its annual meeting at the same time as the ACSM meeting, preventing many sport psychologists from attending both meetings.

On balance, it is my view that the field of sport psychology has continued to operate in a vacuum; it is neither an exercise and sport science nor a psychological science or developed psychological profession. The following are examples of pressing research questions that are rightfully in the domain of sport psychology but that require interdisciplinary or cross-disciplinary tactics to answer. They are practical problems that require theoretical approaches, reliable and valid technologies, and a radical departure from the current wisdom that drives the prevailing culture in sport psychology. It may have been necessary during the scientific impetus of the 1960s for physical educators interested in psychology to splinter from the exercise and sport sciences and adopt the methods and theories of psychology to kindle the spark of a sport psychology culture. But in the 1990s sport psychology as a profession cannot survive without a scientific leap back to the exercise and sport sciences. Licensed psychologists and counselors can legally practice sport psychology. Physical educators cannot. Jack Keogh of the University of California at Los Angeles aptly stated that those who try may be "sports" but they are not psychologists.

Equally true, psychologists are not exercise and sport scientists. Most disturbing, though, most sport psychologists aren't either. A statement by Coleman Griffith, the acknowledged pioneer of America's early era in sport psychology, made to the 1924 annual meeting of the Society of Directors of Physical Education in Colleges, rings painfully true today (sexist language notwithstanding):

> A great many people have the idea that the psychologist is a sort of magician who is ready, for a price, to sell his services to one individual or to one group of men. Nothing could be further from the truth. Psychological facts are universal facts. They belong to whoever will read while he runs. . . . During the last few years and the present time, there have been and are many men, short in psychological training and long in the use of the English language, who are doing psychology damage by advertising that they are ready to answer any and every question that comes up in any and every field. No sane psychologist is deceived by these self-styled apostles of a new day. Coaches and athletes have a right to be wary of such stuff. (Griffith, 1925, pp. 193-194)

Cross-Disciplinary Questions

Although many practical and theoretical questions facing sport psychology and other exercise and sport sciences will be best addressed by a disciplinary approach, many will not. The following are some areas where accelerated efforts of an interdisciplinary or cross-disciplinary nature are required for sport psychology questions.

Overtraining and Staleness

From 1986 to 1988, overtraining was the main topic of concern among U.S. Olympic athletes. Yet the approach taken to the topic in sport psychology was based on nebulous terms such as *stress* and *burnout* and ignored the industrial-organizational psychology literature on job-related stress and the exercise and sport science literature on psychobiological approaches integrating subjective and neuroendocrine markers of stress (Dishman & Landy, 1988). This occurred despite the established syndrome of athletic staleness, which mimics agitated or typical depression and its host of neuroendocrine, immune, and sympathetic nervous system signs of dysregulation (Dishman, in press; Dunn & Dishman, in press).

Determinants of Exercise Adherence

Studies of the determinants of participation in leisure physical activity found in the sport psychology literature have typically been restricted to tests of the generalizability of some variation of decision theory based on outcome expectancy values and/or effectance motivation (Dishman, 1988). The trend has been to read *Psychological Review* or *Psychological Bulletin* or test the general behavior model championed by a colleague in the campus psychology department. Although this has merit, at best the result is some degree of confirmation or rejection of the generalizability of the parent model extended to sport or exercise settings. What is too seldom done, however, is to compare the goodness of fit of competing models, or to explicate the limitations or boundary conditions under which the general model predicts or explains, or to modify the original model.

Failing this, sport psychology does the work for psychology, not for sport psychology; but psychological theory is not changed, nor is sport or exercise behavior, or our understanding of its uniqueness, changed. Moreover, the tests of the models are often incomplete. Most damning is our notorious failure to assess the very behavior we purport to study. Psychology studies of exercise patterns have exclusively relied on self-report estimates of activity without convincing evidence for reliability or validity. Although over 30 different assessment methods exist for measuring physical activity, and a half dozen reviews of the measurement problem have appeared in the literatures of epidemiology, preventive medicine, and sports medicine, this fundamental measurement issue is essentially ignored by sport and exercise psychology.

Stress and Athletic Injury

Studies of psychological predictors of athletic injury and stress among youth athletes have attempted to predict risk with no attention given to elementary principles of epidemiology such as incidence, prevalence, and most astonishingly, person-hours of exposure.

Mental Health

Studies of exercise effects on anxiety and depression show little appreciation for diagnostic issues and essentially treat these diseases as though they were merely self-reports of mood. In fact, large portions of these complex families of disorders have strong biological bases, where plausible neurobiological mechanisms could explain therapeutic effects of exercise (Dunn & Dishman, in press). Yet sport psychology continues to restrict our methods to self-reports and our level of analysis to thoughts and feelings, ignoring that perhaps the only unique aspect of physical exertion is its profound impact on autonomic nervous, neuroendocrine, and possibly limbic function.

We still operate with the 1970s view that circulating beta-endorphin affects postexercise mood, when all evidence from physiology argues it does not. Ignored are brain-imaging studies. Ignored are pharmacological studies. Exercise psychologists have dismissed the complexity and purposes of autonomic and neuroendocrine regulatory responses to exercise, and exercise physiologists have been largely uninterested in studying mechanisms of ''central command'' or ''higher centers'' in ways that will shed light on behavior or psychophysiological aspects of exercise and sport. However, my experience shows me that physiologists are usually more interested in psychology than are psychologists interested in physiology. If this is the case, it must change. The role of autonomic, neuroendocrine, and limbic systems in regulating mental health responses to exercise must be studied by exercise psychologists employing physiological and pharmacological methods or teaming with physiologists and pharmacologists. Psychological responses to exercise cannot be interpreted by social, behavioral, or cognitive methods alone. The physiological and pharmacological responses to the exercise stimulus must be controlled and quantified.

These omissions can have profound ill effects on the body of knowledge. Despite the conclusion of the 1984 NIMH Workshop on Exercise and Mental Health that physical activity and fitness are associated with reduced anxiety and reduced symptoms of moderate depression, and two recent meta-analyses that support this, the recent report on the effectiveness of exercise for primary disease prevention in adults by the U.S. Preventive Services Task Force of the U.S. Office of Disease Prevention and Health Promotion concluded that the quality of this evidence was poor and stated that the relationship was poorly understood (Harris, Caspersen, & DeFriese, 1989). The failure of sport and exercise psychology to employ epidemiological, psychiatric, and psychobiological approaches to the study of mental health has clearly contributed to the unconvincing case made to the field of preventive medicine.

Primary and Secondary Ignorance

Many of the problems I have outlined reflect primary ignorance: No field has answered the questions. I have argued that often this is the case because of the ultimate inadequacy of segregation among the exercise and sport sciences. There also are too many instances of secondary ignorance: Some field has answered the questions, but sport psychology isn't aware of the fact.

A frequently championed anecdote used to support the performance-aiding effects of imagery and autogenic training by applied sport psychologists is the success attributed to famous breath-hold underwater diver Mayol who formerly held the world record at 86 meters or 284 feet. Mayol reportedly has avowed an ability to lower his heart rate during his dives. This has been interpreted as a mental skill by many sport psychologists despite the widely known influence of breath-hold and the mammalian diving reflex on heart rate at depths as shallow as 5 to 20 meters and the dissociation of heart rate and oxygen consumption during depth diving in humans (Lin, 1988). Clearly, anxiety can attenuate the diving reflex in humans, but to attribute heart-rate reductions during breath-hold solely to a nebulous mental skill is naive or misleading.

Similarly, attempts to explain mechanisms purportedly underlying the modest effect of mental practice on motor learning and performance (Feltz, Landers, & Becker, 1988) by invoking a neuromuscular facilitation effect ignore the prevailing theories of motor skill acquisition, which rely on some form of feedback or comparator of feedforward of motor efference. No plausible explanation can currently be mustered for enhancing motor control by imaging in the absence of movement and knowledge of results, yet the practice persists in the literatures of applied sport psychology in isolation from the traditions and methods of what is known about motor skill acquisition and retention.

Moreover, in the imagery literature and the biofeedback literature in sport psychology, very few reports of psychophysiological assessments are made in journals that adhere to the experimental standards and guidelines of the Society for Psychophysiological Research, and the descriptions of methods usually do not permit an evaluation of the accuracy of the measurements reported. It is difficult to believe that imagery-induced EMG signals truly represent low-gain muscle action potentials rather than bracing by the subject, when methods are not described in sufficient detail to permit confidence that surface EMG resolution was even possible under resting conditions. It is difficult to convince exercise physiologists that, as one sport psychology article reported, the practice of meditation by experienced runners performing at 50% of $\dot{V}O_{2peak}$ will lower oxygen consumption at a constant treadmill speed by 10% to 15%, when such an effect would approximate the known coefficient of variation of oxygen consumption across the entire range of economy for ambulatory adults! Average daily variation in oxygen cost for individuals during submaximal treadmill running will approximate just 1 to 2 $ml \cdot kg^{-1} \cdot min^{-1}$.

At present, mainstream sport psychology lacks, or does not use, many of the established measurement technologies, methodologies, and applied theories available to us. This greatly impedes our progress toward our goal of becoming a profession. Some of the means to develop or implement these technologies, methodologies, and theories are available in the traditions of epidemiology, psychiatry, psychometry, psychophysiology, psychopharmacology, nuclear medicine, and the sport and exercise sciences. However, these traditions are not employed by the vast majority of sport psychologists who rely on social psychology or social anthropology theory and methods or clinical principles and techniques largely unvalidated for the sport and exercise settings where they are applied. This is particularly true for top level athletes; very little applied research with top level athletes has been reported in scientific journals. These traditions can be informative and effective, but used exclusively they cannot continue to advance understanding in many areas where psychological and behavioral problems in sport and exercise settings beg for resolution.

A review by Malina (1988) of a recent sport psychology volume is representative of the current state of affairs in sport psychology and offers a solution consistent with my arguments.

> The focus of the volume is, with few exceptions, exclusively behavioral to the neglect of biology. This is puzzling for sport and is unique in that the biological organism must physically perform the neuromuscular skills demanded of a sport in the context of situations which are socially or culturally determined. To exclude the biological is myopic. Sport, like many other aspects of culture, should be treated in a biocultural or biosocial manner. (Malina, 1988, p. 11)

Summary

I view much of the failure of sport psychology in the exercise and sport sciences as stemming from a segregation of questions and methods within the field of sport psychology, so that most questions are asked in the same ways by people of too similar training, using too few and too redundant methods. These methods typically do not include the approaches of other disciplines, yet often other approaches are required to find answers. Students wishing to pursue scholarship or practice in sport psychology need a broader based education with training in methods, theories, and technologies more diverse than social psychology, social anthropology, or nonspecific courses in applied sport psychology.

The professional culture in sport psychology has thrived in some respects, due to a bullish consumer market for practical psychology applications in sport and exercise settings. Many sport psychologists believe that *social validity* (i.e., professional consensus about existing practice coupled with consumer satisfaction) is adequate to justify a profession in the absence of a scientific body of knowledge. I do not. I believe that the profession of sport psychology cannot survive unless its science matures; this cannot occur in isolation from the exercise and sport sciences.

References

DISHMAN, R.K. (1983). Identity crises in North American sport psychology: Academics in professional issues. *Journal of Sport Psychology*, **5**, 123-134.

DISHMAN, R.K. (Ed.) (1988). *Exercise adherence: Its impact on public health*. Champaign, IL: Human Kinetics.

DISHMAN, R.K. (1989). Psychology of sports competition. In A.J. Ryan & F. Allman (Eds.), *Sports medicine* (pp. 129-164). Orlando, FL: Academic Press.

DISHMAN, R.K. (in press). Physiological and psychological effects of overtraining. In K.D. Brownell, J. Rodin, & J.H. Wilmore (Eds.), *Eating, body weight and performance in athletes: Disorders of modern society*. Philadelphia: Lea & Febiger.

DISHMAN, R.K., & Landy, F.J. (1988). Psychological factors and prolonged exercise. In D.A. Lamb & R. Murray (Eds.), *Exercise science and sports medicine: Vol. 1, prolonged exercise* (pp. 140-167). Indianapolis: Benchmark Press.

DUNN, A.L., & Dishman, R.K. (in press). Exercise and the neurobiology of depression. *Exercise and Sport Sciences Reviews*, **19**.

FELTZ, D.L., Landers, D.M., & Becker, B.J. (1988). A revised meta-analysis of the mental practice literature on motor skill learning. In National Research Council (Ed.), *Enhancing human performance, part 3: Improving motor performance*. Washington, DC: National Academy Press.

GRIFFITH, C.R. (1925). Psychology and its relation to athletic competition. *American Physical Education Review*, **30**, 193-198.

HARRIS, S.S., Caspersen, C.J., & DeFriese, G.H. (1989). Physical activity counseling for healthy adults as a primary preventive intervention in the clinical setting. Report for the U.S. Preventive Services Task Force. *JAMA*, **261**, 3588-3598.

HARRISON, R.P., & Feltz, D.L. (1979). The professionalism of sport psychology: Legal considerations. *Journal of Sport Psychology*, **1**, 182-190.

LIN, Y.C. (1988). Applied physiology of diving. *Sports Medicine*, **5**, 41-56.

MALINA, R. (1988). Book review. *Sports Medicine Bulletin*, **12**, 11.

MORGAN, W.P. (1972). Sport psychology. In R.N. Singer (Ed.), *The psychomotor domain: Movement behaviors*. Philadelphia: Lea & Febiger.

SKINNER, J.S., Corbin, C.B., Landers, D.M., Martin, P.E., & Wells, C.L. (Eds.) (1989). *Future directions in exercise and sport science research*. Champaign, IL: Human Kinetics.

SINGER, R.N., Murphey, M., & Tennant, L.K. (Eds.) (in press). *Handbook on research in sport psychology*. New York: Macmillan.

SUINN, R.M. (1985). The 1984 Olympics and sport psychology. *Journal of Sport Psychology*, **7**, 321-329.

New Directions or the Same Old Problem

Susan L. Greendorfer
University of Illinois

Although quite general in nature, the theme "New Possibilities, New Paradigms?" offers the chance to further explore a variety of issues related to the evolving body of knowledge, including the potential of a multidisciplinary field such as ours with respect to the structure of knowledge. Such discussion is not new, as our field is replete with position statements and conceptualizations related to the body of knowledge—the search for a common core, the structure of undergraduate programs, the name of the field, and core-concept identification (Brown, 1967; Corbin, 1990; Newell, 1983, 1989; Thomas, 1985, 1990; Zeigler, 1983)—to mention only a few of our more recent concerns.

Although changing the name of the field to kinesiology is a separate debate in itself, that issue cannot be clearly distinguished from reconceptualization of subject matter. Whether considered independently or in combination, neither issue represents a new debate (Brown, 1967; Metheny, 1965, 1967, 1968; Morehouse, 1965). The name issue extends a familiar philosophical debate that has contributed to disunity in the field for over 90 years. The second issue, how we think about subject matter, also has a familiar ring; it extends the continually debated issue of knowledge structure and objectives. Despite the fact that the name may be slightly different this time around, what is intriguing is the integral relationship between the name of the field and issues related to core-concept identification and subject-matter reconceptualization. Regardless of distinctions made between these issues, however, we should recognize that they both stem from a common source—Cartesian reasoning, or dualistic thinking.

It would seem futile to deny that thinking in terms of mutually exclusive dichotomies, whether real or contrived, has led to a partitioning of knowledge that has mushroomed into some of the more familiar "either-or" debates: mind–body, generalist–specialist, discipline–profession, physical education–sport, teaching–coaching, and bioscience–social science. Unfortunately, this all-too-willing acceptance of a mutually exclusive dichotomous structure of knowledge not only has led to a partitioning of knowledge into the vertical fragmentation represented by the specialized subdisciplines, but it also has created a subtle yet clear hierarchy of knowledge domains that has thus far resisted our attempts at integration (Greendorfer, 1987; Hoffman, 1985; Lawson & Morford, 1979).

Unfortunately, the resultant fragmentation has created another series of debates (Hoffman, 1985; Thomas, 1985), not the least of which involves goals and objectives of curricula (cf., Corbin & Eckert, 1990). Clearly, disagreement about the nature of subject matter leads to a diffuse focus, which in turn creates debate over core concepts. If we fail to agree on subject matter or to arrive at an understanding of underlying concepts, the field's history of debate and disunity will only be extended. In short, we will find ourselves with the same old problem (albeit with a new name) instead of a new direction.

The challenge as well as the foil seem to lie deeply embedded in our recent concerns about reconceptualizing the field. Before going further, however, let me explain what this paper is not. It is not a debate whether to accept the name *kinesiology* or retain the name *physical education*. And despite some superficially critical remarks, it is not an attempt to discredit, devalue, or dismiss conceptual development of core concepts related to subject matter. On the contrary, not only am I supportive of a constructive effort to build a structure of knowledge from a commonly agreed upon set of fundamental concepts, but I also would like to see a broadening as well as shift in focus of current considerations. For this reason, I would like to offer the following caveat: Current attempts at reconceptualization mark only a rudimentary beginning at an enterprise that has lain dormant after being taken seriously some 25 years ago (Brown, 1967; Metheny, 1965, 1968; Zeigler & McCristal, 1967). Therefore, recent efforts should not be viewed as a final or end product. More importantly, to promote inclusion rather than exclusion of conceptual frames of reference, the effort to shape the conceptual substance and content of our knowledge structure must be shared and proportionally representative. As a final note of caution, we need to allow ourselves sufficient time and "hands-on" experience at this enterprise so that we all are able to make the required paradigmatic shift in thinking about subject matter.

In many respects these words of caution could be viewed as a confrontation, because they represent a not-so-subtle challenge to think about our subject matter differently, coupled with a plea to come to grips with a bias that is historically embedded in our knowledge structure. More specifically, this paper challenges the biologistic bias that underlies past as well as present definitions and conceptualizations about subject matter. More simply stated, the time has come to challenge and seriously reevaluate the preeminence given to biological, structural, physiological, mechanical, biochemical, and neuromuscular bases that predominate the micro and macro levels of conceptualizing physical activity and human movement.

To date, our attempts at integration have been feeble, as the knowledge structure seems to characteristically "tack on" factors related to context, social, cognitive, cultural, expressive, and pedagogical processes to the central core of "movement" or physical activity. These efforts representing acknowledgment of alternative knowledge structures are admirable, but they only exacerbate the partitioning and hierarchical knowledge structure that already exists. The time has come to expand our knowledge structure at the core-concept level—to include social, behavioral, expressive, and pedagogical factors in conjunction with biologistic considerations. Before dismissing this challenge as heresy or as something uttered out of sheer ignorance, let's explore this premise a little further.

When we conceptualize fundamental elements of movement or physical activity, we traditionally think of a single (isolated?) individual comprised of cells, tissues, and organs that form a biological structure capable of expending energy to accomplish a motor task involving posture, balance, or a specific motor pattern to project either the body or an object through space. This conceptualization is clearly biologistic, giving precedence to structural, mechanical, neuromuscular, and physiological contingencies. Rarely included as central to the conceptualization or analysis of movement are factors related to presence or absence of others; antecedent factors prior to the task; interpretations, meanings, perceptions, motivations, intentions, and interactions during the task; or contextual factors that shape physical activity or are influenced by physical activity. For the most part, personal, social, and cultural identities, meanings, purposes, or goals related to the movement or its form or style are ignored along with those historical and cultural bases that also influence what goes into the elements of movement. As such, existing conceptualizations of movement and physical activity seem not only exclusionary of pedagogical, social, or expressive components, but through such omission they represent an incomplete conceptualization or definition of our subject matter phenomenon. My argument is simple: A jump is not a jump is not a jump unless components of context such as identity, intention, influence, interaction, and ideology are included in the very definition of *jump* itself!

Although it could be countered that context and environmental contingencies are considered in light of recent formulations of physical activity (Newell, 1983, 1989), typically such contingencies tend to be viewed as constraints to movement somewhat removed from central core notions. For the most part, considerations of ''environment'' are extremely narrow, limited to physical space and laws of gravity. Personal, social, historical, and cultural components of environment are virtually ignored, as evidenced by the fact that with the exception of perspectives taken by those in the social sciences or curriculum, movement and physical activity are treated as having no context, as essentially taking place in a vacuum. By the same token, those of us from the social science and pedagogical end tend to neglect the biological basis of physical activity.

In conceptual terms, however, it appears that only after the basic fundamentals or components of movement have been delineated are other domains considered—specifically, social phenomena typically conceptualized as contexts of physical activity at best and as separate and individual domains far removed from our core concepts at worst. As such, domains of dance, play, games, and sport are viewed in holistic (rather than conceptual) terms and as exclusive and specific subsets of more general forms of human movement and physical activity.

This type of conceptualization is reflective of more traditional orientations that for the most part treat these specific domains as supplemental to core knowledge. Such a partitioning of knowledge tends to give preeminence to the bioscientific basis of physical activity, thereby relegating these other movement domains to second-class status. Moreover, it ignores the contribution that their underlying concepts can make to the fundamental conceptualization of movement and physical activity. Such conceptualization has created a hierarchical knowledge structure, which represents a form of conceptual hypocrisy. Preeminence of biologically based concepts has more than excluded behavioral and expressive concepts of fundamental movement patterns and physical activity, creating the impression that biology is the only or inherent foundation of physical activity. Traditional thinking fails to recognize that without internal context (including cognitions, intentions, learning, and central nervous system impetus, as well as the social and expressive body and physique) and external context (encompassing the social, historical, and cultural, as well as the physical and ecological environment), physical activity and human locomotor forms simply could not take place. The question then is, why are these critical components absent from our basic definitions?

Essentially, three issues have been raised that may need further clarification. First of all, we need to be more cognizant of the underlying biologism that has shaped past and current conceptualizations of our field. Any future attempts made to reconceptualize subject matter should make a concerted effort to remove such bias. One way to remove this primacy is to think of humans engaged in physical activity that emanates from a totality of physical, social, physiological, mechanical, cultural, expressive, and structural forces. The human animal should be conceptualized as a reflective, thinking, social being whose motor skill performance includes learning, meaning, and interpretation.

Second, physical activity is facilitated or constrained as much by meanings, perceptions, and social, psychological, historical, cultural, and pedagogical factors as it is by biochemical, structural physiological, ecological, and neuromuscular factors—and it takes place in the context of all of these. Consequently, it should go without saying that physical activity shapes and is shaped by our interpretations, meanings, expressions, styles, and communicative processes—whether we act alone, in groups, or within institutions, societies, or cultures—as much as it shapes or is shaped by the physiological, biological, mechanical, learning, and coordinative processes that have been called into play to execute such movement.

This leads to the third issue: Any reconceptualization of subject matter is incomplete unless it encompasses integration of concepts at a basic level. The time has come, then, to define our subject matter and core concepts from our multidisciplinary foundations. It is my opinion that integration would be possible without partitioning knowledge and without giving preeminence to any one domain, subdiscipline, or set of concepts (see Figure 1). To achieve this integration, however, we must seek greater representation of concepts at a fundamental level of knowledge from the humanities, social, behavioral, and pedagogical domains.

So the issue is not the name of our field but how we conceptualize its subject matter. The challenge is, how do we become more inclusive instead of exclusive in our conceptualizations; how do we integrate a variety of concepts from multiple inputs; and ultimately, how will we think about our subject matter. In short, how can we incorporate concepts from the social and behavioral sciences, humanities, and pedagogy into the very definition of physical activity itself, instead of treating such concepts as separate addenda or configurations that complement notions emanating from a traditionally biological basis?

If the purpose of a knowledge structure is to make relationships, then some conceptual expansion of theoretical notions seems to be in order. What is needed are some new or different concepts, or new ways to think about existing concepts that traditionally have been treated as peripheral. Of course we could always rediscover our history and more appropriately acknowledge earlier writings by such individuals as Abernathy and Waltz (1964), Brown (1967), Brown and

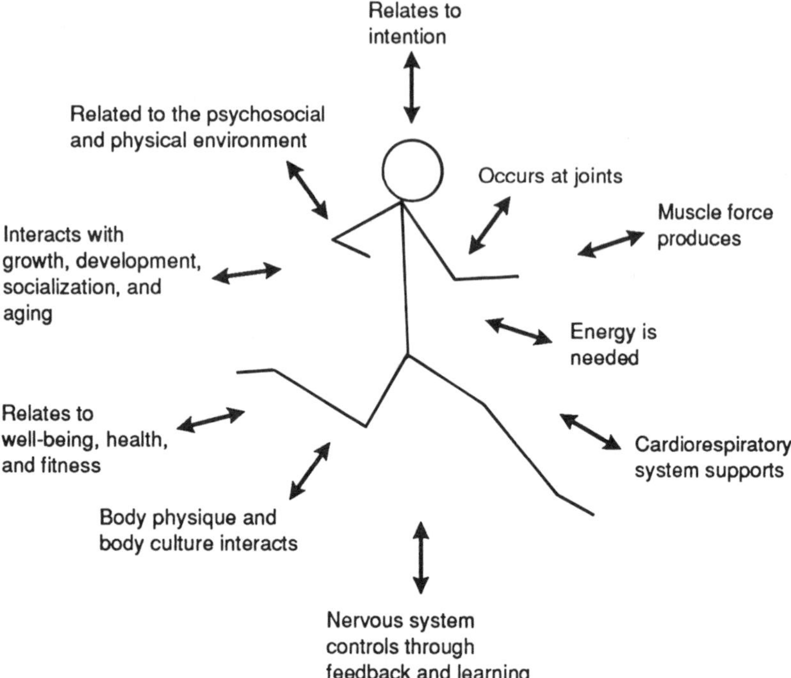

Figure 1 — Involvement in movement. *Note.* The depiction of this figure is an attempt to demonstrate integration and should not be interpreted as a complete representation of core concepts. From *Bioscientific Foundations of Exercise and Sport* (p. 3) by J.B. Teeple and J.E. Misner, 1984, Champaign, IL: Stipes. Copyright 1984 by Stipes Publishing Company. Adapted by permission.

Cassidy (1963), and Metheny (1967), who attempted to deal with expression, aesthetics, and context with respect to concepts of human movement. Perhaps the time has come to dust off this literature and give credit to ideas that once permeated women's physical education.

The notion of context seems to be more than relevant here; it is critical to any conceptualization, because physical activity does not take place in a vacuum. Although some examples in the existing literature have tried to relate aspects of context to physical activity (Brown, 1967), it seems that more recent attempts at the micro level have limited considerations to structural and mechanical features of the body, such as posture (Newell, 1983, 1989), whereas those at the macro level have considered the general social settings in which exercise and sport take place (Harris, 1987). Both approaches represent admirable attempts to include context as a fundamental aspect of physical activity, but neither goes far enough in its attempt to establish context as an overarching link among the biological, psychological, social, and pedagogical components of physical activity. From my perspective, context should be integrated into, instead of separated from, the conceptual foundations of movement and physical activity, not left as a separate concept to be considered by social scientists or teachers and coaches.

As previously suggested, the exclusion of context from theoretical considerations of physical activity and movement may be due in part to the way we have traditionally viewed human potential and capacity for physical activity—from the vantage point of a single individual who exists in a physical environment consisting only of physical space subjected to the force of gravity. Although the failure to consider social, cultural, and historical environments as critical antecedent factors of physical activity represents one shortcoming in previous conceptualizations, I would argue that context represents more than a "mere" external setting. In short, we need to deal with internal as well as external contexts of physical activity. More specifically, cognitive processes involving intention and motivation, personal as well as social identity, personality, perceptions, meanings, and expression could represent dimensions of the internal context that constrains or facilitates physical activity. In fact I would argue that these processes constrain or facilitate physical activity as powerfully as do structure, posture, strength, energy, and skill.

To date, however, such notions have been omitted from any conceptualization of the learner or performer, of the motor task and the interaction between the two. Instead of excluding these notions, our conceptualizations need to become more inclusive and consider the learner (or performer) as more than body structure or physique, cardiorespiratory capacity, neuromuscular status, and physical maturation level. The social construction of the body also should be considered fundamental to physical activity, and notions of power, existing hegemonic definitions of gender, and images and impressions about fitness, health, dominance, identity, and competition should be integral components of our definitions. Self and appearance of the body are not only relational but socially defined and mediated by culture (Desaulniers, 1988). Such notions define our understandings of how the body should look and move; they provide the very means by which we define the body as subject or object (Desaulniers, 1988) and consequently are shaped by as well as shape physical activity meanings, motor skill acquisition, and motor performance. Clearly, then, the vision of the body needs to be expanded beyond notions of a biologically functioning structure coping with forces of inertia and gravity, functioning through sensory motor pathways bridged by synapses and end plates, constrained by features of maturation and growth, body composition, cardiorespiratoration, and physique.

The challenge is to find some way to incorporate all of these notions into conceptualization and analysis of physical activity, because all serve as precursors to and delineators of motor skill acquisition and performance. The trick is to conceptualize our subject matter without further fragmenting it or adding to the existing vertical structure (Greendorfer, 1987). Equally as critical, however, is the necessity to shift our paradigmatic focus to a more broadly based conceptual structure—one more inclusive than the biologistic conceptualization that historically underlies our thinking. An expanded knowledge structure that incorporates identity, intention, influence, ideology, interaction, context, and expression offers the promise of a new direction. Without these integral concepts embedded firmly in our conceptualization of subject matter, we will not have integration; nor will we begin to develop terms, definitions, and concepts that are mutually understood and agreed upon. Without this understanding and agreement, we will continue to partition knowledge. Until we recognize and overcome our biologistic bias, which leads to hierarchical thinking and such partitions, we will not share a common structure of knowledge and will be faced with the same old problem.

References

ABERNATHY, R., & Waltz, M. (1964). Toward a discipline: First steps first. *Quest*, **2**, 1-7.

BROWN, C. (1967). The structure of knowledge of physical education. *Quest*, **9**, 53-67.

BROWN, C., & Cassidy, R. (1963). *Theory in physical education*. Philadelphia: Lea & Febiger.

CORBIN, C.B. (1990). The evolving undergraduate major. In C.B. Corbin & H. Eckert (Eds.), *The Academy Papers: The Evolving Body of Knowledge* (No. 23, pp. 1-4). Champaign, IL: Human Kinetics.

CORBIN, C.B., & Eckert, H.M. (Eds.) (1990). *The Academy Papers: The Evolving Undergraduate Major* (No. 23). Champaign, IL: Human Kinetics.

DESAULNIERS, S. (1988, November). *Sport and the social construction of the gendered body*. Paper presented at the annual meeting of the North American Society for the Sociology of Sport, Cincinnati, OH.

GREENDORFER, S.L. (1987). Specialization, fragmentation, integration, discipline, profession: What is the real issue? *Quest*, **39**(1), 56-64.

HARRIS, J.C. (1987, April). *Social contexts, scholarly inquiry, and physical education*. Paper presented at the NASPE Symposium "Science, Inquiry and Progress: The Future of Physical Education," National Convention of the American Alliance for Health, Physical Education, Recreation and Dance, Las Vegas, NV.

HOFFMAN, S.J. (1985, August). Specialization + fragmentation = extermination: A formula for the demise of graduate education. *Journal of Physical Education, Recreation and Dance*, **56**(6), 19-21.

LAWSON, H., & Morford, W.R. (1979). The cross-disciplinary structure of kinesiology and sports studies: Distinctions, implications and advantages. *Quest*, **31**, 222-230.

METHENY, E. (1965). *Connotations of movement in sport and dance*. Dubuque, IA: Brown.

METHENY, E. (1967). Physical education as an area of study and research. *Quest*, **9**, 73-78.

METHENY, E. (1968). *Movement and meaning*. New York: McGraw-Hill.

MOREHOUSE, L.E. (1965). *A concept of kinesiology and physical education as academic disciplines*. Position paper commissioned by the School of Education at Northwestern University, Chicago.

NEWELL, K.M. (1983). *The department of kinesiology at UIUC: Preliminary proposal*. Unpublished manuscript, University of Illinois, Urbana-Champaign, IL.

NEWELL, K.M. (1989). *Kinesiology: Activity focus, knowledge, types and degree programs*. Unpublished manuscript, University of Illinois, Urbana-Champaign, IL.

THOMAS, J.R. (1985). Are we already in pieces, or just falling apart? *Quest*, **39**(2), 114-121.

THOMAS, J.R. (1990). The body of knowledge: A common core. In C.B. Corbin & H. Eckert (Eds.), *The Academy Papers: The Evolving Body of Knowledge* (No. 23, pp. 5-12). Champaign, IL: Human Kinetics.

ZEIGLER, E.F. (1983). Relating a proposed taxonomy of sport and developmental physical activity to a planned inventory of scientific findings. *Quest*, **35**, 54-65.

ZEIGLER, E.F., & McCristal, K.J. (1967). A history of the Big Ten Body-of-Knowledge Project in physical education. *Quest*, **9**, 79-84.

Teacher Education: Types of Questions and Some Research Answers

Daryl Siedentop
The Ohio State University

It is appropriate that our distinguished president-elect from Berkeley should have arranged the focus for these meetings. A revolution important to our recent history emanated partially from that campus, and although it is too early to tell, another revolution might be forecast from recent postures taken by Berkeley's education school. Two professors from Berkeley published an important book (Clifford & Guthrie, 1988) describing the nearly fatal history of education schools and colleges that have distanced themselves from their professional missions and put the professional constituencies they supposedly served at arm's length to behave in ways that gained acceptance by their arts and science colleagues within the university. Harry Judge (1982) had made a similar analysis in an earlier report, reaching a similar conclusion, namely that education schools, by this behavior, had left themselves isolated from their professional missions and, despite their scientific posturing, largely unaccepted as a mainstream academic unit in research universities. As a reaction to this counterproductive history, Berkeley's dean of education suggested a new motto for education schools, one that would identify clearly their mission and serve to redirect their resources to accomplish that mission—Practice-Oriented Research and Research-Oriented Practice.

Practice-Oriented Research

Practice-oriented research is often misunderstood as focusing on questions raised by practitioners. Practitioner questions are legitimate sources for research, but the questions raised by the systematic study of practice form the main agenda of practice-oriented research. Research programs that focus on questions raised through the systematic study of professional practice are neither theory-oriented nor theory-driven, although in answering them it is not unusual that theories or models are induced. Practice-oriented research exists to improve professional practice, which implies that there are external, professional criteria by which the value of results should be judged once they have satisfied normal research criteria for significance.

My purpose today is to show how practice-oriented research requires multiple research perspectives and an integrative use of conceptual, methodological, and analytic tools from sometimes diverse research traditions. Practice-oriented research needs to have strong ecological validity, which requires that identified problems become dependent variables and that the problems be studied in the places where they occur, under no more experimental control than is necessary and with subjects that represent a fair sample of the population for which the problem is relevant. Results from such research must achieve significance in the standard probabilistic sense despite the noise that results from the study of dependent variables in natural settings, and they must also achieve social significance in ways that typically respond to cost–benefit criteria.

I would like to describe this notion of practice-oriented research by two examples from our research program, highlighting the multiple research perspectives used to answer the questions. The first example is what I view as a microproblem in teaching, that of doing accurate skill analysis as a prerequisite to providing effective skill feedback for learners; the second example is a macroproblem, that of providing teachers with a framework that allows them to interpret the often complex behavioral dynamics of the classes they teach.

Example 1: Skill Analysis

Descriptive research on teaching physical education has shown for some time that rates of specific skill feedback from teacher to student are quite low—alarmingly so, considering the importance attached to specific feedback in the learning and teaching literatures. More recent research, focusing on the types of learning tasks teachers direct their students to engage in, has shown that teachers seldom use what Rink (1985) calls refining tasks, those kinds of learning activities through which students gradually improve the technical characteristics of the skills they are learning. Refining tasks focus on the qualitative improvement of the critical performance elements of motor skills, before the activity is changed slightly and gradually made more complex through what Rink calls extending tasks. Through the cyclical progression of refining and extending tasks, performance improves.

The problem identified through the study of teaching is that specific skill feedback and refining tasks are typically not present in sufficient quantity to reasonably expect improved technical performance of motor skills. Why are these important dimensions of the skill-acquisition setting present only in meager quantities? One good guess seems to be that teachers do not know enough about the critical technical elements of the skills they teach. They don't know what the critical technical elements are and cannot discriminate the presence or absence of these elements in the performances of their students. Put practically, if teachers do not know the four or five technical elements to success for novice learners in the one-hand basketball shot or jump shot, then they can neither provide accurate skill feedback about those elements nor design a series of refining tasks to help students gradually improve those technical elements of shooting.

This is what I call a practice-oriented problem, one defined by the study of teaching practice in schools. The research that derives from the problem is fairly straightforward: how to prepare teachers so they know the critical technical elements of skills they teach and can reliably discriminate the presence and absence of these technical elements in student performance, as it happens, without the aid of technology. There are several research programs in sport pedagogy now investigating this problem, doing what in our programs we call skill analysis research. Our effort has concentrated on a series of related studies that have focused on cost-effective ways for undergraduates to acquire the appropriate discriminative skills.

Conceptually and methodologically we have borrowed from a number of research traditions. Because we have defined the problem primarily as inadequate discriminatory capabilities, the main thrust of our training research has borrowed heavily from the discrimination-training literature in experimental psychology and the concept-formation literature in instructional design and technology. We develop training programs with easily discriminated positive and negative examples of the critical elements, and gradually reduce the differences so that the appropriate discrimination can be learned. We train with sufficient exemplars to reduce the chances of over- or undergeneralization. We might utilize stop-action or slow motion in video training protocols, but the criterion test for heaving acquired the discrimination is typically a full-speed performance from one angle, and often live rather than from tape. Our training programs have borrowed heavily from the applied behavior analysis literature on self-paced instruction, particularly the literature under the Keller model, or PSI (Siedentop, 1975). The experimental designs used to investigate these training programs have been the multiple-probe, multiple-baseline designs from the experimental analysis of behavior (Cooper, Heward, & Heron, 1987).

The training research has been quite successful, mostly, I suspect, because of the strong instructional alignment among training goals, training processes, and testing. The instructional-alignment research literature suggests that well-aligned training programs typically yield performance increments that are 1.5 to 3.0 standard deviations better than standard instruction (Cohen, 1987). What we have learned is as straightforward as the research problem: If you train students to discriminate the critical elements of sport skills, they can do so; but if you do not train them specifically to acquire those discriminations, they will not do so, whether through experience in the sport activity itself or through other, more general means such as courses in kinesiology or biomechanics (Halverson, 1987; Kniffen, 1985; Morton, 1989; Wilkinson, 1986).

So far we have focused on sport-specific skill analysis, simply because there was little support in the literature for the notion that students could be trained to know principles and then apply them accurately. One of our doctoral students is now investigating a program that focuses on elements critical to force production in a number of sport skills. The benefit of such an approach, if it works, is in its cost efficiency. We are also beginning to investigate the extension of skill analysis to skill diagnosis and skill prescriptions, but the training of diagnostic and prescriptive capabilities is substantially more complex and requires skill analysis as a prerequisite anyway.

The skill analysis example is about as micro as practice-oriented research can afford to be—it focuses on a single teaching skill, that of accurately discriminating the presence or absence of critical performance elements as they occur in student performance. To be fully useful in practice (that is, to begin to make some real difference in the effectiveness of a learning setting), skill analysis would have to be used in concert with a broader repertoire of effective teaching skills.

Example 2: The Ecology of Physical Education

A second example moves from a reasonably discrete teaching skill to a more global understanding of the behavioral dynamics of classes. Research has shown that teachers are often influenced dramatically by their students. It has been clear for some time that no understanding of class dynamics can be even partially complete if it ignores the dual-directional influences between teachers and their students. The reform literature in both teaching and teacher education agrees on the need for teachers to be more reflective in their practice. Reflection, however, typically occurs within some framework or model and when done without such an aid tends to be haphazard, lacking particularly in the ability to make connections among events that, on the surface, may appear not to be related.

The model we are investigating in this more global perspective is the ecological paradigm first articulated in education by Walter Doyle (1979). Doyle developed the model from a number of different perspectives, among them information processing theory, cognitive theory, and ecological psychology. Methodologically, Doyle's research has been almost exclusively ethnographic.

Our investigations have focused on understanding better the interactive influences among three task systems in physical education teaching—the managerial, instructional, and student-social systems. We have tried to sort out how changes in one system affect the other systems, and how the three systems come together to form the behavioral ecology of the gymnasium. Our initial investigations (Tinning & Siedentop, 1985; Tousignant & Siedentop, 1983) were ethnographic, because we needed to find out the degree to which the Doyle model fit the dynamics of teaching physical education, and qualitative methodologies have been particularly useful for seeing the forest, even though I believe them to be less useful for clearly analyzing the many habitats that together form the forest.

We needed to ascertain the degree to which Doyle's key findings were replicated in physical education settings, particularly the dynamics through which students negotiate with their teachers to reduce the ambiguity of instructional tasks and to reduce the risks associated with completing those tasks, at least to the point where the risks fall within some acceptable range. Doyle had shown how accountability drove task systems, but we knew that accountability systems in physical education, whatever their forms, differed from the typical grade-exchange systems (quizzes, themes, homework, etc.) that operate in classrooms.

In our first study (Tousignant & Siedentop, 1983) it became clear that although the model did fit, there were important differences in the ecologies of the classroom and gymnasium. The managerial and instructional task systems that Doyle had described were clearly apparent in physical education, as was a student-social system that Doyle had either ignored or underestimated. Physical education students did engage in task negotiations, not by asking questions as in classrooms, but instead by modifying the instructional tasks as they engaged in practice. How the teacher responded to these modified instructional tasks eventually determined what the actual task became. If the teacher supervised practice effectively, responding quickly to task modifications, then the boundaries of the instructional task system stayed near to the tasks as originally described. If, however, the teacher supervised poorly or chose not to respond to task modifications, then students quickly learned that the boundaries of the instructional system were flexible and could be negotiated easily without undue risks. In such cases students routinely modified tasks for many reasons—to make them more challenging, to achieve greater success, to make them easier, or to hide social participation. Some clever students, whom we called *competent bystanders*, managed to avoid nearly all contact with the instructional task system, while always staying completely within the boundaries of the managerial task system.

Our research (Jones, 1989; Marks, 1988; Son, 1989) has also revealed that managerial tasks are typically better taught and enforced than are instructional tasks—and that teachers tacitly (and sometimes overtly) trade reduced demands in the instructional task system for increased cooperation in the managerial system. The student-social system is nearly always present. In some classes we have observed, teachers have allowed the instructional task system to become dominated by student-social tasks, and what follows is best described as supervised recreation. In more effective classes, we have seen teachers cleverly integrate student-social tasks with the instructional tasks in ways that are quite similar to the manner in which sport and fitness participation among adults is accompanied by a strong social element.

Our more recent research has utilized systematic observation, focusing particularly on the instructional task system. We typically judge both the nature of the task instructions and the quality and quantity of responding by more and less skilled students, with the goal of understanding how student response rates are affected by variables such as clarity of presentation, supervision practices, and accountability mechanisms.

This low-inference, systematic-observation methodology is far different from the ethnographic approach with which we began the research program. It is different because we now seek to understand the dynamics of these interrelated systems in a much more specific way. Data sets from these more recent studies provide highly specific maps of the instructional tasks in a unit and the quality and quantity of student response relative to those tasks. Hopefully, we will soon understand more about how response rates and quality of responding are related to task specification, task supervision, and informal accountability mechanisms. This set of lenses not only helps teachers and student-teachers understand more clearly why students behave as they do in class, but more importantly, it also allows them to plan and teach in ways that produce a learning-oriented ecology in their classes.

These, then, are two examples of practice-oriented research. Putting these results to use in a teacher education program represents research-oriented practice of one kind. Putting them to use in the actual practice of teaching physical education represents the final outcome of this process.

The range of conceptual, methodological, and analytic tools needed to investigate these practice-oriented research questions is quite large. It is my experience that practice-oriented research requires this kind of methodological expansiveness, that it requires the bringing together of seemingly diverse conceptual and analytic approaches. As such, I would argue, research rooted in questions derived from the study of practices such as teaching or sport must necessarily be integrative.

References

CLIFFORD, G.J., & Guthrie, J.W. (1988). *Ed school.* Chicago: University of Chicago Press.

COHEN, S.A. (1987). Instructional alignment: Searching for a magic bullet. *Educational Researcher*, **16**(8), 16-20.

COOPER, J., Heward, W., & Heron, T. (1987). *Applied behavior analysis*. Columbus, OH: Merrill.

DOYLE, W. (1979). Classroom tasks and students' abilities. In P. Peterson & H. Walberg (Eds.), *Research on teaching* (pp. 183-209). Berkeley, CA: McCutchan.

HALVERSON, P. (1987). *The effects of peer tutoring on sport skill analytic ability*. Unpublished doctoral dissertation, The Ohio State University, Columbus.

JONES, D. (1989). *Analysis of task structures in elementary physical education*. Unpublished doctoral dissertation, The Ohio State University, Columbus.

JUDGE, H. (1982). *American graduate schools of education: A view from abroad*. New York: Ford Foundation.

KNIFFEN, M. (1985). *The effects of individualized videotape instruction on the ability of undergraduate physical education majors to analyze selected sport skills*. Unpublished doctoral dissertation, The Ohio State University, Columbus.

MARKS, M. (1988). *Development of a system for the observation of task structures in physical education*. Unpublished doctoral dissertation, The Ohio State University, Columbus.

MORTON, P. (1989). *Effects of training in skill analysis on generalization across age levels*. Unpublished doctoral dissertation, The Ohio State University, Columbus.

RINK, J. (1985). *Teaching physical education for learning*. St. Louis: Times Mirror/ Mosby.

SIEDENTOP, D. (1974). How to use personalized systems of instruction in college teaching. In L.L. Gedvilas (Ed.), *NCPEAM-NAPECW proceedings* (pp. 116-125). Chicago: National College Physical Education Association for Men.

SON, C.T. (1989). *Descriptive analysis of task congruence in Korean middle school physical education classes*. Unpublished doctoral dissertation, The Ohio State University, Columbus.

TINNING, R., & Siedentop, D. (1985). The characteristics of tasks and accountability in student teaching. *Journal of Teaching in Physical Education*, **4**(4), 286-299.

TOUSIGNANT, M., & Siedentop, D. (1983). A qualitative analysis of task structures in required secondary physical education classes. *Journal of Teaching in Physical Education*, **3**(1), 47-57.

WILKINSON, S. (1986). *The effects of a visual discrimination training program on the acquisition and maintenance of physical education students' volleyball skill analytic ability*. Unpublished doctoral dissertation, The Ohio State University, Columbus.

Health and Fitness Through Physical Education: Research Directions for the 1990s

Russell R. Pate
University of South Carolina

Enhancement of physical fitness and promotion of health have been stated objectives of physical education since the inception of the profession. The presumed effects of physical education on health and fitness are often used as ammunition in battles to defend school-based physical education programs. Such battles have sometimes been successful, but often they have not. It seems clear that, in most school settings, support for physical education has either stayed the same or decreased in recent decades. Pleas for daily physical education have fallen on deaf ears, and the unfortunate truth is that efforts to reverse the slow trend toward decreased allotment of time to physical education have failed.

How could this happen? How could society reduce its support for physical education at the same time that it is experiencing an adult fitness revolution? How could parents, who seem to care increasingly about their own health and fitness, choose to invest less in an educational process that is designed to promote health and fitness in their children? How could a society that clearly has the highest of hopes for its children fail to provide them with school programs intended to make them healthier and hardier?

In answering these questions I hope not to seem glib or simplistic. Certainly complete answers to these questions are complex. However, with those disclaimers stated, I aim to be direct. I believe that society's support for physical education has waned because it is by no means clear that physical education programs attain the health objectives that are seen by society as critical. Physical educators, when cornered, often resurrect the old arguments about promotion of fitness and health. These arguments sometimes sound good, but under scrutiny they prove to be lacking in substance. The truth is that at present we know a lot about the health and fitness effects of *exercise* (mainly in adults) and almost nothing about the health and fitness effects of *physical education*. I believe that it is not overstated to claim that the future of physical education may depend on an expansion of our knowledge of the effects of physical education (and various components thereof) on the short- and long-term health of students. The purpose of this paper is to present some of my ideas of the relevant research issues that should be addressed in the 1990s.

A Philosophical Position

A research program should lead to the creation of a meaningful, relevant, and coherent body of knowledge. Accordingly, before presenting some specific research ideas that I think are important, I feel compelled to set the stage by briefly describing the philosophical position from which I operate. The key element in my professional philosophy can be stated concisely: I believe that physical education should be viewed as a component of public health education and that it should exist primarily for the purpose of promoting health. It is important to note that I define *health* broadly to include health-related physical fitness and enjoyable, worthy use of leisure time, as well as the traditional absence of disease. Also, I wish to point out that I believe that our major goal should be promotion of lifelong health, not just health during childhood. I have adopted this position for five basic reasons.

1. Health is important—it is critical to the survival and advancement of our society.
2. Health is seen by our society as important and as worthy of a considerable investment of resources.
3. Physical activity is a well-documented and well-recognized component of a healthy lifestyle.
4. It seems likely that childhood experiences with physical activity have an important impact on lifelong physical activity behavior.
5. School-based physical education is a significant component of a child's overall physical activity experience and may represent society's best opportunity to provide youngsters with appropriate physical activity experiences.

So, I believe that physical educators should see themselves as being in the business of promoting lifelong health through physical activity. To the extent that acquisition of motor skills, experience with sporting activities, and short-term gains in fitness may contribute to adoption of a physically active lifestyle, they would be useful. However, I see these traditional objectives as germane only if they in fact contribute to the major goal—regular participation in moderate to vigorous physical activity in adulthood. Proficiency in motor skills, participation in youth sports, and high fitness as a youngster are of dubious value if the individual does not choose to be active as an adult. More detailed discussions of this position appear elsewhere (Pate, 1978; Simons-Morton, O'Hara, Simons-Morton, & Parcel, 1988; Simons-Morton, Parcel, O'Hara, Blair, & Pate, 1988). The research areas discussed in the following passages are those that I feel must be addressed if we are to optimize the effect of physical education on lifelong health and fitness.

Determinants of Adult Physical Activity Behavior

The key element in my philosophy of physical education is adult physical activity behavior, so I feel strongly that we must learn as much as possible about why some adults are physically active and others are sedentary. In recent years considerable attention has been given to this issue, and several excellent review articles have been published (Dishman, 1986; Dishman, Sallis, & Orenstein, 1985). Without exception the authors of these reviews have noted that our knowledge of the determinants of exercise behavior in *free-living* adults is very limited. Future research must, I feel, provide us with a clear and comprehensive picture of why some people choose to be active. In particular, we must learn much more about the effects of various childhood factors on subsequent adult exercise behavior. A few previous studies have attempted to examine this issue (Clarke, 1973; The Perrier Study, 1979), but at present we know very little about the relationship between childhood experiences and adult exercise behavior. In my view, key childhood variables include parental and older sibling behavior, parent–child activity interactions, organized youth-sport experiences, other structured activity experiences (e.g., private lessons, YMCA participation), peer group behavior, and quality and quantity of physical education. Also, personal childhood characteristics such as fitness, developmental status, body size, and motor skill level seem worthy of investigation as possible predictors of future adult activity behavior.

Ideally, investigations of the association between childhood characteristics and adult activity behavior would employ prospective longitudinal epidemiological designs. However, application of such designs would be quite costly, given the large number of subjects and lengthy follow-up period that would be required. Retrospective designs are less desirable, because long-term recall of childhood experiences and status may be unreliable. However, the retrospective design is much less costly than the prospective design and therefore will probably be the method of choice for preliminary studies.

Fitness Status of American Children

Large-scale surveys of fitness status of American youth have been conducted at regular intervals for over 30 years. Until recent years these surveys employed test batteries that emphasized motor performance components such as speed, power, and agility (Reiff et al., 1985). However, in the 1980s the two-phased National Children and Youth Fitness Study (Ross & Gilbert, 1985; Ross & Pate, 1987) employed measures of health-related fitness in national random-sample surveys of American youngsters aged 6 to 10 years. As a result of this study we have a good sense of the *absolute* health-fitness level of the typical American child. Unfortunately, we are very limited in our capacity to interpret and evaluate these absolute fitness levels.

There are several key questions. Are American children as fit as they should be, for both short- and long-term health purposes? Are American children more or less fit than children of previous decades? How do the fitness levels of American youngsters compare with those of children in other societies, and how do they vary across segments of our own society? Regrettably, at the present time we have, at best, limited knowledge of these issues. Yet it seems critical that we find answers to these questions, because, collectively, they will answer the big question: Are American children as fit as they ought to be?

In my estimation, we will not arrive at a definitive answer to this question (or to the component questions) in the near future. At present we are simply too far from accumulating the ideal body of knowledge upon which to base the answers. We are only beginning to understand the associations among physical activity, fitness, and health in childhood, and currently we know very little about the relationships between childhood activity and fitness and adult health (Blair, Clark, Cureton, & Powell, 1989). Without knowledge of these associations we will only be able to guess at the fitness standards children should attain for health purposes. An entire array of small-group experimental and large-group epidemiological studies are needed.

Cross-cultural studies of youth fitness could be conducted if sufficient funding were available. However, to date carefully standardized comparative studies have not been undertaken, and as a consequence we are currently very limited in our capacity to compare American youth with those in other countries (Pate & Shephard, 1989). Furthermore, a comprehensive health-fitness comparison of contemporary American youth with those of previous generations is not possible. Earlier surveys used test batteries that emphasized motor performance, not health-related fitness. An exception is in the area of body composition, where some skinfold-thickness data indicate that children are fatter than they used to be (Gortmaker, Dietz, Sobol, & Weber, 1987; Ross & Pate, 1987). In my view, health fitness should be monitored in our population just as we track changes in height, weight, blood pressure, serum cholesterol concentration, and alcohol consumption. It is hoped that surveys like NCYFS will be replicated in future decades and that an effort will be made to maintain consistency in procedures.

Fitness Testing Issues

Although there is merit in maintaining consistent approaches to fitness measurement, I believe strongly that testing procedures should be modified in accordance with emerging research findings. Failure to change in response to new knowledge produces discord and confusion like that experienced in the fitness testing field during the decade between 1975 and 1985. Because fitness testing is a very common practice in school physical fitness programs, I believe that we should be striving to learn the best ways to conduct fitness tests.

The transition from motor performance testing to health-related fitness testing became nearly complete in the late 1980s with the adoption of new test batteries by AAHPERD (1988), the Institute for Aerobics Research (1987), the President's Council on Physical Fitness and Sports (1987), and other organizations (American Health and Fitness Foundation, 1986; Chrysler Fund–Amateur Athletic Union, 1987; Franks, 1989). All these batteries include test items that are thought to measure the components of health fitness (Pate, 1978). But which components are really health related? It seems clear that body composition and cardiorespiratory endurance are associated with important health outcomes (Bouchard, Shephard, Stephens, Sutton, & MacPherson, 1990), but the evidence linking upper body strength, abdominal strength, and low back/hamstring flexibility with health is much less compelling (Bouchard et al., 1990). A regular reexamination of the presumed health-related components of fitness should be conducted at least every 5 years for the foreseeable future.

Likewise, our techniques for measurement of the health-fitness components are based on far less than the ideal research base. The common measures are known to be reliable, but relatively little is known about their validity (Safrit,

1990; Safrit & Wood, 1987). This deficiency is particularly problematic when the tests are used with children, who have been used rather infrequently as subjects in validity studies. Validity studies in youngsters are entirely feasible, but few have been undertaken to date.

Given the high prevalence of fitness testing in the schools, it seems important that we know the effects of this process on youngsters. There are several relevant questions. Does participation in a fitness test motivate youngsters to improve their fitness? Do children acquire knowledge about fitness through participation in fitness tests? Is the testing process enjoyable for youngsters? From a pedagogical standpoint, what is the optimal approach to administration of fitness tests? Are award systems productive or counterproductive? To date scant research had addressed these questions, and this deficiency must be overcome. In many physical education programs fitness testing constitutes a component of the curriculum to which much time, energy, and expense is allocated. This expenditure of resources may be warranted, but at present we know little about the cost–benefit ratio for fitness testing programs.

Effects of Physical Education on Physical Activity and Fitness

The statements I make in this section of the paper will probably not make me any friends. However, I would ask the reader to keep in mind that I apply the indictments that follow to myself as well as to others in the physical education research community. As was noted in the introduction to this paper, I believe that we know very little about the effects of physical education. We do know a lot about the effects of acute exercise. We have learned a great deal about techniques for motor skill instruction. We know something about the adaptations to exercise training in youngsters. Truly, there is much that we do know about exercise, physical activity, and sport participation in youngsters, and this has been catalogued in many sources (Bar-Or, 1983; Rowland, 1990; Seefeldt, 1986). But I feel that we must acknowledge that we have tiptoed around the question that is the most important for those who care about physical education: Does professionally delivered, school-based physical education enhance the quality of life of the students to whom it is delivered?

The excellent and extensive review article by Vogel (1986) demonstrates very clearly that the potential effects of physical education on physical fitness and related outcomes have not been ignored by researchers in our field. In that paper Vogel cites 30 primary research articles in which the effects of physical education on various outcome measures were studied. In almost all cases the cited studies employed a research design in which a modified approach to physical education was compared with a normal or control physical education program. Based on his review of these studies, Vogel concludes that there is evidence that participation in physical education can influence body composition, flexibility, health variables such as blood lipids and blood pressure, and how children feel about physical activity and health fitness. Further, he concludes that there is convincing evidence that participation in physical education can influence student physical activity levels, aerobic fitness, muscular endurance, muscular strength, and knowledge related to healthy lifestyles.

So, if the evidence referred to by Vogel exists, how can I conclude that we know very little about the effects of physical education? My conclusion is based on the view that the existing research base, though moderately voluminous, *in toto* is markedly weakened by three major limitations. First, as noted above, most of the relevant studies employed a design in which a modified physical education program was compared with a standard one. Of course, this design has its attractive elements, but it also has its problems. The major concern is that this design helps us learn about what physical education *could* accomplish if it were implemented as it was in a particular study. But such designs tell us little about what physical education accomplishes when it is implemented in the normal (and much more prevalent) fashion. A second problem relates to the overall quality of the completed research in this area. In concluding his review paper, Vogel states: "The discouraging aspects of the review are the inferior scientific quality of the studies that have investigated the association between physical education programs and their outcomes." I concur with this conclusion, but I hasten to add that those investigators who have worked in this area are to be commended for their efforts to study very complex issues with, usually, very limited resources.

Third, I am struck by the fact we have directed so little attention to studying the effects of physical education as it currently exists in this country. Most of us probably feel that existing physical education programs are lacking in both quality and quantity, but the fact is that the taxpayers of America make an enormous annual investment in school physical education. Is this money well spent? I do not think that we know, because we have never systematically studied the outcomes of the various types of programs that currently exist. In my view, major studies employing epidemiological designs are required.

It is my sense that at least three types of epidemiological studies are needed. Initially, cross-sectional studies in youngsters who are and have been enrolled in various kinds of existing physical education programs should be compared in terms of fitness, health, motor performance, and other variables. Of course, potential confounding variables should be controlled in this design. Second, prospective studies should be performed for the purpose of tracking changes in fitness, health, motor performance, and other variables in youngsters enrolled in various types of physical education programs. Third, the long-term effects of physical education should be examined by studying adults who as youngsters participated in various types of physical education programs. This would probably necessitate retrospective reporting of physical education experiences, a procedure that clearly has its limitations. The ideal would be a long-term prospective study that tracks youngsters into adulthood and examines the relationships among physical education experiences and adult exercise behavior, fitness, health, and other outcomes. This latter approach would, of course, be quite costly.

Summary

Physical education is an institution in American schools, and nationally, vast sums of money are expended annually to support it. I do not predict that support for physical education will fade away or even be markedly curtailed in the foreseeable future. However, I do believe that there is a risk that our nation's investment in physical education may be gradually reduced over the coming decades. In my view, that would be tragic, because it would mean that a wonderful opportunity will have been lost.

The solution, I feel, lies in an expanded body of knowledge concerning the effects of physical education on health and fitness. Physical education should be in the schools only if it works. It is my sense that society would be satisfied that physical education works if it could be demonstrated that at least certain types of physical education provide students with valuable short- and, most importantly, long-term benefits with regard to health and fitness. This paper constitutes an effort to outline some of the types of research that will be needed to establish the efficacy of physical education as a truly important public-health promotion strategy.

References

AMERICAN Alliance for Health, Physical Education, Recreation and Dance. (1988). *The AAHPERD Physical Test Program*. Reston, VA: Author.

AMERICAN Health and Fitness Foundation. (1986). *Fit Youth Today*. Austin, TX: Author.

BAR-OR, O. (1983). *Pediatric sports medicine for the practitioner*. New York: Springer-Verlag.

BLAIR, S.N., Clark, D.G., Cureton, K.J., & Powell, K.E. (1989). Exercise and fitness in childhood: Implications for a lifetime of health. In C.V. Gisolfi & D.R. Lamb (Eds.), *Perspectives in exercise science and sports medicine. Volume 2, youth, exercise, and sport* (pp. 401-430). Indianapolis: Benchmark Press.

BOUCHARD, C., Shephard, R.J., Stephens, T., Sutton, J.R., & MacPherson, B.O. (1990). *Exercise, fitness and health*. Champaign, IL: Human Kinetics.

CHRYSLER Fund–Amateur Athletic Union. (1987). *Physical Fitness Program*. Bloomington, IN: Author.

CLARKE, H.H. (Ed.) (1973, May). National adult physical fitness survey. *President's Council on Physical Fitness and Sports Newsletter*, pp. 1-27.

DISHMAN, R.K. (Ed.) (1986). *Exercise adherence: Its impact on public health*. Champaign, IL: Human Kinetics.

DISHMAN, R.K., Sallis, J.F., & Orenstein, D.R. (1985). The determinants of physical activity and exercise. *Public Health Reports*, **100**, 158-171.

FRANKS, B.D. (1989). *YMCA youth fitness test manual*. Champaign, IL: Human Kinetics.

GORTMAKER, S.L., Dietz, W.H., Sobol, A.M., & Weber, C.A. (1987). Increasing pediatric obesity in the U.S. *American Journal of Diseases in Children*, **14**, 535-540.

INSTITUTE for Aerobics Research. (1987). *FITNESSGRAM user's manual*. Dallas, TX: Author.

PATE, R.R. (1978). A new definition in youth fitness. *The Physician and Sportsmedicine*, **11**, 77-83.

PATE, R.R., Corbin, C.B., Simons-Morton, B.G., & Ross, J.G. (1987). School physical education. *Journal of School Health*, **57**, 445-450.

PATE, R.R., & Shephard, R.J. (1989). Characteristics of physical fitness in youth. In C.V. Gisolfi & D.R. Lamb (Eds.), *Perspectives in exercise science and sports medicine. Vol. 2, youth, exercise, and sport* (pp. 1-45). Indianapolis: Benchmark Press.

THE Perrier Study: Fitness in America. (1979). New York: Author.

PRESIDENT'S Council on Physical Fitness and Sports. (1987). *The president's physical fitness award program*. Washington, DC: Author.

REIFF, G.G., Dixon, W.R., Jacoby, D., Ye, G.X., Spain, C.G., & Hunsicker, P.A. (1985). *National school population fitness survey*. Washington, DC: President's Council on Physical Fitness and Sports.

ROSS, J.G., & Gilbert, G.G. (1985). The national children and youth fitness study: A summary of findings. *Journal of Physical Education and Recreation*, **56**, 45-50.

ROSS, J.G., & Pate, R.R. (1987). The national children and youth fitness study II: A summary of findings. *Journal of Physical Education and Recreation*, **58**, 51-56.

ROWLAND, T.W. (1990). *Exercise and children's health*. Champaign, IL: Human Kinetics.

SAFRIT, M.J. (1990). The validity and reliability of fitness tests for children: A review. *Pediatric Exercise Science*, **2**, 9-28.

SAFRIT, M.J., & Wood, T.M. (1987). The test battery reliability of the health-related physical fitness test. *Research Quarterly for Exercise and Sport*, **58**, 160-167.

SEEFELDT, V. (Ed.) (1986). *Physical activity and well-being*. Reston, VA: American Alliance for Health, Physical Education, Recreation and Dance.

SIMONS-MORTON, B.G., O'Hara, N.M., Simons-Morton, D.G., & Parcel, G.S. (1988). Children and fitness: A public health perspective. *Research Quarterly for Exercise and Sport*, **58**, 295-302.

SIMONS-MORTON, B.G., Parcel, G.S., O'Hara, N.M., Clair, S.N., & Pate, R.R. (1988). Health-related physical fitness in childhood: Status and recommendations. *Annual Review of Public Health*, **9**, 403-425.

VOGEL, P. (1986). Effects of physical education programs on children. In V. Seefeldt (Ed.), *Physical activity and well-being* (pp. 455-509). Reston, VA: American Alliance for Health, Physical Education, Recreation and Dance.

Science, Social Science, and the "Hunger for Wonders" in Physical Education: Moving Toward a Future Healthy Society

Patricia Vertinsky
University of British Columbia

The relationship between a profession and science, said Walter Kroll (1971, p. 133), is complex, for the dynamics are fueled by shifting market demands and the ability of science to inform and be molded by the professional response to those demands. If a science is important to society, it is drawn into a profession (as in psychology). If a profession is important to society, it is drawn into a science (as in medicine). Physical education, like medicine, has been pressed by society's needs to give birth to a scientific discipline, and both professions have flourished or floundered based in large part on their ability to satisfy market forces derived from changing conceptions of health and the body.

In turn, the ability of the physical education profession to cope with shifting market demands has rested upon the involvement of and relative balance between the contributions of the biological and the social sciences to the formation of its scientific discipline. It is my intention, therefore, to illustrate how changing market forces and opportunities for the profession to regulate the supply and demand for its services in the health-promotion field have partially molded the links among physical education, the sciences, and the social sciences, creating a professional, and consequently a disciplinary, life cycle that is about to return, in some respects at least, to its late-19th-century origins (Park, 1989a).[1]

At the same time, I want to address how the context from which demands for professional services arose has undergone significant transformations that must be dealt with by strategies not contemplated by the founding members of the profession. Changing demographic trends in North America show that a population that is becoming older, more heterogeneous, disproportionately fe-

[1]Clearly other important facets of the demands for physical education services, such as coaching and sport administration, also influenced the disciplinary life cycle. This paper, however, focuses attention upon changing health-related demands and professional opportunities.

male, and, by some current norms, healthy and vigorous, will demand a vast array of preventive health services both in the public sector and through private retailing (Ellis, 1988). The shift to a leisure- and service-oriented society presses us to focus upon entrepreneurial activities related to human resource development and quality-of-life indices such as health enhancement and the thirst for adventure and "ultra" experiences.

There are signs that the demands of popular culture for personal meaning and transcendent experiences (often sought through health regimens or the pursuit of high-level performance) now portray an increasingly strong reaction to the repressive and mystifying role of scientific rationality, or what the poet William Blake called "single vision." This sense of longing for extraordinary experience through health and bodily practices, present as superstitious beliefs and quackery in days gone by, has become, in the late 20th century, a more subtle phenomenon aptly termed by Theodore Roszak (1980) a "hunger for wonders," or by some health seekers, athletes, and runners the desire to find the "mystique that borders on the metaphysical" (Kostrubala, 1976), "an escape to the higher self" (Sheehan, 1980). The hunger for wonders has fed particularly upon the current promises of health promotion and physical performance as they are projected through the mass media and distorted by sensational advertising.

In this paper I explore how, over the past century and a half, particular changes in health concepts have opened and closed opportunities for the profession of physical education, and how the profession has employed its scientific roots to exploit these opportunities. I conclude with an analysis concerning how the profession can meet the new demands for health promotion and cope with the challenges of the hunger for wonders without abandoning its legitimacy as a profession rooted in science. Rather than accept John Lucas's (1986) proposition that physical education will have vanished from higher education by the year 2000, my suggestion is that the application of improved methodologies of learning by doing, a systems approach, and the development of methodologies that merge value judgments with scientific inquiry present the chance for physical education, clothed as a domain of applied health science, to become what Park (1989a) has envisioned as the renaissance field of the 21st century.

The Profession, the Discipline, and the Marketplace: The Historical Response to Science and Changing Conceptions of Health

The aspirations of physical educators and their ability to respond to the perceived needs of the marketplace have been intimately connected to society's conceptions of health and the body. Indeed, anyone who would understand the nature of the present-day relationship of physical education and health promotion and the past problems and future responsibilities for professional growth in this domain can derive important insights from the professional and preprofessional responses of early physical educators to broad social concerns about health and physical well-being. (See Tables 1 and 2.)

Table 1

Changing Views of the Body

Period	Proponents	View of body
Mid 19th Century	Preachers and reformers	Organic
Late 19th Century	Positivistic scientists	Mechanistic
First half of 20th Century	Public health advocates	Atomistic
Mid 20th Century	Journalists and educators	Holistic
Late 20th Century	Advocates	Socioecological

Table 2

Encyclopedia Definitions of Health

Source	Definition
Chambers (1887)	The state of body or mind opposed to disease and characterized by the integrity of soundness. Health is understood as referring chiefly to the body and as indicating that perfect and harmonious play of all the functions which permits a man to be all that his creator intended.
Britannica (1911)	A condition of physical soundness or well-being, in which an organism discharges its functions efficiently.
Americana (1935)	The state of health depends upon the normal functioning of the body. The modern movement in medicine is in the direction of preventive medicine through hygiene.
Americana (1973)	State of complete physical, mental, and social well-being, and not merely the absence of disease.
Britannica (1985)	The extent of an individual's continuing physical, emotional, mental, and social ability to cope with his or her environment.

The 19th Century: An Organic View of the Body

Popular concepts of health in North America have changed significantly since colonial times, when disease was viewed as inevitable and as divine retribution in a world of sin (Verbrugge, 1988). By the 19th century such fatalism was beginning to give way to a growing belief that physical well-being was possible through personal effort and that Americans had a moral responsibility to pursue self-improvement in the drive to a better society. Such beliefs were certainly not stimulated by the emerging profession of medicine, which was largely characterized in the first half of the 19th century by ineffective heroic measures more likely to kill than to cure (Vertinsky, 1987). On the contrary, democratic and antiauthoritarian trends in society generated a wave of health reform predicated upon the belief that people caused their own diseases by living unhealthily and with right behavior could achieve health and grace.

The idea that personal health could be improved by obeying natural laws (exercise, diet, sleep, sanguinity) has its roots in classical Greek civilization, nourished in part by ancient convictions about the close connection between mind and body, but its blossoming in the first half of the 19th century attended that era's fascination with nature and personal freedom (Tesh, 1988, p. 21). By promulgating the belief that physical Arminianism went hand in hand with moral purity, health-reform crusaders evoked an alliance between religion and science in the drive toward hygienic reform (Vertinsky, 1986). Because their concepts of health tended to be oriented toward science more than medicine, it was an approach to prevention that revolved around a natural, organic view of the body.

The personal behavior theory, while denying the legitimacy of medical authority, promoted prevention in the form of health-based physical education as a legitimate area for professional intervention. Physical education implied a full education about one's body, and knowledge about one's body was deemed crucial to a well-educated and healthy individual. It was, therefore, tantamount to an entire system of hygiene embracing "every thing that by bearing in any way on the human body, might injure or benefit in its health, vigor and fitness of action" (Berryman, 1989, p. 544).

Mechanistic View of the Body

Late-19th-century Americans were less confident about the perfectability of individuals and society. The stresses and strains caused by industrialization and urbanization laid bare personal and social problems that seemed to require new responses to health and physical well-being. Popular physiologists, doctors, and physical educators joined to advise Americans on how to adjust to modern society by using new scientific information to understand how to balance the internal needs of the body with the newly perceived demands of the environment.

Convinced by earlier health-reform ideology of the reformative powers of health and physical education, the late-19th-century proponents of physical education identified morality with muscularity, and hence efficiency, in their crusade to stave off what they perceived as the imminent degeneration of American society. Regular exercise was the way to improve muscle power and therefore generate the brainpower needed to advance society (Whorton, 1982, p. 286). Industrial society provided the central metaphors and goals of health. The body, like society, resembled a machine, and scientific study showed how the machine could be maintained and even improved to seek greater efficiency. If health was the ability to perform, then it was a measurable phenomenon that physical educators could systematically pursue through scientifically informed practice.

Early physical education professionals thus played a powerful role in articulating a new model of health that focused upon a reciprocal relationship between individual and social well-being. Health was a technique of personal adjustment and social management—and physical education was to help in its attainment by focusing upon fitness—"fitness for work, fitness for play, fitness for anything a man may be called upon to do" (Sargent, 1906, p. 297).

The close connection between physical fitness and social health was a clarion call of those medically oriented professionals with a preventive bent who dedicated their careers in the latter part of the 19th century to what Whorton has called the "birthing of the modern physical education movement" (Whorton, 1982, p. 282). Doctors all, Luther Gulick, Edward Hitchcock, Jr., Dudley Allen Sargent, Edward Hartwell, William Anderson, and R. Tait McKenzie collectively sought to combine the new religion of science with the growing authority of medicine and place both at the disposal of the physical education profession. Few scientific fields, said Gulick, "offered opportunities for the study of problems of greater value to the human race" (Gulick, 1890, p. 65). Furthermore, only scientifically oriented professionals would have the expertise necessary to control or limit the consequences of social problems caused by a rapid industrialization and urbanization (Riska & Vinten-Johansen, 1981). To this end they worked to build a profession that would turn physical education into a patriotic duty, and physical educators into what Gulick claimed would be "biological engineers" (Gulick, 1903). Despite this rather presumptuous claim, says Whorton, early professionals sensibly "gave the bulk of their attention to improvement of the body; the physical improvements [they] anticipated were plausible, and they did not break in any major way with established scientific opinion" (Whorton, 1982, p. 295).

Roberta Park has convincingly shown how physical educators' activities broadened as, increasingly influenced by the social sciences, they formalized the profession's stance toward the achievement of twin hygienic (health promotion) and educational (proper habit formation) goals through the study and care of the body (Park, 1987). Although they were at first concerned with the establishment and maintenance of personal health through attention to the findings of the biological sciences, as the 20th century got under way physical educators demonstrated the influence of the burgeoning social sciences by professing to be involved with the social, psychological, and moral development of the individual.

In tandem with the tendencies of other fields of study to seek professional authority based upon specialized knowledge and intensive preparation, the physical education profession sought to harness scientific study to practice. George W. Fitz of Harvard, for example, was a leading exponent of the demand for specialized scientific knowledge underpinning the practices of the developing physical education profession. His desire was to form a profession that could draw upon a knowledge structure in making practical decisions—to substitute why for how, intellect for emotion, and fact for fancy. Give physical educators a strong scientific, biological, and medical orientation, he said, and they would then seek scientific facts to support their physiological theories instead of relying on ideas and cherished opinions that were "simple, entirely logical, very superficial, delightfully fantastic and mostly absurd" (Fitz, 1896, p. 178).

Like other scientists of his time, Fitz was intensely aware of the dangers of ignorance and superstition among credulous people where matters of health and exercise were concerned, as well as the need to put science to work against the business of quackery and the desire for miracles. William Hammond had couched the problem nicely in 1883 when he commented about the

> inherent tendency in the mind of man to ascribe to supernatural agencies those events the causes of which are beyond his knowledge . . . [yet] as his intellect becomes more thoroughly trained, and as science advances in its developments, the range of his credulity becomes more and more circum-

> scribed, his doubts are multiplied, and he at length reaches that condition of 'healthy skepticism' which allows of no belief without the proof. (p. 229)

Scientific authority was needed to combat the isolated beliefs of superstition and provide a logical, systematic context for thinking about health and physical activity. The scientific method applied to the study and application of physical education would provide this authority, which was especially important, noted Edward M. Hartwell (1894), "since physical training, on its theoretical side, belongs to a class of questions that fascinate doctrinaires and dabblers" (pp. 619-20). Thomas Dennison Wood reaffirmed this point: "The idea of the science should exist first in the minds of the profession, and then in the minds of the laity" (Wood, 1894, p. 621).

The 20th Century—An Atomistic View of the Body

It was mainly a market opportunity outside the health field, however, that was to influence the direction and nature of professional practice in the next half century. The possibility that physical education would develop in tandem with the biological sciences or take responsibility for popular health education faded in light of the influence of the social sciences and professional education dictates that encouraged play, games, and sports for the youth in the nation's schools (Kroll, 1971; Park, 1989b).

Health promotion and physical education followed increasingly divergent paths in the first half of the 20th century. The influx of public health measures, by contributing to a growing acceptance that the environment and social conditions played a substantial role in health and disease, led away from a dominant concern with individual responsibility for health and toward an emphasis upon public health measures and professional medical care. The germ theory, in particular, rapidly overtook other theories of health and disease, intensifying social pressures for cleanliness and hygienic behavior. When added to evidence, such as the efficacy of endocrine systems, that the body consisted of complex systems in delicate balance, and that each body cell had power on its own, the view of the body as a machine began to give way to a more fragmented, atomistic model of the human body (Allen, 1975).

Sanitarian views embodied the rapidly developing sciences and provided an entry for not only scientists and physicians but other professionals and paraprofessionals to the field of health education, thus eroding the specialized role of physical education in the provision of health-related activities. The physical educator with his or her specialized training had no comparative advantage in dealing with "clean air, clean bodies and clean clothes" (Means, 1962, p. 142). The reliance on physical education as a guarantor of physical development and physical fitness diminished and was replaced by an increasing dependence for health maintenance upon the curative powers and new wonder drugs of the medical profession. Indeed, the discovery of specific causes of infectious diseases and specific cures made following a generally healthy lifestyle strategy seem less urgent and fomented a growing dependency upon the wonders of technology. Other professionals, especially the medical profession, moved in to assert authority over the health and fitness affairs of youth, and in all substantive matters of health the teachers deferred to the physicians and nurses upon whose expertise they believed the health of the nation depended.

Where physical educators were concerned, health and fitness objectives often came out second best. The importance attributed by social scientists to the role of play and games in the physical and mental development of children, as well as the growing popularity of athletics, caused physical educators to focus upon the social dimensions of physical activity and sport in the drive for compulsory school physical education programs. Medically oriented physical educators diminished in numbers as health and physical activity concerns became less a focus in school programs, this in spite of the influence of both world wars in centering attention upon the poor state of physical fitness of recruits (Reiser, 1978). As the "new" developmental physical education promoted education of the whole child "through" rather than "of" the physical, the links of physical educators to the medical scientists and the scientific method weakened (Wedgwood, 1924). "Twenty-five centuries of good experience with emphasis on the physical abandoned over-night," complained Charles McCloy. "We forgot most of the fundamentals; we didn't want to be strong" (McCloy, 1936, p. 6). By 1933, James Frederick Rogers was able to claim that "there is no correlation between interest in physical activities and interest in science and it is little wonder that the average teacher in physical education, excellent as he may be, is neither adept nor interested in teaching hygiene" (Rogers, 1933, p. 17).

While the opportunities in the health field contracted, mandated physical education programs built upon the social objectives of games and play offered the profession a stable market niche protected by requirements for teacher certification. Teacher education soon came to constitute the major activity of physical education departments in higher education. Physical education was a teaching profession, insisted Clark W. Hetherington (1925), first, last, and all the time. As a result of occupying such a narrow and protected environment, physical education developed structures, philosophies, and technologies that were supportable only so long as the nation's population was predominantly youthful and the citizenry were happy to vote taxes to support their mission (Ellis, 1988, p. 12). Only while these conditions were sustained could the educational establishment remain secure.

A Holistic View of the Body

As we now know, both of the latter conditions proved to be transitory. During the 1950s the Kraus-Weber test results elicited a public uproar by drawing attention to the lack of physical fitness of American youth (Report, 1956). President John F. Kennedy complained that an increasingly large number of young Americans were neglecting their bodies, getting soft, and destroying the vitality of the nation (Kennedy, 1973). The professional posture of physical education was to turn attention to health-related physical fitness but only as one among many other objectives. This resulted in a poorly defined public image and the further challenge of physical education as the guardian of physical fitness. As scientific information increasingly illustrated the links between physical activity and health, and as exercise came to be seen as prophylaxis against coronary heart disease (Wenger, 1978), school physical education was castigated for having failed both to improve the health of American children and to prepare them for a lifetime participation in sports and physical pursuits.

The profession's myopic stance toward the public's realization that all was not well with physical education in the schools led to a general confusion as to what was the appropriate mission of physical education and to vigorous (Greendorfer, 1987, would say renewed) questioning by academics about the lack of a carefully defined domain of content in physical education. In an indictment of what he saw as the physical education profession's inability to identify and support a clearly focused mission, Franklin Henry called in 1964 for renewal through the development of an academic discipline of human movement. Though his plan led to a concerted and partly successful effort by academics to build a systematic body of knowledge about the fundamental process of human movement in all its forms, physical educators in the schools remained tied to educational goals and committed for some time to making contributions to a set of objectives that were nearly impossible to achieve (see Kroll, 1971, p. 91).

The public's disenchantment with their experience and understanding of the health and fitness objectives of school physical education reflected the profession's inability to articulate and deliver a recognizable product even in a captive marketplace. Public disapprobation of school physical education, however, was also part of a broader cultural disorientation during which every aspect of the American system came under radical and sustained attack, including the educational enterprise, which was accused of betraying its basic social purpose, and the medical care system, which was assailed by widespread consumer dissatisfaction (Geison, 1983; Stevens, 1971).

Serious doubts were cast upon the relevance of mechanistic and atomistic models to the problem of health, as it became increasingly evident that human health was not determined predominantly by medical intervention (McKeown, 1978). Health was being redefined from the mere absence of disease to the existence of a positive state of wellness in the whole person. The new holistic approach to health particularly acknowledged the powerful role of the mind in the prevention and healing of disease and the critical importance of personal lifestyle measures.

Just as happened in the late 19th century, the cure for the nation's ills was seen in a return to personal responsibility for healthy lifestyles, with physical activity taking an important role. "It is time," said William Kannel in a comment reminiscent of Luther Gulick's notion of "biological engineers," "to consider engineering physical activity back into daily living to counter the sloth and gluttony promulgated by modern technology and changing mores" (Kannel, 1970, p. 1153). As social concern shifted the preoccupation with curing illness to a parallel concern for promoting health and its potential for restoring order and control to society and individuals, the growing enthusiasm for holistic health claimed "to restructure the way we think about health and illness, revolutionize the health-care delivery system and vastly improve our health" (Tesh, 1988, p. 2).

The 1970s and 1980s saw an exponential growth in concern for and discussion of health and what individuals could do to promote and improve their own health. Spurred on by classic publications such as, in Canada, Lalonde's *New Perspectives on the Health of Canadians* (1974) and, the U.S. government's

Healthy People (1979) and *Promoting Health/Preventing Disease* (1980), as well as the compilation and mass distribution of lists of health objectives for the 1990s, health became a national obsession, and "self-help" and "self-care" the major slogans.

The emphasis on health was seen in the strenuous pursuit of healthy lifestyles and in widespread attempts to reduce risk factors. Fully 87% of adults claimed to have attempted to make healthy changes in their lifestyles (Barsky, 1988). Indeed, one could hardly exaggerate the revival of interest among many Americans in taking responsibility for their health by pursuing personal lifestyle behaviors such as jogging, bicycling, diet, sports, exercise, and so on (Kimble, 1980). The pursuit of physical fitness, in particular, took a leading role in the drive for biological self-betterment. From the romance with running to the exercise boom, tens of millions of Americans starved, stretched, and monitored their vital signs in pursuit of high-level wellness, and fueled an economic juggernaut by spending billions of dollars on natural foods, vitamins, athletic equipment, health resorts, and health club memberships (Ardell, 1977; Glassner, 1989; Liles, 1979; Naisbitt, 1982).

Within the drive for holism as a reaction to the medical model and its implications emerged the enlarged notion of health as a commodity, and, with it, undreamed-of opportunities for both health-related professionals and peddlers of a wide variety of "magic bullets." The increasing popularity of the wellness concept led to the belief that lifestyle-modification practices and programs held the key to transforming North Americans into a society of healthy people. This opened new vistas of professional opportunities to physical education, medicine, and other established professions, but it also became a fertile and highly competitive field for a new type of health-related professional who rapidly turned health promotion into a subclinical domain requiring specialized preparation and the development of a whole new set of operational concepts and regulations (Ellis, 1988; Vertinsky, 1985).

This window of opportunity for physical education re reengage its professional concerns with broad exercise- and health-related matters in a mass market of unprecedented proportions was not, however, quite as accessible as might at first have been believed. An overabundance of physicians seeking new roles and new clients vied for business with other health professionals, using their historical authority to advantage. Doctors put their own muscle behind the exercise bandwagon, says Solomon (1984), leaped aboard as it got rolling, and provided further legitimacy for medical involvement in exercise schemes. In addition, the concept of holistic health and the progressive medicalization of daily life brought unrealistically high expectations about both the potential benefits of preventive health activities and the range of techniques that could be expected to lead to health enhancement and high-level wellness experiences (Cresswell, 1982). The professions, tied by ethical constraints and professional requirements built upon their underlying scientific paradigms, were not able to meet vicarious market demands for miracles through body sculpting, drug-induced performance, rapid weight-control, excessive risk-taking, and superendurance feats, leaving that market to a potpourri of entrepreneurs and nonprofessionals.

Nor were the increased professional opportunities presented by the epidemic of overuse injuries, gynecological difficulties, and eating disorders, resulting from an obsessive pursuit of fitness activities, accessible to the physical education profession. A booming market opened up for sports medicine specialists and rehabilitation experts, who occupied a recuperative niche that physical education was not able to penetrate.

> Replete with their own clinics, their own journal, and their own courses, sports medicine orthopedics cater[ed] not only to professional athletes but also to the running public who develop[ed] significant injuries at the rate of 35 per cent per year. (Gillick, 1984, p. 378).

Sports gynecology developed a growing following. Because national attention focused on a perceived epidemic of anorexia nervosa among adolescent girls resulting from obsessive dieting and exercise, a veritable army of health professionals became involved in the treatment of eating disorders, especially private-for-profit marketing of medical services (Brumberg, 1988). To the academic discipline of physical education, the opportunities afforded by the growing market for sports medicine and rehabilitative services, and the monies available for research to support those activities, led to a shift in focus and the development of specializations in epidemiology, ergonomics, and rehabilitation.

Furthermore, the settings in which physical educators had traditionally worked, and had been trained to work in, changed in nature and scope. The demography of North America shifted to an older population. As the median age of the population increased and concern for health enhancement grew among populations at risk, the market for health and fitness activities targeted at an adult and older adult market rapidly expanded. Presented with a new and challenging market, the profession required a new set of entrepreneurial skills and counseling abilities to successfully compete in the private sector as well as new knowledge to inform appropriate practice for diverse populations.

The number of Americans of school age also declined, resulting in a shrinking market for physical educators accustomed to working with youth in educational settings and in public sport organizations. Not only were there fewer youth to fill the schools, the public enthusiasm for school physical education programs was at a low ebb. School physical education was seen to be "in sad disarray as it fail[ed] in its major missions" (Ellis, 1988, p. 13).

Fearing that school education, which had been an important focus of the profession since its inception, had failed in both its hygienic and its educative goals by virtue of its sustained emphasis upon social goals of games and play, and strongly influenced by the health and fitness boom of the '70s and '80s, many in the profession called for a reemphasis upon hygiene in physical education practices. Allensworth and Wolford (1988) suggested that fundamental to achieving the 1990 national health objectives in the key area of physical fitness and exercise was a physical education program that met daily, focused on activities promoting cardiorespiratory fitness, and established periodic screening and remedial prescriptions regarding the physical fitness of students. Supporting this focus, Jack Wilmore commented that

> the objectives for the nation speak for physical education professionals. We have a job to do—now. . . . We must join in the national effort to reach the articulated goals for 1990. We must be dedicated to helping others, from the

> cradle to the grave, to understand that good health is more choice than chance. We are obliged as professionals to ensure a proper foundation of knowledge on which to make this choice. (Wilmore, 1982, pp. 41-43)

The profession attempted to respond and refocus. A renewed emphasis on health-related physical fitness commenced in 1980 with the publication of the American Alliance for Health, Physical Education, Recreation and Dance *Health-Related Fitness Manual* (see AAHPERD, 1980; Pate, 1983; Petray & Cortese, 1988). The aim, said Corbin, was to help people "achieve an optimal level of physical fitness, increase their capacity to feel good, look good, enjoy life, work efficiently, and handle life's emergencies" (Corbin, 1986, p. 82).

Dudley Sargent (1906) could not have said it better. Yet it was also clear, as Wilmore (1982) had shown, that the profession urgently needed support from its academic discipline. The discipline, however, was stretched. A review of the section titles of *Research Quarterly for Exercise and Sport* over the decade 1980 to 1990, for example, shows an expansion of subdisciplinary headings up to 16 in 1982 followed by a reduction and simplification in the years that followed (see Figure 1). Significantly, the category *health* became *health behavior* in 1981, reflecting the emphasis of the time, in the medical and other health-related professions, upon behavioral determinants of health. In 1986, *health behavior* became *exercise epidemiology*, illustrating the expansion of the concept of health into social, economic, and environmental concerns, but also strongly reflecting medical and scientific terminology.

The Challenge of the 1990s

As the profession moves to meet the health and fitness demands of a changing marketplace, the concept of health and the interpretation of health promotion have begun to shift once more. Pundits increasingly underline the downside of a health-promotion philosophy built upon personal responsibility for health, claiming that the lifestyle approach has ignored the more difficult but equally important problem of the social environment, which both creates some lifestyles and inhibits the maintenance of others (Crawford, 1980).

Excessive emphasis upon individual lifestyles has been shown to exacerbate a "blaming the victim" mentality where individuals are accused of becoming unhealthy through irresponsible behavior and a lack of personal effort (Kilwein, 1989; Vertinsky, 1985). Failure to act preventively becomes a sign of social as well as individual responsibility (Knowles, 1977). Wrist-slapping messages by physical education professionals "to run, jump, and be fit" have not given due consideration to the important effects of the social environment upon health status, health attitudes, and health behavior. By no means do all the strands of scientific evidence point to causal links between healthy lifestyles and health status, hence professionals have been accused of exaggerating the connection because of their economic and intellectual investment in this theory (Epstein & Swartz, 1981; Ingham, 1985). Overenthusiasm of the profession in promoting individual imperatives for pursuing healthy lifestyles has thus led both to confusion about what constitutes proper evidence for professional practice and, at times, to an unhealthy and narcissistic preoccupation with the body that has sent clients back to the medical profession (Alster, 1989).

1980	1981	1982	1986	1990
Biomechanics				
Growth and Development				
Health	Health Behavior		Exercise Epidemiology	
History and Philosophy				
Measurement and Research Design	Measurement and Evaluation			
Motor Learning	Motor Control —behavior —neuromuscular	Motor Control and Learning		
Multidisciplinary				
Neurophysiology				
Physiology of Exercise: Strength and Endurance	Physiology —neuromuscular —metabolic & circulatory	Physiology		
Psychology of Sport	Psychology —behavioral —psychobiology	Psychology		
Recreation				
Sociology of Sport		Social and Cultural Anthropology		
Teacher Preparation: C&I	Pedagogy			
	Activities for Special Populations			

Figure 1 — A decade of section headings in *Research Quarterly for Exercise and Sport.*

As the definition of health has expanded to feeling good, wellness, and in turn high-level wellness, it has become increasingly difficult for people to know how to reach that state. Bodily awareness, self-consciousness, and introspection are associated with a tendency to amplify somatic symptoms, and increased awareness has sometimes brought more negative assessments. People are living better but worrying themselves sick (Barsky, 1988; Becker, 1986). How is it, said McKnight (1986, p. 78) in a speech to the American Academy for the Advancement of Science, "that as we open each door to health, at the end of the corridor we find we have re-entered the medical chamber."

The mass media have played a particularly important role in commercializing health and fitness and amplifying the public's sense of somatic vulnerability, with media hype exaggerating the risks posed by health hazards, portraying preliminary research findings as major breakthroughs, and attributing certainty to unproven health claims and techniques. Commercial exploitation of health fads, fitness fancies, and risky physical pursuits has also brought fast relief to the public's hunger for wonders, those restless spiritual longings that generate an eager but indiscriminate appetite for "self enslavement to easy absolutes" while "blithely suspending the authority of the hard sciences" (Roszak, 1980, p. 305). This loose use of scientific ideas to appease an essentially religious appetite, claims Roszak, may suggest that our scientific worldview has simply not taken, and that our culture remains as divided as ever in its metaphysical convictions. Unable to understand the increasingly subtle and technical aspects of modern experimental science or the exotic, theoretical realms of some social sciences that often defy common sense and the evidence of ordinary experience, the public has turned instead to a search for personal meaning and experience in the extraordinary. Long-distance runners claim euphoric experiences and a sense of unrealness, a "refreshment of the soul" and "a form of worship, an attempt to find God, a means to the transcendent." More health seekers seek in exercise programs and holistic health practices, altered perceptions, cosmic affirmation, "unity with nature," and "the integration of mind, body and spirit for the attainment of whole health" (Mrozek, 1987, p. 85; Solomon, 1984).

Media sensationalism and claims by gurus of transport to the exotic and the extraordinary through health and fitness experiences thus pose a particular problem to a conscientious profession bent on using the scientific knowledge provided by its discipline to combat unscrupulous or well-meaning claims of miracles for the gullible. If indeed exercise is to be seen as a path to euphoria, says Solomon (1984), the reward is only too often bought at the expense of exertion becoming one more path back to the doctor's office.

Although the public of the 1990s is more sophisticated and demanding for the health and fitness objectives of physical education professionals, many are still susceptible to overexpectation and the hunger for wonders. Burnham suggests that the conditions that foster superstition and unhealthy credulity about health have changed dramatically since the late 19th century and not for the better. When one attempts to compare the history of scientific ideas and institutions with the popularization of health and scientific ideas, a certain cognitive dissonance arises. Though the evolution of scientific ideas about health may well be progressive, the history of their popularization could equally be seen as retrogressive. The record shows, Burnham suggests, "that changes in the way in which ideas about health came to be popularized, in fact, ultimately reduced and frustrated the cultural impact of both science and scientists" (Burnham, 1987, p. 4). Far from eradicating unhealthy credulity and irrational beliefs about health and fitness in favor of a knowledge of health contributing to a broad and coherent worldview, scientists and health-related professionals unwittingly exacerbated the former. Specialization caused a loss of interest in presenting accurate scientific health information to the public. This left the field of health popularization to the world of the media, where sensationalism and disjointed facts were exactly those elements of superstition that had been attacked by scientific skeptics of an earlier day. Whether or not one agrees with Burnham that "superstition has won and science lost," today's physical education professional, hemmed in with regulations and institutional liabilities, cannot afford to involve herself or himself with nonscientific practices while competing in the health and exercise market, but neither can public demands be ignored.

Again, as in the 1890s, the physical education profession is at a crossroads, facing both opportunities and challenges. But though the situations appear similar, the circumstances of the 1990s are quite different. The profession in the 1890s was in its infancy, so it did not have the baggage of size and complexity of today's profession. Society was much less market oriented, and the roles of economics and organization were of much less importance than the role of ideas. Now we are dealing with a huge, multifaceted profession in an age characterized by the need for cooperative efforts to confront global problems.

Socioecological Views of Health

A new, socioecological paradigm of health is emerging. The current approach to health focuses less on individual lifestyles and more on the ability of the environment to influence people's health in both positive and negative ways. Health is increasingly understood to be a social commodity, much like other social commodities such as housing and education, that is differentially distributed. Some get more of it, some get less, and those at the top of the social stratification tend to do better than those at the bottom. Too many are, in current government parlance, underserved. For this reason, new strategies for empowerment, social support, and community-based services are advocated as broad and powerful strategies for health. The broadened concept of health promotion is usefully described in the recent Canadian landmark publication, *Achieving Health for All* (Epp, 1986).

> Health promotion implies a commitment to dealing with the challenges of reducing inequities, extending the scope of prevention, and helping people to cope with their circumstances. It means fostering public participation, strengthening community health services, and co-ordinating healthy public policy. Moreover it means creating environments conducive to health in which people are better able to take care of themselves and to offer each other support in solving and managing collective health problems. (p. 12)

Here we have a new paradigm of health marked by a socioecological, multidisciplinary orientation, which provides a broader environmental perspective for health-promotion efforts and allows an increasingly wide range of actors to participate in the process of nurturing health. In the new thinking, health has become the concern and responsibility of the collective as well as of the individual, inviting the involvement and bridge building of a broad range of disciplines and emphasizing the necessity for collaboration and coordination across a number of political and professional boundaries (Draper, 1986; Minkler, 1989). Health, in fact, has become the concern of everybody and everything.

Moving Toward a Future Healthy Society

In the 1990s, individual aspirations and demands are higher than ever, with a new insistence upon individual rights and an increasing desire to achieve a healthy, leisured, and satisfying style of life. There is again a growing disbelief in the ability of institutions to solve personal and environmental problems and enhance quality of life. There is also an emerging belief that markets are the major mechanism of social control that permits direct individual involvement without the need for bureaucratic, institutional controls. Yet success for markets requires informed consumers and responsible and flexible producers.

The profession of physical education, if it is to succeed in exploiting new windows of opportunity in the area of health promotion, must satisfy an impatient public, hungry for more wonders, that wants to know that new knowledge is continuously being generated and employed and that progress is being made. There is a growing need for decision making rooted in science but appropriate to an age characterized by high levels of uncertainty with respect to the determinants of health and the risks and benefits associated with physical activity. The framework for generating knowledge within the traditional science paradigm, with its quest for certainty of knowledge and its demands for controls and a nonreactive experimental environment, provides inadequate support for decision making under uncertainty. This presents a continuing challenge for the academic discipline of physical education and the potential for the development of a niche that will differentiate it from the traditional disciplines.

Decision making under uncertainty involves some value judgments. These include

1. judgments with respect to the inferences one can draw from an incomplete knowledge base (i.e., judgments that use the full experience and knowledge of a scientist and a professional), and
2. judgments with respect to the values held by stakeholders in a decision process: values that must decide the choice among alternatives, and the levels of acceptable risks.

The biological scientists in the academic field of physical education must develop methodologies and techniques for improving probability judgments necessary for the diagnostic and prognostic tasks faced by the profession in prescribing physical activity for health and fitness. The social scientists must address two major areas of judgment: They must develop the means for deciding upon levels of acceptable risks for individuals and society, and for determining how individuals' preferences should shape the judgments of the professionals who serve them. Indeed, this arena of meshing value judgments with the application of science and scientific principle, what Weinberg (1972) has called the domain of trans-science, will increasingly characterize the development of policies and practices of health-related professions.

Finally, to achieve greater success in improving the specialized knowledge base of the profession, the academic discipline must develop and employ new paradigms of experimentation. The principle of learning by doing is one that can assist the development of a knowledge base in a rapidly changing environment. Schemes can be designed (such as the evolutionary operations practiced by some industries) that can induce professional practice to supply data that can be used to improve practice (see, for example, Box & Draper, 1969). Such practices, of course, require a close alignment between the profession and its academic discipline.

For the professional, this means accepting experimentation as a valuable tool for improved practice. For the academic, it means leaving the comfort of the highly controlled laboratory and engaging in field experiments with their demanding constraints and requirements for collaborative team research. New ways of thinking, valuing, and experimenting make interdependence between professionals and researchers the critical key to any proposal for a renaissance of physical education in the next century—certainly where its health-related dimensions are concerned.

References

ALLEN, G.E. (1975). *Life science in the twentieth century*. New York: Wiley.

ALLENSWORTH, D.D., & Wolford, C.A. (1988). Schools as agents for achieving the 1990 health objectives for the nation. *Health Education Quarterly*, **15**(1), 3-15.

ALSTER, K.B. (1989). *The holistic health movement*. Tuscaloosa, AL: The University of Alabama Press.

AMERICAN Alliance for Health, Physical Education, Recreation and Dance (AAPHERD). (1980). *AAPHERD health related physical fitness test manual*. Washington, DC: Author.

ARDELL, D.B. (1977). *High level wellness: An alternative to doctors, drugs and disease*. Emmons, PA: Rodale Press.

BARSKY, A.J. (1988). The paradox of health. *The New England Journal of Medicine*, **318**, 414-418.

BECKER, M.H. (1986). The tyranny of health promotion. *Public Health*, **14**, 15-25.

BERRYMAN, J.W. (1989). The tradition of "six things non natural": Exercise and medicine from Hippocrates through ante-bellum America. *Exercise and Sport Sciences Review*, **17**, 515-559.

BOX, G.E.P., & Draper, N.R. (1969). *Evolutionary operations*. New York: Wiley.

BRUMBERG, J.J. (1988). *Fasting girls: The emergence of anorexia nervosa as a modern disease*. Cambridge, MA: Harvard University Press.

BURNHAM, J.C. (1987). *How superstition won and science lost. Popularizing science and health in the United States*. New Brunswick, NJ: Rutgers University Press.

CORBIN, C. (1986). Fitness is for children. *Journal of the American Alliance for Physical Education, Health, Recreation and Dance*, **57**(5), 82-85.

CRAWFORD, R. (1980). Healthism and the medicalization of everyday life. *International Journal of Health Services*, **10**(13), 365-388.

CRESSWELL, W.H., Jr. (1982). Quo vadis—health education? *Health Education*, **13**(4), 12-17.

DRAPER, P. (1986). Nancy Milio's work and its importance for the development of health promotion. *Health Promotion*, **1**(1), 101-105.

ELLIS, M.J. (1988). *The business of physical education: Future of the profession*. Champaign, IL: Human Kinetics.

EPP, J. (1986). *Achieving health for all: A framework for health promotion*. Ottawa, Canada: Health and Welfare Canada.

EPSTEIN, S.S., & Swartz, J.B. (1981). Fallacies of lifestyle cancer theories. *Nature*, **289**, 127-130.

FITZ, G.W. (1896). Report of the tenth annual meeting of the American Association for the Advancement of Physical Education. American Association for the Advancement of Physical Education.

GEISON, G.L. (1983). *Professions and professional ideologies in America*. Chapel Hill: University of North Carolina Press.

GILLICK, M.R. (1984). Health promotion, jogging and the pursuit of the moral life. *Journal of Health Politics, Policy and Law*, **9**(3), 369-387.

GLASSNER, B. (1989). Fitness and the post modern self. *Journal of Health and Social Behavior* , **30**, 180-191.

GREENDORFER, S.L. (1987). Specialization, fragmentation, integration, discipline, profession: What is the real issue? *Quest*, **39**, 56-64.

GULICK, L.H. (1890). Physical education: A new profession. *Proceedings of the American Association for the Advancement of Physical Education*, **5**, 59-66.

GULICK, L.H. (1903). The problem of physical training in the modern city. *American Physical Education Review*, **8**, 29-34.

HAMMOND, W.A. (1883). *On certain conditions of nervous derangement, somnambulism—hypnotism—hysteria and hysterical affection, etc.* New York: G.P. Putnam's Sons.

HARTWELL, E.M. (1894). Physical education. Opening address of the Chairman. *Proceedings of the International Congress of Education of the World's Columbian Exposition*, (**32**, 618-620).

HETHERINGTON, C.W. (1925). Graduate work in physical education. *American Physical Education Review*, **30**, 207-210, 262-268.

INGHAM, A.G. (1985). From public issue to personal trouble: Well-being and the fiscal crisis of the state. *Sociology of Sport Journal*, **2**, 43-55.

KANNEL, W. (1970). Physical exercise and lethal arteriosclerotic disease. *The New England Journal of Medicine*, **282**, 1153-1154.

KENNEDY, J.F. (1973). The soft American. In J. Talamini & C. Page (Eds.), *Sport and society* (p. 369). Boston: Little, Brown.

KILWEIN, J.H. (1989). No pain, no gain: A puritan legacy. *Health Education Quarterly*, **16**(1), 9-12.

KIMBLE, C. (1980). In pursuit of well-being. *Wilson Quarterly*, **4**, 60-74.

KNOWLES, J. (1977). *Doing better and feeling worse: Health in the United States*. New York: Norton.

KOSTRUBALA, T. (1976). *The joy of running*. New York: Pocket Books.

KROLL, W.P. (1971). *Perspectives in physical education*. New York: Academic Press.

LALONDE, M. (1974). *A new perspective on the health of Canadians*. Ottawa: Government of Canada Printing Office.

LILES, R. (1979, July). To jog or not to jog: The pains and the pleasures. *Good Housekeeping*, p. 188.

LUCAS, J. (1986). Open forum. *The American Academy of Physical Education News*, **6**(3), 8.

McCLOY, C.H. (1936). How about some muscle? *Journal of Health and Physical Education*, **3**(4), 6-8.

McKEOWN, T. (1978). Behavioral and environmental determinants of health and their implication for public policy. In R.C. Carlson & R. Cunningham (Eds.), *Future directions in health care* (pp. 21-38). Cambridge, MA: Ballinger.

McKNIGHT, J.L. (1986). Well-being: The new threshold to the old medicine. *Health Promotion*, **1**(1), 77-80.

MEANS, R.K. (1962). *A history of health education in the United States*. Philadelphia: Lea & Febiger.

MINKLER, M. (1989). Health education, health promotion, and the open society: An historical perspective. *Health Education Quarterly*, **16**(1), 17-30.

MROZEK, D.J. (1987). The scientific quest for physical culture and the persistent appeal of quackery. *Journal of Sport History*, **14**(1), 76-86.

NAISBITT, J. (1982). *Megatrends*. New York: Warner Books.

PARK, R.J. (1987). Physiologists, physicians and physical educators: Nineteenth century biology and exercise, hygienic and educative. *Journal of Sport History*, **14**(1), 28-60.

PARK, R.J. (1989a). The second 100 years: Or, can physical education become the renaissance field of the 21st century? *Quest*, **41**, 1-27.

PARK, R.J. (1989b). Healthy, moral and strong: Educational views of exercise and athletics in nineteenth-century America. In K. Grover (Ed.), *Fitness in American culture. Images of health, sport, and the body, 1830-1940* (pp. 123-168). Amherst, MA: University of Massachusetts Press.

PATE, R. (1983). A new definition of youth fitness. *The Physician and Sports Medicine*, **11**(4), 77-83.

PETRAY, C.K., & Cortese, P.A. (1988). Physical fitness: A vital component of the school health education curriculum. *Health Education*, **19**(5), 4-7.

REISER, S. (1978). The emergence of the concept of screening for disease. *Milbank Memorial Fund Quarterly*, **56**(4), 408.

REPORT of the President of the United States on the Annapolis Conference. (1956). *President's Conference on Fitness of American Youth, President's Council on Youth Fitness* (pp. 1-52). Washington, DC: U.S. Government Printing Office.

RISKA, E., & Vinten-Johansen, P. (1981). The involvement of the behavioral sciences in American medicine: A historical perspective. *International Journal of Health Services*, **11**(4), 583-595.

ROGERS, J.F. (1933). *Health instruction in grades 9-12*, (U.S. Department of the Interior, Office of Education Pamphlet No. 43). Washington, DC: U.S. Government Printing Office.

ROSZAK, T. (1980). On the contemporary hunger for wonders. *The Michigan Quarterly Review*, **19**, 303-321.

SARGENT, D.A. (1906). *Physical education*. Boston: Ginn.

SHEEHAN, G. (1978). *Running and being: The total experience*. New York: Warner Books.

SHEEHAN, G.A. (1980). The moral equivalent of war. *The Physician and Sports Medicine*, **8**(12), 37.

SOLOMON, H.A. (1984). *The exercise myth*. New York: Harcourt Brace Jovanovich.

STEVENS, R. (1971). *American medicine and the public interest*. New Haven, CT: Yale University Press.

TESH, S.N. (1988). *Hidden arguments: Political ideology and disease prevention policy*. New Brunswick, NJ: Rutgers University Press.

U.S. Department of Health and Human Services. (1980). *Promoting health/preventing disease*. Washington, DC: U.S. Government Printing Office.

U.S. Department of Health, Education and Welfare. (1979). *Healthy people: The surgeon general's report on health promotion and disease prevention*. Washington, DC: U.S. Government Printing Office.

VERBRUGGE, M.H. (1988). *Able-bodied womanhood. Personal health and social change in nineteenth century Boston*. Oxford: Oxford University Press.

VERTINSKY, P. (1985). Risk benefit analysis of health promotion: Opportunities and threats for physical education. *Quest*, **37**, 71-83.

VERTINSKY, P. (1986). God, science and the marketplace: The bases for exercise prescriptions for females in nineteenth century North America. *Canadian Journal of History of Sport*, **17**(1), 38-46.

VERTINSKY, P. (1987). Body shapes: The role of the medical establishment in informing female exercise in nineteenth century North America. In J.A. Mangan & R.J. Park (Eds.), *From fair sex to feminism: Sport and the socialization of women in the industrial and post industrial eras* (pp. 256-281). London: Frank Cass.

WEDGWOOD, H. (1924). *Recognition of health as an objective*, (U.S. Department of the Interior, Bureau of Education, School Health Studies Pamphlet No. 7). Washington, DC: U.S. Government Printing Office.

WEINBERG, A.M. (1972). Science and trans-science. *Minerva*, **10**, 209-22.

WENGER, N. (1978). The physiological basis for early ambulation after myocardial infarction. In N. Wenger (Ed.), *Exercise and the heart*, (pp. 107-115). Philadelphia: Davis.

WHORTON, J.C. (1982). *Crusaders for fitness: The history of American health reformers*. Princeton, NJ: Princeton University Press.

WILMORE, J.H. (1982). Objectives for the nation—physical fitness and exercise. *Journal of Physical Education, Recreation and Dance*, **53**(3), 41-43.

WOOD, T.D. (1894). Some unresolved problems in physical education. *Addresses and Proceedings of the International Congress of Education*, **3**, 621-623.

Physical Education in American Higher Education

Gary S. Krahenbuhl
Arizona State University

Physical education is a discipline in transition. A look back suggests that the momentum of change has been gathering for some time. It is not clear whether a collective view of what the discipline will become has been established. The purpose of this paper is to examine the discipline of physical education in the context of the culture of American higher education. It is hoped that, by looking at the discipline from this perspective, the problems and issues now being debated by its leaders will come into sharper focus, the many impressive accomplishments will be appreciated, and the opportunities for further change will be more apparent.

There have been numerous attempts to classify the cultures of higher education (Kuh & Whitt, 1988). I utilize here the disciplinary groupings suggested by Becher (1987). This approach features a two-by-two matrix; one dimension separates disciplines into hard and soft; the other dimension divides disciplines into academic and professional. The four cells produced by this two-by-two table are the hard-pure disciplines such as the natural sciences, the soft-pure disciplines such as the social sciences and humanities, the hard-applied disciplines such as engineering, and the soft-applied disciplines such as education. Becher (1987) contends that members of each cell of this matrix exhibit unique academic cultures specific to such things as the knowledge base, the mode of graduate training, and faculty characteristics. This particular approach to considering the cultural characteristics of the disciplines was especially attractive because of the tendency of physical education research to fragment along the lines of traditional disciplines in the academic community.

According to Becher (1987) the knowledge base of the pure disciplines is characterized by concern over substance. The knowledge base of the applied or professional disciplines is characterized by concern over process. The hard-pure disciplines (which include individuals in physical education doing basic work in exercise physiology and exercise biochemistry) exhibit concern with knowing and understanding universalities, treat knowledge as cumulative, and are characterized by the subdivision of problems. The soft-pure disciplines (which include physical education researchers involved in psychology, history, philosophy, and sociology of sport) feature a reiterative style wherein the same material and questions are reviewed from different perspectives. There is more concern about the particular instance than about establishing universalities, and considerable attention is paid to understanding complexities, especially as they apply to the psychological and social dimensions of a problem or question. The nature of knowledge in the hard-applied disciplines (which include individuals working in the field of biomechanics) is cumulative, with special attention to products and techniques. The knowledge base in the soft-applied fields (which include individuals in teacher education, educational administration, and the like) tend to be more eclectic, drawing basic material from other fields and focusing on protocols and procedures.

Graduate training is quite different for students in these different cultures of the academic community. In the hard-pure area, research typically is a collective enterprise featuring teams of investigators that collaborate on projects and coauthor published results. As with most team efforts the work hours are regimented. A student's research topic is frequently determined by the mentor. Students trained in these areas frequently have limited exposure to teaching as part of their graduate experience. Postdoctoral research experiences are the norm. This model matches very closely the graduate training being provided at many of the better institutions in the area of exercise physiology.

Graduate training in the soft-pure areas reflects the fact that research in those areas is a more independent enterprise. Because it is more individual, the work hours are more flexible, and collaboration is less common. Graduate students have greater latitude in the selection of research themes and are more likely to be the sole author of publications that result from the work. These conditions are perhaps more true for the more humanistic aspects of physical education, such as history or philosophy of sport, but also fit many students studying in sociology and psychology of sport. (The remainder would exist in conditions more closely resembling the hard-pure model.)

Graduate training in the hard-applied area is very similar to that found in the hard-pure area; thus the training of students in biomechanics looks very much like the training of students in exercise physiology, except for a reduced likelihood of postdoctoral training opportunities.

Students trained in the soft-applied areas tend to be very different from those in the previous three areas. They typically begin graduate study with few specific ideas about what they wish to study or who might serve as an effective mentor for their graduate training. These questions usually sort themselves out during the first few semesters of course work. The definition of the work is not nearly so tightly bound to the mentor's expertise as in the other cases. Thus, individuals gaining physical education degrees in elementary physical education, secondary physical education, adapted physical education, educational administration, and so on are likely to have very different experiences than typical students working in the hard-pure, soft-pure, and hard-applied areas. The ability of individuals who gain degrees in the soft-applied area to gain tenure and promotion at the nation's comprehensive research universities seems to be sharply lower than for those trained in the other cultures.

One might expect a discipline in transition to call no single place its home, and that is indeed the case for physical education. A recent review of *Peterson's*

Guide (Von Vorys, 1990) reveals that of the 290 institutions granting graduate degrees in physical education, 37 (13%) are housed in liberal arts colleges, 70 (24%) in professional colleges of various names such as Health, Physical Education and Recreation or Allied Health, and 183 (63%) in education colleges.

If a department were strictly bound to operating in a manner consistent with the administrative unit in which it were housed, programs would take three forms. When housed in a college of education, physical education would be limited to professional preparation of teachers for positions in education. When housed in a professional college (such as allied health) separate from education, the discipline could legitimately prepare individuals for a professional life within or outside of education. When the discipline of physical education is located in an academic college such as a college of liberal arts and sciences, it can appropriately enjoy a full complement of academic possibilities. Such departments can legitimately offer both academic and professional degrees. When physical education exists outside a professional school setting, it is accepted as a legitimate liberal arts discipline, an integral part of a comprehensive general education. As an academic (as opposed to a professional) major, it offers the possibility for study without the constraints of specific career expectations. This is education in its purest form: knowing, not because one necessarily can or need do anything with the knowledge, but because it is important in and by itself, because knowledge is better than ignorance (Schaefer, 1990).

In universities where departments of physical education are housed in colleges of liberal arts and sciences, the popularity of the bachelor of arts degree has been growing steadily. For example, at Arizona State University most undergraduate students now major in the B.A. degree program. The percentage of students majoring in the professional degree program has dropped from nearly 100% in 1980 to approximately 30% in 1990—in spite of the fact that B.A. students must fulfill a much more intense general studies requirement that includes 2 years of a foreign language.

From my perspective it is clear that what is happening in physical education has happened to many disciplines. Late in the last century, psychology formed as a body of knowledge from various disciplines interested in the study of the mind and behavior. Early in this century biochemistry grew out of biology and chemistry. The discipline of political science grew out of early education programs preparing high school teachers of government and academic programs in political philosophy. At the moment, cellular and molecular biology programs are being formed around the advances in biotechnology. Just as these disciplines have taken shape as their knowledge base became established (Kash, 1987; Kates, 1989; Sproull & Hall, 1987), the discipline of physical education is taking shape as knowledge related to human movement continues to accumulate and take form.

As we consider how disparate knowledge coalesced in these earlier academic experiments, and look ahead to consider ideas to advance the discipline of physical education, one thing is clear. The discipline has made dramatic gains against incredible odds. Until recently, virtually everyone outside physical education held the view that the discipline was nonacademic. Now, in spite of the fact that hundreds of individuals are making significant contributions to the knowledge base, progress in being recognized as a significant player in the academic world is lagging (Aronson, 1989; Mawby, 1987). I believe that the delay in recognition is contributed to by the lack of

1. a common name for departments of physical education across universities,
2. a common location within administrative organizations of higher education,
3. a common preparation across the various areas of graduate study within physical education, and
4. common expectations for faculty seeking promotion and tenure across the various subject matter areas within physical education and across institutions.

Progress in these four areas will be slow. Educational institutions are among society's most conservative organizations, and there are years of misunderstanding to overcome. Nevertheless, if the leaders of the field can agree on the future directions of physical education in these four areas, then the most significant obstacle will be overcome. We are clearly headed in the right direction. I believe it is only a matter of time before the discipline of physical education receives the recognition it deserves and becomes a full partner in the academic enterprise.

References

ARONSON, R.M. (1989). Denial of promotion to administrative positions in higher education for physical educators. *Journal of the International Council for Health, Physical Education, and Recreation*, **26**(1), 26-29.

BECHER, T. (1987). The disciplinary shaping of the profession. In B.R. Clark (Ed.), *The academic profession* (pp. 271-303). Berkeley: University of California.

KASH, D.E. (1987). Intellectual need versus institutional resistance: Interdisciplinary centers. *Proceedings of the 27th Annual Meeting of the Council of Graduate Schools*, **27**, 83-90.

KATES, R.W. (1989, May 17). The great questions of science and society do not fit neatly into single disciplines. *The Chronicle of Higher Education*, pp. B1-B3.

KUH, G.D., & Whitt, E.J. (1988). The invisible tapestry: Culture in American colleges and universities. *ASHE-ERIC Higher Education Report No. 1*. Association for the Study of Higher Education, Washington, DC.

MAWBY, R.G. (1987). University-based public service. *Science*, **238**, 1491.

SCHAEFER, W.D. (1990). *Education without compromise*. San Francisco: Jossey-Bass.

SPROULL, R.L., & Hall, H.H. (1987, December). Multidisciplinary research and education programs in universities: Making them work. *Government–University–Industry Research Roundtable*, National Academy of Sciences, Washington, DC.

VON VORYS, B. (Ed.) (1990). *Peterson's guide to graduate programs in business, education, health and law*. Princeton, NJ: Peterson's Guides.

Knowledge Problems in Physical Education

Rainer Martens
Human Kinetics Publishers

Information As a Resource

You would have to be living in the dark ages not to know we are now well into the information age. We are beyond the "gee whiz, by golly" stage of how computers can manipulate information. Yet we sense, from the most recent and rapid changes, that much more is to come. This appears to be especially so as we move information around by linking computers with our global telecommunications systems, and as light rather than electricity becomes the primary means of manipulating bits of information.

The information age has dawned the knowledge economy where information is a commodity to be bought, traded, and sold. It is estimated that 40% to 65% of the U.S. labor force is employed in the knowledge industry. Information is a major resource; those who have it have the competitive advantage. Historically Americans have had this advantage, but now we are rightfully concerned about losing it. It's been said that we are moving from a world of the survival of the fittest into a world of the survival of the best informed. Next to our human resources, I believe information is our greatest resource. And yet it is a resource so different from human and material resources.

- It expands even as it is used.
- It cannot be exchanged, only shared.
- It can be compressed through synthesis and integration.
- It leaks easily and moves at the speed of light.
- It is substitutable and transplantable.

Knowledge Problems

The explosion of information in physical education has created several significant "knowledge problems," including those associated with the production, dissemination, and utilization of knowledge. In this brief essay I shall discuss three of these problems.

To begin I need definitions for three terms—*data, information*, and *knowledge*. I like the definitions given by Harlan Cleveland (1985) in *The Knowledge Executive*. He defines data as "undigested observations; unvarnished facts." Information, according to Cleveland, "is organized data," and knowledge "is organized information, internalized by me, integrated with everything else I know, and therefore is useful" (p. 22). Information is narrower in scope, whereas knowledge embraces both empirical facts and facts derived by inference and interpretation.

For example, newspapers provide streams of data, but John Naisbitt (1982) in *Megatrends* connected these data into information. For this information to become knowledge, you and I must "internalize" it, or come to "know" it, and then integrate it with everything else we know to use it in some way. To most of society, access to vast amounts of undigested facts is of little value. These facts need to be organized into principles, generalizations, guidelines, models, theories, and so on. To say it another way, knowledge is not knowledge unless it is usable by society.

This leads me to the three most significant knowledge problems in physical education today.

1. The foremost knowledge problem in physical education is not the production of more information, but the production of knowledge from information.
2. The second most significant knowledge problem is the poor utilization of this knowledge by our society.
3. The third most pressing knowledge problem is scientism—the misplaced faith in the current paradigm for acquiring information via the scientific method.

I will briefly comment on the third problem first, and then discuss problems 1 and 2.

Scientism

Despite all the evidence that the use of the scientific method as developed for the natural sciences does not work well in studying human behavior, we continue to employ the rules and procedures of what I call orthodox science in acquiring information in physical education. Orthodox science is based on the conception of objectivity as a fundamental assumption—scientific information is objective information unlike other sources of information, and this is what makes it a superior source of information.

Stated in an oversimplified way, orthodox science attempts to develop controls and procedures that remove the bias that may be introduced by the investigator. But of course this is not possible, as has been repeatedly proven. No scientist investigates a problem without bias. The selection of the problem to be studied and the methods used to investigate the problem are major biases at the outset.

A great deal of evidence argues against the current methods of science—especially those principles that try to impose objectivity by removing the scientist as an active part of the process of knowing. From any serious study of the practice of science, it is obvious that scientists play an active role in what they observe, and that the reality they report is shaped by their perceptions. Space does not permit me to develop a sufficient argument about my objections to scientism, but I have made that case elsewhere (see Martens, 1987).

My purpose here is to at least repeat my warning: Orthodox science is not the only source of knowledge, and it often is not the source of more valid knowledge that it often is touted to be. Furthermore, the blind belief in orthodox science is destructive, because it prevents us from moving toward a better scientific paradigm for studying human behavior. To be branded "unscientific," especially in academe, is likely to lead to excommunication from the hallowed halls and ivoried towers. Young scientists simply cannot succeed in academe unless they accept the dogmatic doctrine of objectivity as prescribed by the current paradigm of the scientific method. The information gatekeepers—the editors and editorial board members of journals, conference organizers, and peers in the tenure and promotion review process—simply do not accept alternative sources of information and knowledge, and thus those who do not play "the game of science" are certain to fail in academe.

This unjustified belief in orthodox science leads to many destructive practices, including the following.

1. The denigration of other sources of knowledge. Scientists all too often condemn the work of practitioners or professionals because their knowledge is not based exclusively on information acquired by orthodox science. This often creates animosity between scientists and professionals, which prevents them from integrating scientific and experiential information.
2. Studying problems not because they are important but because the available methods lend themselves to studying the question objectively. That is, scientists study problems that do not require solutions.
3. The overreliance upon statistics to replace sound judgment and tacit knowledge.
4. The belief that the peer review process provides objectivity to research; that is, the reviewers are unbiased. Of course they are not; they are usually colleagues or competitors of the scientist and have a vested interest in what they review.

I am happy to report that there is a paradigm shift beginning to occur in the behavioral and social sciences that recognizes that knowledge acquisition is not an objective process, but optimally one that involves the perceptions of a responsible scientist. Michael Polanyi (1958) refers to this new paradigm as the heuristic paradigm of knowledge; it acknowledges the importance of the scientist's tacit knowledge—the totality of what a person knows through his or her subsidiary awareness. The process of integrating data into information, and information into knowledge, is a human process, and we wisely should not attempt to remove the scientist from the process in order to be objective.

Please understand, I am not opposed to science. I firmly believe science is essential for information and knowledge acquisition. My comments are made to advocate a better science, one that recognizes the human qualities of scientists in acquiring knowledge.

Converting Information Into Knowledge

Information is in chronic surplus, but knowledge is scarce. The proliferation of data and the glut of information place a premium on the synthesis and integration of information to produce knowledge. Of course, there is still plenty for scientists to find out, but the most significant knowledge problem in physical education, and in almost every other field, is the need to convert information into knowledge.

The process of converting information into knowledge is often extremely difficult. It requires knowledge integrators to synthesize vast amounts of information into coherent generalizations, principles, models, and theories. There is no useless information, only people who have not learned how to use it—to convert it into knowledge. This demanding process requires the creative and intellectual feat of making sense of what seems nonsensical, and it often requires integration across fields of study and integration of scientific information with experiential information.

A major factor that has had adverse influence on the conversion of information into knowledge is that the responsibility for doing so has not been embraced by either scientist or practitioner. Should the responsibility lie with scientists who produce information and are experts in a particular field? Should it be with practitioners who understand the real-world problems for which the knowledge is needed? It is easy to make a case that both scientists and practitioners should take responsibility for converting information into knowledge, and both do to a limited extent, but each group makes conversions at very different levels of knowledge. The scientist most often seeks synthesis of scientific information into the form of theory or models, in the absence of practical considerations. The practitioner most often seeks to meld diverse experiential information into knowledge that directly influences the practice of her or his profession, without considering the scientific evidence.

What often does not happen is the integration of scientific and experiential information into useful knowledge by scientists or practitioners, and for obvious reasons. Scientists often are not interested in this task, are not rewarded for it in academe, and have little understanding of how the information they have may be applied to real-world problems. The practitioner, on the other hand, often is unable to understand the scientific literature and lacks time to sort through the voluminous information to integrate it with experiential information.

This is why a new breed of scholar is emerging, the *knowledge integrator*—the rebirth of the generalist, the get-it-all-together person. This person must be well educated in science, often being a former scientist, and must be well educated about the real-world demands faced by the practitioner. Furthermore, the person must be motivated to synthesize both sources of information into useful knowledge.

Unfortunately, knowledge integrators are in short supply, mostly because academe does not recognize the worth of this type of significant scholarship. Academe tends to reward foremost the production of information and to a lesser extent the production of knowledge. Academicians know all too well that they had best be full professors before deciding to become knowledge integrators. Young academics who primarily convert information into knowledge will find their writings difficult to publish, invitations to speak at prestigious meetings meager, and the promotion ladder out of reach. Knowledge integrators, who are often master teachers, are second-class citizens by most standards in academe.

I assure you this will change. The continued avalanche of information, the enormous chaos in the brickyard, the demand by society that academe pay its dues to those who pay its salaries, will elevate the knowledge broker to first-class citizenship—and this shall come to pass sooner rather than later. It already is so in business and industry. In "high tech" fields, those who can convert science (information) into technology (knowledge) are the heroes and heroines of the day. Those in academe who can do this successfully now have enormous opportunity in consulting with business and industry.

I see another problem here that concerns me. We all recognize that real-world problems are inherently interdisciplinary. Consequently, as information becomes more and more specialized, the more the specialists from different subdisciplines within our field need to work together to understand the whole. Thus more cross-disciplinary and interdisciplinary work is needed, and scientists need to have a greater understanding and appreciation for the other disciplines. This is one reason it is time we provide forums for transdisciplinary information exchange so that we can produce more knowledge about the whole. We need to dispose of the disciplinary pecking order and lack of respect by some scientists for the work of other scientists.

Of course not all scientists should be expected to learn about all the subdisciplines in our field. And not all research should be interdisciplinary. Therefore, the value of having knowledge integrators should become obvious to these specialized scientists. Knowledge integrators put scientists' information to use; they add value to this information and therefore to the work of scientists. Yet we so often see scientists condemning the work of knowledge integrators when they extend their information beyond the limited scientific conclusions to application in the real world. When such application is done poorly, it warrants condemnation; but often it is condemned when done well, simply because the integration requires filling gaps that are not yet bridged scientifically. The condemnation also is based on the assumption that scientific information is always more accurate than other information, an assumption that is often invalid.

Isaac Stern, the famous violinist, was asked what distinguished the great musician from the ordinary, given that all competent musicians play the same notes in the same order. After a thoughtful moment, he replied: "It's the intervals between the notes." Analogously, it is not our capacity to dig out facts and compile information, but rather the educated intuition and the practical experience to integrate these facts into meaningful knowledge—to fill the gaps—that warrants at least equal recognition.

Universities especially need to address these issues. The emphasis on the production only of information is too narrow in responding to society's needs. The rewards for scholarship must recognize all aspects of the information–knowledge process, especially knowledge production, dissemination, and implementation. Universities especially need to adapt their disciplinary structures to the inherently interdisciplinary nature of the real world. Universities need to see extension programs not as extension programs but as programs that are essential and central to their mission.

Knowledge Utilization

Of course, producing knowledge and not utilizing it is a great waste of a resource. Knowledge utilization requires, first, the effective dissemination of the knowledge, and second, action to implement the knowledge.

When I was an academician, I assumed that when I produced information it would automatically become knowledge, and the knowledge would readily be utilized. When I developed the American Coaching Effectiveness Program (ACEP), which has had more than 100,000 coaches participate in its courses, I thought that once we converted the information from the sport sciences and our coaching experience into practical knowledge, every sport organization responsible for coaches would leap at the opportunity to utilize this knowledge. Ten years later and 2 million dollars invested, I can tell you it doesn't happen that way.

Producing knowledge is only one step. Then you have to convince people that they should use this knowledge, and once they are convinced, you have to show them how to utilize it effectively. As we all know, many people do not readily embrace knowledge they know is good for them. People continue to smoke, overeat, and underexercise, even though they know better. Organizations often resist implementing available knowledge because they do not like to cope with change or they fear loss of control. Much knowledge is not utilized because it costs considerable money to disseminate the knowledge and to implement the changes prescribed by the new knowledge.

The ACEP example is relevant here. We spent several years with a small staff of four producing knowledge from sport science and medicine that we thought would benefit coaches. I was certain that producing this knowledge was the hardest part, but soon discovered that we had only begun in the battle to educate coaches. As we recognized the problem, we began to employ individuals who came from the coaching ranks and who we called ACEP implementors. As distasteful as it might sound, they had to *sell* ACEP by convincing sport organizations and coaches that knowing a little something about sport physiology, sport psychology, sport pedagogy, and sports medicine would be good for them. Once we convinced them, then we had to show them step by step how to deliver the education.

Although academic institutions and scholarly societies are well prepared to produce and disseminate information, they are less well prepared to produce and disseminate knowledge. And they are poorly equipped to actively implement change. Typically, when academics see a problem, they issue a position statement, circulate it (usually amongst themselves) and then proudly declare that they have done all that's possible to solve the problem. And perhaps this is appropriate; academe is the source of information and the producer of some knowledge, but other institutions in our society may need to assume the greater responsibility for producing and implementing this knowledge.

A major barrier for academics to overcome in implementing knowledge is that their information is often not trusted by practitioners to be practical knowledge. And often practitioners are right. Furthermore, practitioners are skeptical of academics, because they perceive that academics do not respect their experiential knowledge base and do not appreciate the challenges they face when dealing with real-world problems.

It especially concerns me that almost none of our organizations in physical education are structured to be effective in implementing change. The 10 or so scholarly societies are not, NAPEHE is not, and certainly the Academy is not. AAHPERD comes closest, but it spends the vast majority of its resources on maintaining itself rather than helping to implement new knowledge into society's institutions. Physical education cannot hope to realize its potential as a profession until it develops organizations that do more than disseminate information. Physical education needs action-oriented organizations that produce, disseminate, and implement knowledge in our society.

References

CLEVELAND, H. (1985). *The knowledge executive*. New York: Truman Talley Books.

MARTENS, R. (1987). Science, knowledge, and sport psychology. *The Sport Psychologist*, **1**, 29-55.

NAISBITT, J. (1982). *Megatrends*. New York: Warner Books.

POLANYI, M. (1958). *Personal knowledge: Towards a post-critical philosophy*. Chicago: University of Chicago Press.

Homo Movens: In Search of Paradigms for the Study of Humans in Movement

Roland Renson
Institute of Physical Education, Belgium

The Challenge and Responsibility

Let me begin on a personal note, a look back at my own experiences as a physical education student in the early '60s in Belgium. At that time, the Institute of Physical Education was still a subsection of the Faculty of Medicine of the University of Leuven. The physical education curriculum was characterized by a strong dualistic division between theory and practice. Both moieties lived separate lives without any trading posts present to establish a rapprochement. Moreover, the curriculum entailed the juxtaposition of a variety of disciplines, ranging from philosophy to physics. These different pieces of the physical education jigsaw puzzle were offered without a master plan or model to integrate them. The really difficult task of integrating knowledge was left to the individual students, without giving them any guidelines for doing so—a situation comparable to an academic game of blindman's bluff.

The same held true when I combined physical education with studies in physical therapy: Pathology was taught without any reference to physical therapy practice. My decision to study social and cultural anthropology was inspired by the specific topic of my PhD thesis in physical education, *Sociocultural Determinants of Growth, Motor Fitness and Sport Participation of 13 Year Old Belgian Boys* (Renson, 1973a).

This refreshing immersion in anthropology certainly encouraged me to develop a new look at the picture of humans in movement during sport and play (Renson, 1973b). However, a feeling remained that this picture was still incomplete and needed better focusing. The fact, for instance, that sociocultural anthropology had split off from physical anthropology seriously jeopardized the so-called holistic approach to the study of humans. At that time, I felt happy that the biological dimension had been part and parcel of the truly humanistic physical education curriculum.

The foregoing has not been mentioned to criticize my former teachers' neglect of integration. Some of them, like Pierre-Paul De Nayer, MD, and Mik Ostyn, MD, have been real pioneers who—sometimes against all odds—have claimed and obtained an independent status for the discipline of physical education within the university. However, the situation has evolved so drastically that our discipline is now in desperate need of a better flag to cover the full range of its cargo. Indeed, from the 1960s onward, physical education has gone through a stage of progressive differentiation, characterized by specialization and the establishment of various subdisciplines. This process has not only caused dissatisfaction with the term *physical education*; it has also shown the need for new paradigms to integrate the evolving body of knowledge. In this context, the present contribution seeks to provide some concepts in an attempt to construct a more coherent approach to the study of humans in movement.

First, the concept of Homo movens is presented as the central theme that (re)unites all those who study humans in movement. Second, a taxonomy is developed to integrate different aspects of Homo movens from a biocultural perspective. Finally, the concept of kinanthropology is proposed as an integrative paradigm and an epistemological charter for the study of humans in movement.

The Concept of Homo Movens

> Like all higher animals, man is basically designed for mobility. Consequently, our locomotive apparatus and service organs constitute the main part of our total body mass. (Åstrand, 1989, p. xx)

The study of Homo movens, or the science of humans in movement, is a cross-disciplinary, theme-oriented approach, and it is therefore of the highest importance to define the central theme correctly.

I was first confronted with this definitional problem in 1974 when I tried to conceptualize an undergraduate course on the history of physical education. Historically speaking, the term *physical education* is of fairly recent origin, a cultural product of the Enlightenment put into practice by the 18th-century pedagogical school of the Philanthropinists, of which GutsMuths (1759-1839) was the most important contributor to physical education. The term *sport* is also relatively new, and therefore to speak of, for instance, sport in antiquity or during the Middle Ages is to commit an anachronism. Mutatis mutandis these two characteristic concepts of Western civilization, physical education and sport, cannot be transplanted to the movement activities of other cultures without running the risk of crude ethnocentrism.

Ever since the appearance of the pioneering works of Huizinga (1938) on the meaning of play and Caillois (1958) on games, the prime movers of modern sport sociology (Loy & Kenyon, 1969; McIntosh, 1963) and sport anthropology (Blanchard & Cheska, 1985; Harris & Park, 1983) have rightly recognized this problem of definition. They have further explored and clarified the meaning of concepts such as play, game, physical activity, and sport (see, e.g., Guttmann's analysis in his book *From Ritual to Record: The Nature of Modern Sports*, 1978). All the sources cited have adopted *sport* as a generic term for all the playful or competitive movement activities of humankind. And I must admit to having made the same compromise in my publication *History of Sport in Antiquity* (Renson, 1980a), in which I situated sport in the intersection of the two Venn diagrams of *physical culture* on the one hand and *play* on the other hand. Today I slightly retouch this picture by introducing the concept of Homo movens (see Figure 1).

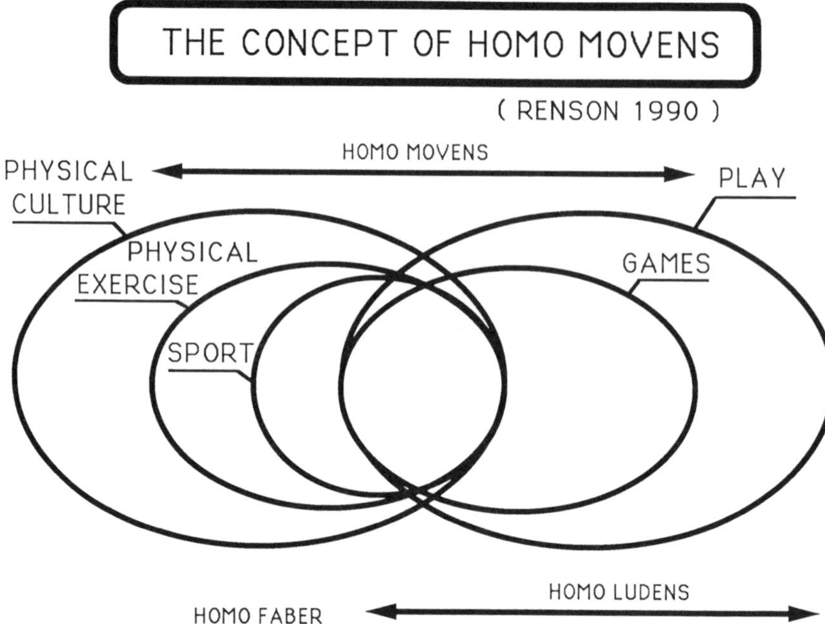

Figure 1 — The concept of Homo movens.

The concept of physical culture—and not work—was chosen as one of the two major components of the concept of Homo movens, the other being play. Physical culture has been for years the umbrella concept for physical education in countries with Marxist ideologies (Riordan, 1977). The French anthropologist Mauss (1935) has justly qualified this neglected area in anthropology as "the techniques of the body." Physical culture has an instrumental undertone and refers to humans performing physical exercises during work, rehabilitation, or leisure. Play, on the other hand, is *autotelic*, a nonutilitarian activity for its own sake. Homo movens thus embraces the related but antithetical concepts of both *Homo faber* (the artisan) and *Homo ludens* (the player), at least as far as movement is involved. It encompasses a wide scale of movement activities, ranging from physical exercise in all its forms (including work, rehabilitation, calisthenics, and dance) to sport, movement games, and motor play. Physical education as such does not appear in this list of movement activities; it constitutes the (ped)agogical dimension of homo movens, which makes use of the entire range of movement activities for reaching its biocultural goals. Homo movens cannot be studied in a purely biological manner or in a purely cultural manner; it necessarily requires a multidisciplinary, biocultural approach, as has been stressed before by Malina (1980).

A Taxonomy for Studying Humans in Movement

The biocultural study of Homo movens is of such a wide scope that diversified knowledge from various disciplines must be organized in an integrated framework. Tendencies toward specialization have too often driven scholars apart into secluded scientific subcultures. This process of fragmentation through specialization has happened not only in physical education but also in other fields that focus on human beings, such as medicine. But more and more voices now claim that it is time to reconstruct a holistic picture of humankind: A macroscopic approach is needed to (re)integrate the narrow microscopic views (Engel, 1982; Nabel, 1985).

When I was approached some years ago to write a review on the topic of limits to sport performance, I decided to take up the challenge to construct a taxonomy for studying humans in movement (Renson, 1983). Bateson's *Steps to an Ecology of Mind* (1973) acted as a stimulating source of inspiration. This field anthropologist, who later did research in psychiatry and ethology, was deeply concerned with the nature of order in living systems. As a modest tribute to Bateson, therefore, this chapter might be subtitled "Steps to a Taxonomy of Homo Movens."

A series of explanatory models were chosen from the literature to cover the broad spectrum of humans in movement. Lüschen's (1969) social action system model served as starting point. This model is based on the sociological theory of Parsons (1961), and it clearly identifies four different subsystems that both control and condition sport behavior. These subsystems are

1. culture,
2. the social system,
3. the personality, and
4. the behavioral organism.

Lüschen stated moreover that the general action system is related to the physical organic environment, most directly through the behavioral organism. However, little was said about how these subsystems interact and how they function as a whole. In an attempt to touch up Lüschen's model, nine other models were selected from the literature (see Figure 2). In this rearranged and completed model, the individual, with her or his biological organism and personality, is presented in interaction with the social, the cultural, and the physical environments. The physical environment was transplanted from the base of Lüschen's model to the top of our taxonomy. Further, conceptual bypasses are added to integrate the five different blocks more functionally. These connection systems consist of energy, symbol, role, and the motor system. Figure 2 presents a kind of concise topographical anatomy of the taxonomic model, going vertically from head to toe.

The interaction between human beings and their physical environment has recently been given considerable attention. Certain outdoor sports have damaged our natural environment, causing in turn an ecological reflex. As a first SOS signal, the research section of the 21st International Council for Health, Physical Education and Recreation (ICHPER) congress of 1981 in Manila was entirely dedicated to ecological factors affecting the physical activity of children.

The concept of energy is employed to bridge physical environment and culture. As Leslie White stated,

> culture is but a means of carrying on the life process of a particular species, homo sapiens. It is a mechanism for providing man with subsistence, protec-

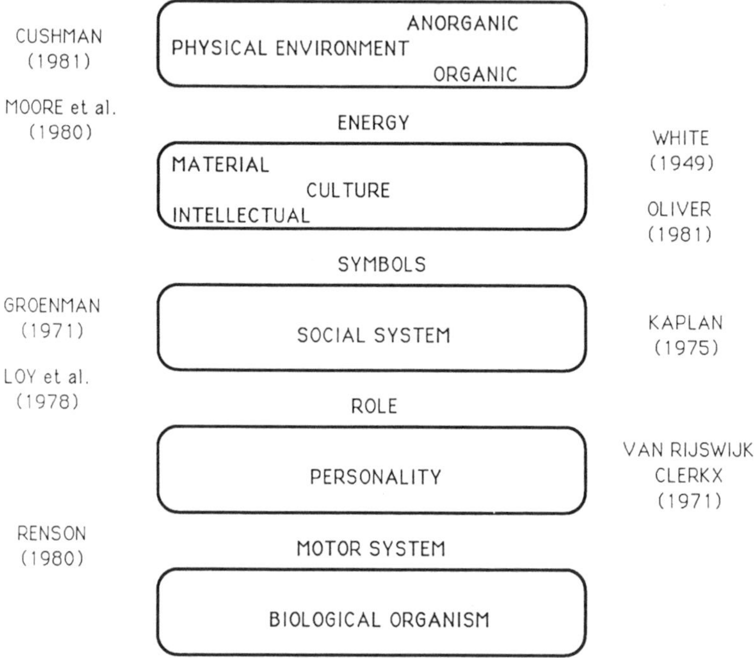

Figure 2 — A taxonomy for studying humans in movement (Renson, 1983).

> tion, offense and defense, social regulation, cosmic adjustment, and recreation. But to serve these needs of man energy is required. It becomes the primary function of culture, therefore, to harness and control energy so that it may be put to work in man's service. (White, 1949, p. 367)

Although the anthropological school of cultural ecology, to which White belongs, thus stresses the importance of material culture (technology and economy), these material aspects cannot be seen independently from aspects of intellectual culture. Both constitute our human-made environment. Furthermore, the intellectual aspects of the cultural system, such as norms, values, and beliefs, are related to the structural elements of the social system. The different organs within the social system, such as social categories, groups, organizations, and institutions (Loy, 1972), make use of symbols to identify themselves as a body and to manifest themselves to the outside world.

"The world is a stage, everybody plays his role and gets his part." The role concept reflected in this well-known quotation from the Dutch writer Joost van den Vondel (1587-1679) appears in the taxonomic model as the link between the society and the individual. This individual, Homo movens, is presented here by the personality system and the biological organism, which are connected through the motor system. Human movement is the most important research domain of the science of Homo movens. However, this science should not be restricted to a single disciplinary approach to human movement (kinesiology or human kinetics) but should encompass a cross-disciplinary approach to humans in movement (kinanthropology).

Kinanthropology: An Integrative Paradigm for the Study of Humans in Movement

In a recent article in *Quest* (Renson, 1989), I attempted to trace and interpret the origins of the dissatisfaction with the term *physical education*, giving a retrospective-comparative overview of the major conceptual trends and structural developments that have arisen since the academic status of physical education has been questioned. Our quest, in the medieval sense of an adventurous journey (here, through the international literature), started in the United States in 1964, from where it moved to the francophone sphere, then to Germany and Great Britain, to end up in the Low Countries. The outcome of this search revealed four major conceptual trends (see Table 1).

Traditionally, a *discipline* is characterized by

1. a particular focus or object of study,
2. a specialized method of inquiry, and
3. a unique body of knowledge.

The study of human movement, not humans in movement, has been claimed as such a unique scientific domain, a field of knowledge not explored by other disciplines.

A *multidisciplinary* approach consists of the study of one central topic, for example, sport, from separate disciplinary perspectives, without a unifying concept. It is vertically oriented, and therefore the outcome is the sum of various disciplinary approaches (the so-called applied sciences). Knowledge is borrowed from parent disciplines and applied to the practical problems of physical activity or physical education. The sport sciences, or physical activity sciences, represent this conceptual trend.

An *interdisciplinary* approach consists of the interaction between two or more different disciplines in the form of the communication of ideas leading to the mutual integration of the respective fields. Because an integrative paradigm is lacking, the orientation remains vertical, and thematical integration is only partial. The concept of sport science can be viewed as such an interdisciplinary attempt.

A *cross-disciplinary* science is oriented horizontally because it transcends disciplinary boundaries. Although certain portions are borrowed from the traditional disciplines, a unifying concept exists that generates its thematically integrated subject matter. Such a cross-disciplinary approach is informed by, though

Table 1

Comparative Overview of Major Conceptual Trends, Authors, Terminology, and Journals in the Scientific Approach to Humans in Movement (Renson, 1989)

Geographical areas	Conceptual trends	Investigations, epistemological contributions, and conceptual propositions	Terminology	Journals
North America	Cross-disciplinary	Henry, 1964	Physical education	*Quest*, 1964
		Ross, 1974, 1978, 1981	Physical education	
		Lawson & Morford, 1979	Kinesiology and sport studies	
	Multidisciplinary	Zeigler, 1985	Sport and physical education	
Francophone Canada	Cross-disciplinary	Meynard, 1966	Kinanthropology	*Kinanthropologie,* 1969-1974
		Sheedy, 1967, 1974a, 1974b	Physical education	
France		Parlebas, 1971	Physical education	

Canada		Bouchard, 1974	Physical activity sciences	
France		Parlebas, 1981	Science of motor action	*Science et Motricité*, 1987
Germany				
GDR	Multidisciplinary	Erbach, 1964, 1966	Sport science	
FRG		Schmitz, 1966	Sport science	
	Interdisciplinary	Willimczik, 1968, 1980, 1985	Sport science	
		Grupe, 1971	Sport science	*Sportwissenschaft*, 1971
	Multidisciplinary	Willimczik, 1974	Sport sciences	
	Interdisciplinary	Haag, 1979	Sport science	
Great Britain	Disciplinary	Brooke & Whiting, 1973	Human movement studies	
		Curl, 1973; Renshaw, 1973, 1975	Human movement studies	*J. Human Movement Studies*, 1975
		Whiting, 1982	Human movement science	*J. Human Movement Science*, 1982
	Interdisciplinary	Reilly, 1983	Sport sciences	*J. Sports Sciences*, 1983
Low Countries				
Netherlands	Cross-disciplinary	Rijsdorp, 1971, 1974	Gymnology	
Belgium		Renson, 1975	Kinanthropology	
		Renson, 1980	Kinanthropology	

not subordinated to, the propositions and theories of the traditional disciplines. Kinanthropology is presented here as a holistic, integrated, cross-disciplinary science of humans in movement.

In the francophone world of physical education, the Canadian Roch Meynard introduced the term *kinanthropologie* in 1967. The term *kinanthropology* is an etymological combination of the Greek *kinein* (to move), *anthropos* (human), and *logos* (science), thus indicating the science of humans in movement.

Kinanthropologists, or specialists in the area of humans in movement, represent the holistic physical education tradition. Epistemological and professional arguments for this claim are presented in a two-dimensional model in Table 2. The disciplinary approaches are positioned on the vertical axis, and the cross-disciplinary approach of kinanthropology is positioned on the horizontal axis. The different disciplines on the vertical axis range from the natural sciences through the human sciences. Human kinetics (or human movement science) falls midway on the scale as a natural bridge. Whereas the subdiscipline of kinesiology links with the natural sciences, motor learning links with the behavioral sciences. Kinanthropometry occupies a position in between. The different sport sciences are presented as applied disciplines on a parallel vertical axis. It should be mentioned that, just as with "sport sciences," one can speak of "rehabilitation sciences" when knowledge of a parent discipline is applied to the process of rehabilitating people. The term *physical activity sciences* (Bouchard, 1974) therefore seems to be a more appropriate common denominator for this multidisciplinary or interdisciplinary vertical category.

Kinanthropology, the science of humans in movement in the context of sport, play, dance, physical exercise, work, or rehabilitation, is featured as a cross-disciplinary science on the horizontal axis. Instead of mere application of knowledge borrowed from so-called parent disciplines, this holistic approach integrates the physical-organic, the motor, and the behavioral components. These three components, represented in Figure 3 as an integrated triad, form the fundamental subject matter of the science of humans in movement (Renson, 1987).

Five different approaches, or areas of specialization, are identified within the cross-disciplinary science of kinanthropology (Renson, 1980b).

1. *Developmental* kinanthropology studies the dynamic processes of physical growth, motor development, and sport socialization in their mutual interaction.
2. *Differential* kinanthropology studies the structure of physical, motor, and behavioral characteristics in their mutual interaction as well as the differentiation of these factors among different groups or categories.
3. *Social-cultural* kinanthropology studies to what extent social and cultural determinants affect physical, motor, and behavioral aspects in their mutual interaction.
4. *Clinical* kinanthropology studies the therapeutic applications of human movement in the interrelated areas of physical, motor, and behavioral disorders.
5. *Agogical* kinanthropology studies the educational process in the interrelated areas of physical/health education, movement/safety education, and sport/dance/outdoor education.

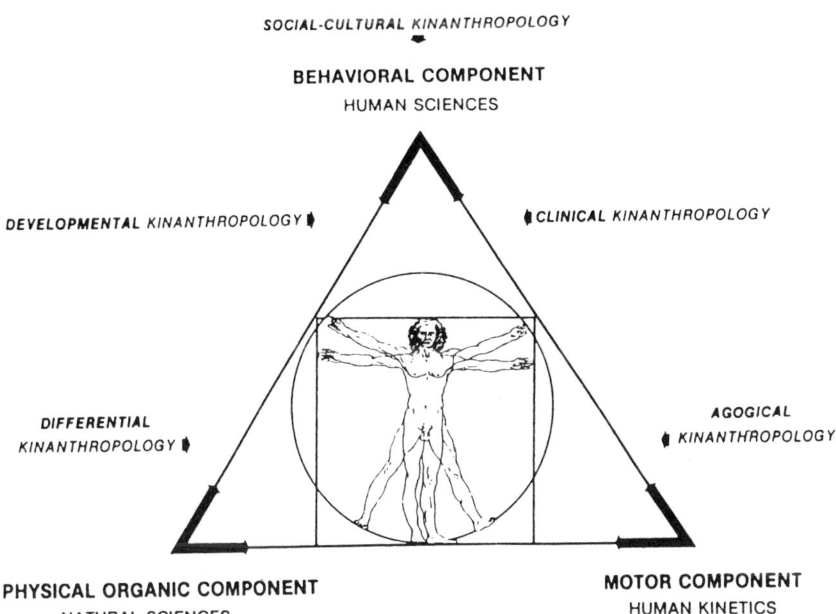

Figure 3 — The kinanthropology triad and five different approaches or kinanthropological subdisciplines (Renson, 1987).

Each of the five kinanthropological subdisciplines focuses on the physical–motor–behavioral trinity, although from a somewhat different perspective. The perspectives, however, are complementary and constantly interact. A holistic kinanthropological approach necessitates both specialization and teamwork and is therefore essentially both disciplinary and cross-disciplinary in nature. Indeed, human kinetics, or the science of human movement, can be viewed as the disciplinary entrance, and physical activity sciences as the multi- and interdisciplinary entrances, of the kinanthropology model.

Conclusion: The Problem of Integration and Terminology

The cross-disciplinary "horizontal" science of kinanthropology cannot be isolated from the disciplinary "vertical" physical activity sciences, from which knowledge is borrowed. However, without integration through one of the five mentioned kinanthropological approaches, knowledge runs the risk of being sectarian-disciplinary, fragmented, and often irrelevant for or unapplicable to human beings in a movement context.

The viability of the kinanthropology paradigm and the benefits of cross-disciplinary research were demonstrated in two major projects undertaken at the University of Leuven. The team that carried out both the Leuven Growth Study of Belgian boys (Ostyn, Simons, Beunen, Renson, & Van Gerven, 1980) and the Leuven Growth Study of Flemish Girls (Simons et al., 1990) was composed of research workers who looked at physical fitness from several kinanthropological perspectives. Physical fitness evaluation included anthropometric dimensions,

Table 2

Kinanthropology: An Integrated Paradigm for the Study of Humans in Movement (Renson, 1989)

Sciences (disciplines)	Physical activity sciences (sport and rehabilitation) (applied disciplines)	Kinanthropology (cross-disciplinary science)				
		Developmental	Differential	Social-cultural	Clinical	Agogical
		Natural sciences				
Physics Chemistry Biology Physiology Medical sciences	Biomechanics of sport & rehabilitation Biochemistry of sport & rehabilitation Human biology of sport & rehabilitation Exercise physiology Sport & rehabilitative medicine	Physical growth	Physical characteristics	Social-cultural determinants of physique	Physical therapy	Physical education
		Human movement science				
Human kinetics	Kinesiology Kinanthropometry Motor learning	Motor development	Motor characteristics	Social-cultural determinants of movement patterns	Psychomotor therapy	Movement education

Human sciences						
Psychology	Sport & rehabilitative psychology	Psychosocial development	Psychosocial characteristics	Social-cultural determinants of sport & play	Adapted physical education	Sport and leisure education
Pedagogy	Sport & rehabilitative pedagogy					
Sociology and cultural anthropology	Sport & rehabilitative sociology					
Economics	Sport & rehabilitative administration					
Law	Sport and rehabilitative law					
History	Sport & rehabilitative history and comparative studies					
Philosophy	Sport and rehabilitative philosophy					
Professional applications						
		Physical performance evaluation and guidance	Training and coaching ergonomics	Sport and recreation management	Physical therapy Psychomotor therapy Adapted physical education	Physical and health education Movement and safety education Sport/dance/outdoor education

physiological and motor ability tests, sport and physical activity inventories, health knowledge, personality assessment, and sociocultural information. These data sets were not, however, broken down into isolated disciplines of physical anthropology, exercise physiology, motor fitness, sport psychology, sport sociology, and so on. Rather, a cross-disciplinary biocultural approach was adopted. The impact of the social determinants, for instance, was not limited to the sociological area of sport participation, but also included the social differentiation of physical growth and motor characteristics (Renson et al., 1980).

Academic education in kinanthropology supposes a well-balanced and systematically built-up curriculum. It should start with a relevant selection from the disciplinary natural sciences and human sciences (see the first column in Table 2), followed by the disciplinary human movement sciences (kinesiology, kinanthropometry, and motor learning) and the applied physical activity sciences (see the second column in Table 2), to be completed by the integrated kinanthropology paradigm (developmental, differential, sociocultural, clinical, and agogical). Incipient specialization in one of these five kinanthropological fields can start at the graduate level (optional courses or thesis), but true specialization seems to be indicated at the postgraduate level.

Each of the five kinanthropological approaches outlined in the model provides specific professional outlets. Developmental kinanthropology opens professional perspectives in physical performance evaluation and guidance. Differential kinanthropology is applied in training and coaching. Social-cultural kinanthropology forms the basis for sport and recreation management. Clinical kinanthropology leads to the professional areas of physical therapy, psychomotor rehabilitation, and adapted physical education. Agogical kinanthropology is translated into the practice of physical education (in the strict sense of the word) and health education, movement and safety education, and sport/dance/outdoor education.

Brooks (1981) stated that a discipline stands or falls in its accomplishments and not in its name, but it is my opinion that a unifying paradigm and a common denominator is a sine qua non for profiling the specific cross-disciplinary body of knowledge of humans in movement and its various professional possibilities. *Nomen sit omen* is an appropriate Latin expression: Let the name *kinanthropology* be an omen to overcome the anachronistic neglect of our academic and professional identification. Just as do physicists, biologists, psychologists, sociologists, and so on, we have a need for an internationally uniform and etymologically sound identity. Whether they are active in research, in teaching, or in therapy, the heirs apparent to the legacy of physical education should stand up and make known their common denominator: kin-anthropo-logy!

References

ÅSTRAND, P.O. (1989). Keynote lecture: Exercise and sports for all—our biological heritage. In J.S. Skinner, C.B. Corbin, D.M. Landers, P.E. Martin, & C.L. Wells (Eds.), *Future directions in exercise and sport science research* (pp. xv-xxiii). Champaign, IL: Human Kinetics.

BATESON, G. (1973). *Steps to an ecology of mind*. London: Granada.

BLANCHARD, K., & Cheska, A. (1985). *The anthropology of sport: An introduction*. South Hadley, MA: Bergin & Garvey.

BOUCHARD, C. (1974). Les sciences de l'activité physique: Un concept fondamental dans notre organisation disciplinaire et professionelle. *Mouvement*, **9**, 117-129.

BROOKS, G.A. (1981). What is the discipline of physical education? In G.A. Brooks (Ed.), *Perspectives on the academic discipline of physical education: A tribute to G.L. Rarick* (pp. 3-9). Champaign, IL: Human Kinetics.

CAILLOIS, R. (1958). *Les jeux et les hommes*. Paris: Gallimard.

CUSHMAN, G. (1981). *Ecological factors affecting the physical activity of children*. Paper presented at the 24th World Congress on Health, Physical Education and Recreation, Manila, Philippines.

ENGEL, G.L. (1982). The biopsychosocial model and medical education. *The New England Journal of Medicine*, **306**, 802-805.

GROENMAN, S. (1971). *Social behavior and environment: An introduction to sociology* (in Dutch). Assen, the Netherlands: Van Gorcum.

GUTTMANN, A. (1978). *From ritual to record: The nature of modern sports*. New York: Columbia University Press.

HARRIS, J.C., & Park, R.J. (Eds.) (1983). *Play, games & sports in cultural contexts*. Champaign, IL: Human Kinetics.

HUIZINGA, J. (1938). *Homo ludens: Proeve eener bepaling van het spelelement der cultuur*. Groningen: Tjeenk Willink.

KAPLAN, M. (1975). *Leisure: Theory and policy*. New York: Wiley.

LOY, J.W. (1972). Sociology and physical education. In R. Singer et al. (Eds.), *Physical education: An interdisciplinary approach* (pp. 168-236). New York: Macmillan.

LOY, J.W., & Kenyon, G.S. (Eds.) (1969). *Sport, culture and society: A reader on the sociology of sport*. New York: Macmillan.

LOY, J.W., McPherson, B.D., & Kenyon, G. (1978). *Sport and social systems*. Menlo Park: Addison-Wesley.

LÜSCHEN, G. (1969). Small group research and the group in sport. In G.S. Kenyon (Ed.), *Aspects of contemporary sport sociology: Proceedings of C.I.C. symposium on the sociology of sport* (pp. 57-66). Chicago: Athletic Institute.

MALINA, R.M. (1980). A multidisciplinary, biocultural approach to physical performance. In M. Ostyn, G. Beunen, & J. Simons (Eds.), *Kinanthropometry 2* (pp. 33-68). Baltimore: University Park Press.

MAUSS, M. (1935). Les techniques du corps. *Journal de Psychologie*, **32**, 271-293.

McINTOSH, O. (1963). *Sport in society*. London: Watts.

MEYNARD, R. (1967). *Kinanthropologie*. Unpublished manuscript.

MOORE, L.G., Van Arsdale, P.W., Glittenberg, J.A., & Aldrich, R.A. (1980). *The biocultural basis of health*. St. Louis: Mosby.

NABEL, G.J. (1985). Order and human biology. *The American Journal of Medicine*, **78**, 545-548.

OLIVER, C. (1981). *The discovery of humanity: An introduction to anthropology*. Cambridge, MA: Harper & Row.

OSTYN, M., Simons, J., Beunen, G., Renson, R., & Van Gerven, D. (Eds.) (1980). *Somatic and motor development of Belgian secondary schoolboys*. Leuven: Leuven University Press.

PARSONS, T. (1961). An outline of the social system. In T. Parsons (Ed.), *Theories of society: Foundations of modern sociological theory* (Vol. 1, pp. 30-48). New York: Glencoe.

RENSON, R. (1973a). *Sociocultural determinants of growth, motor fitness and sport participation of 13 year old Belgian boys* (in Dutch). Unpublished doctoral dissertation, K.U. Leuven.

RENSON, R. (1973b). *Sport and play from a Western and non-Western perspective: An anthropological approach* (in Dutch). Unpublished master thesis, K.U. Leuven.

RENSON, R. (1980a). *History of sport in antiquity* (in Dutch). Leuven, Belgium: Acco.

RENSON, R. (1980b). *Proposals for classification of projects into 19 "special fields."* (Committee on Sport Research, DS-SR(80)10, pp. 1-9). Strasbourg: Council of Europe.

RENSON, R. (1983). Limits to sport performance: A theoretical framework (in Dutch). *Sportcahiers*, **15**, 21-34.

RENSON, R. (1987). Selection and rationale for the Eurofit motor ability tests. In Council of Europe (Ed.), *5th European Research Seminar on Testing Physical Fitness* (Formia 1986, pp. 86-114). Strasbourg: Committee for the Development of Sport.

RENSON, R. (1989). From physical education to kinanthropology: A quest for academic and professional identity. *Quest*, **41**, 235-256.

RENSON, R., Beunen, G., De Witte, L., Ostyn, M., Simons, J., & Van Gerven, D. (1980). The social spectrum of physical fitness of 12- to 19-year old boys. In M. Ostyn, G. Beunen, & J. Simons (Eds.), *Kinanthropology 2* (pp. 104-118). Baltimore: University Park Press.

RIORDAN, J. (1977). *Sport in Soviet society*. Cambridge: Cambridge University Press.

SIMONS, J., Beunen, G., Renson, R., Claessens, A.L.M., Vanreusel, B., & Lefevre, J. (Eds.) (1990). *Growth and fitness of Flemish girls: The Leuven growth study* (Sport science monograph series 3). Champaign, IL: Human Kinetics.

VAN RIJSWIJK-CLERKX, L. (1971). *Child and environment* (in Dutch). Assen, the Netherlands: Van Gorcum.

WHITE, L. (1949). *The science of culture*. New York: Grove.

Studying Human Movement: Research Questions Should Drive Assignment of Labels

Jerry R. Thomas
Arizona State University

Locomotion: Swimming in the Pteropod Mollusc

An odd way to begin a paper with this title is to discuss swimming in the pteropod mollusc (*Clione Limacina*), yet that is exactly what I intend to do. R.A. Satterlie, associate professor of zoology at Arizona State University, conducts this line of research (Satterlie, 1989; Satterlie, LaBarbera, & Spencer, 1985; Satterlie & Spencer, 1985), and the value is that this mollusc "may serve as an excellent model for the examination of locomotion from the level of pattern generation and descending control from higher centres, through motor output and muscle activation. Interneurones, motor neurones and muscle cells are simultaneously available for microelectrode recording" (Satterlie & Spencer, 1985, p. 220). It also exhibits many of the intricacies of locomotor control in higher animals, including premotor central pattern generation, descending control and peripheral sensory modulation of pattern generation, motor neuron recruitment, and distinct "gear" changes during changes in locomotor speed (possibly resembling gait changes in higher animals). Figure 1 shows this mollusc in hovering behavior in the water from dorsal, ventral, and lateral views.

Those of you familiar with the motor control area will note that it has a number of terms and concepts in common with Dr. Satterlie's work. In fact it seems logical that work of this sort might have considerable implications for locomotor gait changes in humans (e.g., walking to running). Figure 2 presents the organization of the central ganglia of the mollusc. The central nervous system includes the cerebrals (labeled *C* in Figure 2) and the pedals (*Pe*) with the major nerve leading to each wing (*W*). When the connection between the cerebrals and the pedals is cut, normal swimming behavior continues; thus the totally isolated pedals generate the swimming movements, including the "gear" changes in speed, and the two wings maintain synchrony. However, when the pedal commissure was cut, each pedal ganglion continued to produce control of the wing on its side, but the movements were out of synchrony. Thus, each pedal ganglion contains the pattern generators for the ipsilateral wing, and the pedal central pattern generators are tightly coupled through the pedal commissure. Here is a

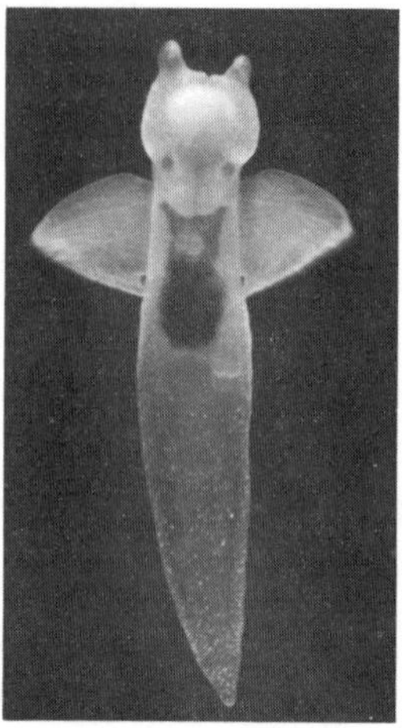

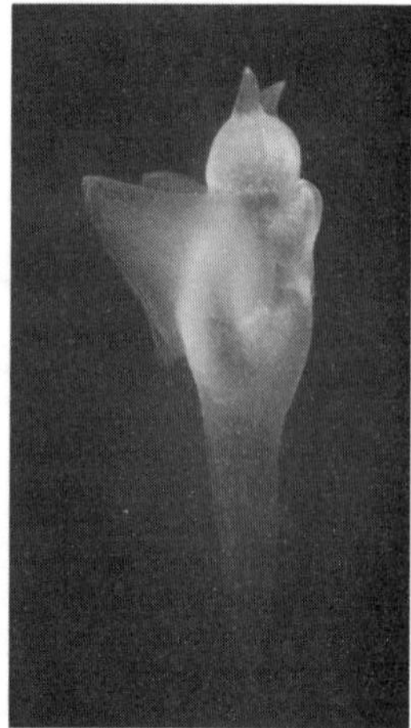

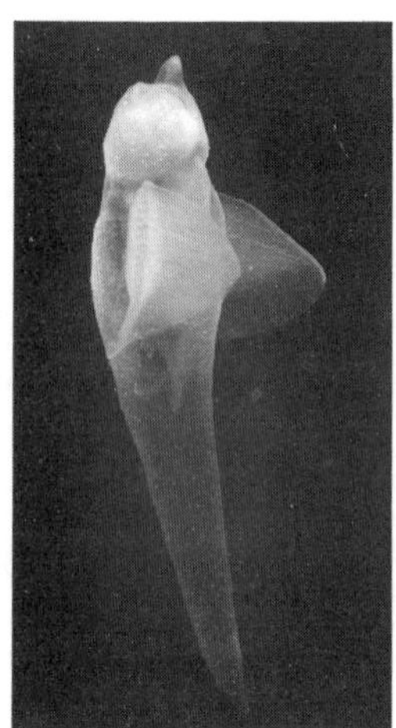

Figure 1 — Hovering swimming in the pteropod mollusc. (Used with permission from Dr. Richard Satterlie, Department of Zoology, Arizona State University, Tempe, AZ.)

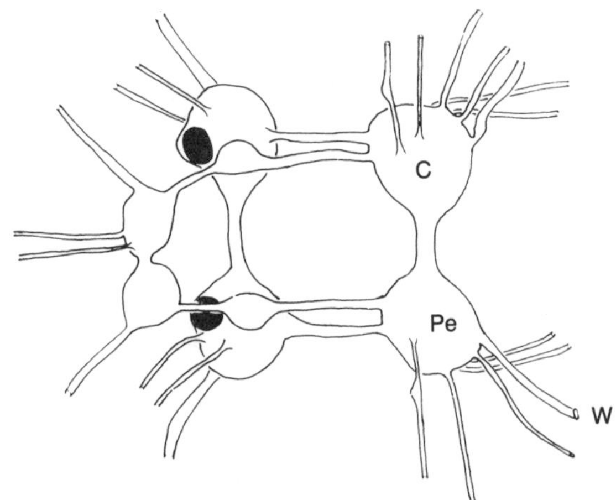

Figure 2 — Dorsal view of the central ring of ganglia of the pteropod mollusc with major nerves. *C*, cerebrals; *Pe*, pedals; *W*, major wing nerve. Scale bar = 100 *u*m. (Used with permission from Dr. Richard Satterlie, Department of Zoology, Arizona State University, Tempe, AZ.)

descriptive example of the central pattern generator, its connection to higher centers, and how alternating limb movements are coupled—topics that have been of considerable interest to motor control researchers as they have attempted to understand how locomotion is controlled.

Can Pathological Gait Problems Be Changed?

What has that to do with the topic of this paper? I intend to answer that question, but first I want to provide a second example. G.T. Yamaguchi is an assistant professor of chemical, biological, and materials engineering at Arizona State University; this second example comes from his work (Yamaguchi, in press; Yamaguchi, Pandy, & Zajac, in press; Yamaguchi & Zajac, 1989, in press), which asked the question, In individuals with pathological gait problems, how can the system be altered to improve walking? A specific example of their work should demonstrate its potential. They are interested in using computer modeling of gait. Assuming that a computer could provide the correct stimulation (intensity, frequency, and order) to the muscles that control walking, what is the minimum number of muscles and joints needed for ambulation? Their technique used principles of direct dynamics—force inputs for specific motor outputs, as compared to the inverse dynamics—looking at motion and trying to determine the muscular force outputs used, a technique typically observed in biomechanics. Using the appropriate mathematical models, Yamaguchi attempted to determine the number of degrees of freedom required for upright locomotion and the associated musculature needed. Figure 3 shows the 8-degrees-of-freedom model

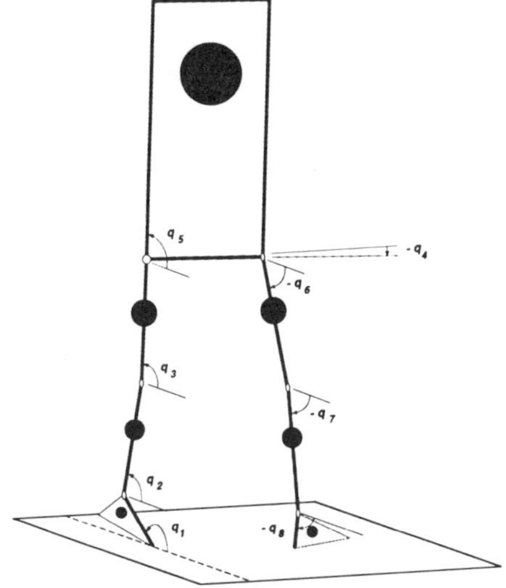

Figure 3 — The 8-degrees-of-freedom model. Angles q1 to q3 are defined in the sagittal plane; angle q4 is defined in the frontal plane. Remaining angles q5 to q8 are defined in the tilted plane inclined from vertical by angle q4. (Used with permission from Dr. Gary Yamaguchi, Department of Chemical, Bio, and Material Engineering, Arizona State University, Tempe, AZ. From "Restoring Unassisted Natural Gait to Paraplegics via Functional Neuromuscular Stimulation: A Computer Simulation Study" by G.T. Yamaguchi and F.E. Zajac, in press, *IEEE Transactions on Biomechanical Engineering*. Copyright © 1990 by IEEE. Reprinted by permission.)

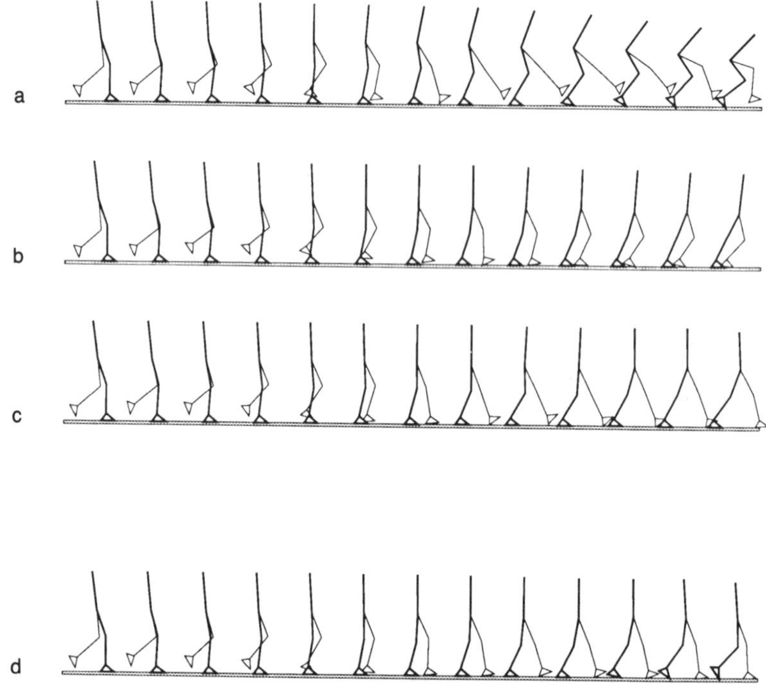

Figure 4 — Stick-figure sequences of selected computer runs, illustrating these common failure modes: *a*, stance leg collapse; *b*, premature heel contact; and *c*, an excessively long step length/duration. Several hundred simulations were required before the sequence shown in *d* was obtained. (Used with permission from Dr. Gary Yamaguchi, Department of Chemical, Bio, and Material Engineering, Arizona State University, Tempe, AZ. From "Restoring Unassisted Natural Gait to Paraplegics via Functional Neuromuscular Stimulation: A Computer Simulation Study" by G.T. Yamaguchi and F.E. Zajac, in press, *IEEE Transactions on Biomedical Engineering*. Copyright © 1990 by IEEE. Reprinted by permission.)

required, as determined from many computer simulations. Figure 4 presents stick figure models for unsuccessful attempts (*a-c*) and for a successful sequence (*d*). The significance of this work should be obvious; people who cannot locomote can be assisted in becoming ambulatory from work like this, if the computer can be developed to handle the stimulation required.

Why Are Questions Like These of Relevance to This Paper?

Human movement can be examined from many perspectives. For example, movement is often categorized by types—movements used in sports, such as striking, kicking, throwing, and catching; types of swimming strokes; types of gymnastics skills; and so on. Sometimes movements are examined simply as forms of vigorous exercise—running, swimming, cycling, or jumping rope.

Movements may also be examined in many settings that are not considered sport or vigorous exercise, such as piano playing, surgery, or dentistry.

Often the scientist with an interest in these movements asks questions about systems that control the movements, or ways that we learn the movements. A scientist might be interested in systems that allow a form of exercise to continue for extended periods of time or the mechanics that lead to the most efficient movements.

Scholars interested in types of movements or systems that control or influence movement often frame their questions in theories that have psychobiological bases. For instance, how do the brain, nervous system, cardiovascular system, muscular system, and hormonal system interact to produce movements and respond to exercise? Psychobiological theories and models are developed and tested in various settings by many individuals with interests in movement.

Often animal models are used to evaluate these psychobiological theories, because they allow better control of intersubject differences and environments as well as the use of invasive techniques that are not used in human experimentation. In addition, animals may offer more simple examples of responses that are very complex in humans. Yet animal findings provide considerable insight into the understanding of human movement and exercise.

The types of movements to be studied, the nature of the systems that control these movements, and the psychobiological theories that describe and explain exercise and movement are all driven by the nature of the research questions. This leads to the setting for the experimentation, as well as the level of analysis that is required for the study of human movement. Thus, research questions should drive how human movement is examined, not merely provide structures or labels for how this research is to be organized within the research community.

Can We Create a "Discipline" of Human Movement?

Our field has been discussing the nature of human movement, how it should be studied, subareas it comprises, and how it should be structured since Henry's (1964) classic paper over 25 years ago (for recent examples see *The Academy Papers* [Corbin & Eckert, 1990] and *Quest* [Hoffman & Morford, 1987]). Our newest claim is that the body of knowledge from the study of human movement is to be called *kinesiology* and might best be subsumed in departments of kinesiology on university campuses (last year's meeting). The basic suggestion is that the study of human movement is a discipline and, like other disciplines, should be located in a relevant academic department.

That is a most arrogant statement. Yet if we had proposed it 30 years ago, we might have brought it off. This is much like departments of psychology claiming they are the source for the study of cognition. If claims like this were believed, universities would need only three academic units: those for the study of cognition, affect, and movement. I suppose we could be generous and add a couple more academic units, maybe one for the study of everything else that grows as well as one for inanimate objects.

The point here is that to claim ownership of a discipline called kinesiology for the study of human movement (or physical activity) is absurd. The study of human movement is so broad in scope and of such great interest in society, it is by definition interdisciplinary, as are such other areas as cognition and affect. How one studies human movement, under what circumstances, and at what level of analysis depends on the research questions, not artificial labels to circumscribe the field of study—particularly if these labels are held out as disciplines.

I believe Satterlie and Yamaguchi would argue that they have focused (and will continue to focus) much of their research careers on movement and are not restrained by the boundaries of a discipline called kinesiology or by departments that use that name. That does not mean that they have no interest in working with other scholars, even in departments of kinesiology or exercise science, who study movement. In fact, both Satterlie and Yamaguchi are members of the interdisciplinary exercise science area at Arizona State University and have begun cooperative ventures with our faculty. However, that is interdisciplinary cooperation in the study of movement, not their admission that our department contains the academic content of what they propose to study. One department cannot, and should not, claim as its exclusive territory the content of movement, any more than one department has as its exclusive territory the content of cognition.

Have Disciplinary Boundaries Outlived Their Usefulness?

Universities still have traditional disciplinary divisions. However, these lines are rapidly blurring. How many of your universities now have departments like biochemistry, biophysics, and bioengineering? How many have centers or institutes for the study of cognitive science, developmental research, women's issues, black studies, and many others. The restructuring of universities along these lines is acknowledgment that research is increasingly interdisciplinary and should drive the labels used for organization.

Will traditional academic units dissolve? If so, how will students be educated if more theme-related issues drive research questions and academic structure? These are difficult questions that departments and universities are now facing. But given that we can observe this trend toward boundary blurring, how can we propose to create a "new discipline" circumscribing the study of human movement? I argue that a university that takes your work seriously will never allow this to happen. Pandora's box is open; the cat is out of the bag; we cannot, and would be foolish to attempt to, create a discipline with clear boundaries, when the rest of the academic community is seeking to identify important research themes for interdisciplinary study. Human movement is that sort of theme, as are more delimited versions like exercise and sport science. A lot of scholars are interested in studying physical activity. They bring unique perspectives, models, and methodologies to the study of movement. Let us help them by cooperatively investigating phenomena of interest and not cut off communication by trying to claim the study of human movement as our turf.

References

CORBIN, C.B., & Eckert, H.M. (Eds.) (1990). *The Academy Papers. The Evolving Undergraduate Major* (No. 23). Champaign, IL: Human Kinetics.

HENRY, F.M. (1964). Physical education: An academic discipline. *Journal of Health, Physical Education and Recreation*, **35**, 32-33.

HOFFMAN, S.J., & Morford, R. (Eds.) (1987). The future of graduate study in physical education. *Quest*, **39**, 79-226.

SATTERLIE, R.A. (1989). Reciprocal inhibition and rhythmicity: Swimming in a pteropod mollusk. In J.W. Jacklet (Ed.), *Neuronal and cellular oscillators* (pp. 151-171). New York: Marcel Dekker.

SATTERLIE, R.A., LaBarbera, M., & Spencer, A.N. (1985). Swimming in the pteropod mollusc, *Clione Limacina: 1*. Behavior and morphology. *Journal of Experimental Biology*, **116**, 189-204.

SATTERLIE, R.A., & Spencer, A.N. (1985). Swimming in the pteropod mollusc, *Clione Limacina: 2*. Physiology. *Journal of Experimental Biology*, **116**, 205-222.

YAMAGUCHI, G.T. (in press). Performing whole-body simulations of gait with 3-D, dynamic musculoskeletal models. In J. Winter & S. L-Y. Woo (Eds.), *Multiple muscle systems*. New York: Springer-Verlag.

YAMAGUCHI, G.T., Pandy, M.G., & Zajac, F.E. (in press). Dynamic musculoskeletal models of human locomotion: Perspectives on model formulation and control. In A. Patla (Ed.), *Adaptability of human gait: Implications for the control of locomotion*. Amsterdam, Holland: North-Holland.

YAMAGUCHI, G.T., & Zajac, F.E. (1989). A planar model of the knee joint to characterize the knee extensor mechanism. *Journal of Biomechanics*, **22**, 1-10.

YAMAGUCHI, G.T., & Zajac, F.E. (in press). Restoring unassisted natural gait to paraplegics via functional neuromuscular stimulation: A computer simulation study. *IEEE Transactions on Biomedical Engineering*.

Research in Current Context

Michael J. Ellis
University of Illinois

For this paper I originally planned to consider what questions ought to be addressed by the researchers in the field of kinesiology and physical education during the near future. I intended to make recommendations with some force in order to constrain the behavior of researchers in the field; to restrict their academic freedom. This is an unpopular idea, and so before telling you what to tell your colleagues to study, I have decided to first justify the telling.

Academic Freedom

A rational society's foundation is widespread recognition that knowledge is dynamic and that today's truth may well be proven otherwise later. It is necessary to cast doubt systematically to prove or test currently held truths. As knowledge is found wanting, it is discarded, and new discoveries replace it. In this way we struggle to progressively refine our understanding of the real world. This testing occurs throughout the society, but of late a class of citizens—scholars—is maintained with the express purpose of forcing the process.

Changing the knowledge used in a society naturally disturbs the status quo. There are often strong counterforces with interests vested in maintaining adherence to current ways of knowing. If large financial, social, or political interests are threatened and react to inhibit the process of refining knowledge, then the revolutionary thinker is a risk. Such thinkers, scientists, scholars require protection if the rational society is to progress.

Tenure as Protection for Academic Freedom

The protection of academic freedom is a right granted to scholars. It is a refinement of the First Amendment and is a protection necessary to encourage the pursuit of truth no matter how unpopular the result. Academic freedom for university scholars is operationalized in the granting of tenure. Tenure is granted not as the reward of an employment contract for life (read, until 70 years of age), but to protect the right of the scholar to pursue unpopular truths. It is not granted lightly, and it is not granted to protect the scholar from the consequences of any action. It is granted to permit the scholarly pursuit of truth in those areas in which the scholar is qualified to extend knowledge.

Limits to Academic Freedom

It has proved so difficult to determine the limits of the protection charted by a scholar's expertise that academic freedom has widened into a kind of academic diplomatic immunity (e.g., I am told that no tenured professor in the history of the University of Illinois has ever been fired). Thus, the granting of tenure to protect the creation and dissemination of unpopular truths comes at great cost.

As this conference considers only research, the creation of knowledge, I will ignore the costs of academic freedom to the curriculum and deal only with the costs to the research enterprise. Those costs stem from the fact that in both professional and disciplinary programs there are real restrictions imposed by the resources available. There are not enough people or funds to permit a search for answers to all extant questions, so choices among questions are necessary. We cannot afford to license our scarce personnel to pursue just any line of inquiry that takes their fancy. We must as leaders assume responsibility for directing the process.

Frequently the choices of questions to study are made on the basis of expediency. It is rare that a path is laid out to a goal of significant professional import, for two reasons. First, there looms the question of whether we should constrict a scholar's academic freedom, and second, looms the question of who should decide.

Constricting Academic Freedom. Answering the first question is difficult. It is clear that many discoveries were not results of some orderly plan but created by unpredictable combinations of events. A major report for the National Science Foundation entitled *Technology in Retrospect and Critical Events in Science* (TRACES) charted the flow of understanding to several major technologies (Illinois Institute of Technology, 1968). It was clear that the assembly of the fundamental knowledge upon which technologies like the ferrite core, the oral contraceptive, the VCR were based followed multiple paths. It was only when the application was glimpsed that the research could be directed, the applications developed, and the product prepared for market. For simplicity's sake, the report divided research into three broad categories.

- Nonmission research—motivated by the search for knowledge without special regard for its application
- Mission-oriented research—motivated by the desire to develop information for specific application
- Developmental research—motivated by the desire to create prototypes and demonstrate efficacy prior to production

It is obvious that these categories arrange themselves along a continuum. At the nonmission-oriented pole it is least possible to chart the course of scholarship. Here academic freedom, curiosity, the examination of phenomena simply because they are there, are most necessary. The TRACES document shows that there is typically about a 30-year lag between a critical event in science and its finding some application. There is no clear method that can guarantee prescience over a period of 30 years; consequently, to constrain the academic freedom of those pursuing nonmission research is to mortgage the future.

However, as soon as professional goals are determined or critical applications for fundamental theory are understood, the weight of the goal requires disciplined, organized, cooperative action by researchers who follow a path to the goal rather than their nose. This requires choices determined by the actions needed to achieve the goal rather than the inclinations of the researchers. This is necessary and desirable. Thus, at the applied end of the research spectrum academic freedom is restricted.

Responsibility for Directing Research. I argue that academic leaders in the professional schools and departments have hidden behind the blanket application of the principle of academic freedom designed to protect research at the nonmission pole of the continuum. We have not accepted the responsibility of asking whether the time and effort expended on research advances the profession or not. We have assumed that a university professor has academic freedom and that it is inappropriate to ask whether a research venture should have been undertaken. We rarely make judgments as to whether research activities moved us toward a goal and were important for the profession. We are prepared to judge method but rarely content. I argue that we should be willing to influence the course of mission-oriented and developmental research and not leave it to chance.

The judgmental process has passed into the hands of those controlling the flow of extramural funds from foundations and the agencies administering grants and contracts. We bewail that influence as we scramble to meet their criteria for their funds. Yet we have vested in them the determination of what is important, the order in which we wish to study things, and the applications that are to be pursued. Some time back, the National Cancer Institute published its critical-path analysis for the national cancer research effort. This was a blueprint that rationalized the process and informed the choices of myriad scientists as to what they should study. The Human Genome Mapping Project currently attempts to direct the work of many using a grand plan. Cancer will not be understood, nor will the human genome be mapped, without some overall guidance.

Thus we need balance between the various types of research. We need the fundamental work that will underpin the future health of the field some 30 years ahead, and we also need a major effort to turn the work of the past into useful applications for our professionals in service.

Goals for Research in Physical Education

At last year's meeting I addressed this same concern from a different viewpoint. I opened my paper with the following words.

> In my scheme of things the needs of the professions drive the nature and content of scholarly activity in the field. The field and its attendant disciplines exist because of a compact struck between our society and members of the field. Resources are directed to us with the expectation that we will alter the likelihood that people will live higher quality lives and that the nation's stock of human capital will be improved. Our support will depend directly on the extent to which we can reliably produce desired effects. We are, as are all professions, charged with the responsibility for engineering effects, not simply knowing.

> The current and future needs of the professions should thus dictate the kinds of questions asked by the researchers associated with the field. (Ellis, 1990, p. 13)

This indicates that in professional departments and schools, the principal mission for the research effort should be to find reliable applications of fundamental theory to the questions of the profession. Effort should be directed toward applications, technologies, methods, content. There should be a close tie to the world of practice, with research results finding easy application and the research questions being derived from the field.

It is only in those departments and schools adopting a disciplinary orientation that research may be conducted freely under the protection of total academic freedom. Even here,

> researchers and scholars should be forever mindful that their work is only justified by the potential understanding the fundamental processes of human movement bring to the practice of countless professionals. The building of the body of theory should address human movement and be informed by its potential for possible use. The targetless efforts to simply understand phenomena may, and I say may, be supported in the colleges and arts and sciences without expectation of use. (However, in my university I note increasing attention is given to those areas in the arts and sciences that are believed to be potentially valuable, e.g., optics, theater, artificial intelligence, materials science, etc.). Those who wish to explore phenomena in isolation of any responsibility for benefiting the professions are best located in the cognate disciplines in the colleges of arts and sciences. We have such scarce resources in our own departments that we cannot afford to support people who would be more comfortable without some responsibility for underpinning the professions. (Ellis, 1990, p. 13)

In our fields I believe there should be two kinds of judgments made. There should be discriminations made concerning the nature of the research effort mounted at different types of institutions, and in all institutions there should be some attempt to influence the nature of the questions addressed. Only in the major research universities with departments with disciplinary orientations should some be granted freedom to follow any line of inquiry they wish. In the professional departments, and those departments falling outside the prior definition, the research should be consciously biased toward the development of applications and technologies exploiting our understanding of human movement. In the teaching institutions, research should be targeted toward methods and techniques that directly improve practice.

Continuum of Goals for Scholarship

Thus, in the same way that there is a continuum of research from basic to applied, there should be a continuum of targets for the various kinds of institutions in higher education. It is not in the best long-term interests of the field that all universities and colleges ape the major research institutions by trying to conduct fundamental or basic research. In my experience far too many institutions parrot the language of the major research institutions, declaring that research is their most important mission.

Research and scholarship should reflect the differing missions of the institutions in which they are conducted. We have great need for improved technologies, methods, and techniques that empower practitioners. The number of people working at the various points along the basic-versus-applied continuum should increase as the applied pole is approached. Fortunately the demography of the faculty in higher education mirrors this. There are many more institutions with restricted missions, and thus most physical education faculty in higher education find themselves working in settings where applications and developments should be prized. Unfortunately, it seems that far too many institutions declare themselves to be major research universities, thus missing the opportunity to exert direct powerful influence on practice.

I believe that among the most critical needs for our field today are research-based practice and practice-based research.[1] Meeting this need will require that we accept responsibility for directing the available talent toward questions of importance to practice. This direction will require the abridgement of academic freedoms and the development of strategic plans to bring some coherence to the collective research effort. In the closely related area of health promotion there have been efforts to direct the efforts of the scholarly community by laying out targets/objectives for the enterprise. The Surgeon General produced two reports that started this process (Richmond, 1979, 1980) by establishing health-promotion objectives for the nation, and The Department of Health and Human Services hosted a major conference entitled "Achieving the Nation's Health Promotion Objectives" (U.S. Department of HHS, 1984). Some small attempts have been made to iterate these goals for the field of human movement studies and the physical activity professions by Wilmore (1982); Skinner, Corbin, Landers, Martin, and Wells (1989); and Ellis (1988). I believe that it is time to address the problem of trying to determine what is important and what is largely irrelevant and giving guidance to our colleagues. We should, in Lawson's words, be heavily engaged in "problem setting" rather than problem solving (Lawson, 1984).

There is now only time to point the way with one example of the kind of direction I have in mind. My suggestions take one theme from exercise physiology and lay out a prescription and rationale for a program of research—and then assign different aspects of the research effort to different types of institutions in the American system of higher education.

Nonmission Research in Movement Physiology

The first area is the broad one of the effects of activity on human physiology. At the basic end of the spectrum, research should search for understanding of the fundamental mechanisms of muscle contractions and their energetics, together with the energy-supply and waste-removal systems as they are involved in move-

---

[1]This idea is drawn from the manifesto of the College of Education at UC Berkeley, which used the words "Research based education, and education based research" to define its overarching goal.

ment. We need also to understand the basic physiological mechanisms of flexibility, bone density, and strength, and the generation and maintenance of muscular strength.

Mission-Oriented Research in Movement Physiology

However, relatively few people should dedicate their energy to this, because other issues are more pressing and important. Perhaps the most important question involves the development of families of activity/dosage effect curves to permit us to determine how little activity is enough to produce a beneficial effect. For too long the field has been concerned with how much activity, strength, endurance, and so on is possible. (For example, see Clarke & Eckert, 1985.) It is clear that we are making little headway in achieving the Surgeon General's goal for exercise-generated fitness across the nation. The activity goal was set so high that only 10% to 15% of the population have reached the goal by this, the target, year. We have great need to examine the belief that even very small amounts of exercise influence beneficially the most sedentary fraction of the population—for if this is true, then the total marginal benefits to health enhancement will come by encouraging very large numbers of people to exercise a little, rather than encouraging very few to exercise intensely. We have no economic models of the cost–benefit curves as they affect the total population. We have only an all-or-none threshold at the upper ends of the intensity and duration scales that are unachievable by most.

This process should be extended to develop the same dosage/effect curves for the traditional aspects of fitness (endurance, flexibility, strength) as well as bone health.

Further, there is a great need for simple techniques for measuring dose and assessing effect in the field. There needs to be a reliable and cheap array of methods to support the work of those investigating the effects of their practice—those practicing developmental research.

Developmental Research in Movement Physiology

The understanding of the mechanisms needs to be applied to the day-to-day practice in the field so that it can influence most of the population. A large number of reliable techniques, recipes, activities need to be developed to underwrite the prescription of activity to the various segments in the population in their different settings. We need to know what the activities are that most reliably and enjoyably involve different age groups in activities conducive to their health. We need to know how each activity influences local and central endurance, strength of the major muscle groups, flexibility of the joints, and bone mineralization. This will require meta-analysis of the vast array of work already done, and then filling in the gaps.

Allocation of Responsibility

There are few major research universities, and they should generally be staffed with people charged with working at any point of the nonmission–development–research continuum. These scholars should have the greatest freedom to conduct research on the fundamental processes where it is most difficult to predict the importance of any eventual findings. These scholars provide the seminal principles upon which the future health of the field is dependent.

The next tier of institutions should dedicate the majority of their efforts to the development of mission-oriented research. Regional universities, colleges with high teaching loads, community colleges, and practitioners should be actively encouraged to engage in research that brings developments into practice.

To differentiate the goals of the scholarly enterprise and to allocate expectations will be unpopular. However, I still believe we should encourage different approaches. Those who spend most of their time in teaching and various kinds of clinical service have the setting in which development can take place under their immediate control. They are teaching, leading, and assessing the effects of their work continually. We should reward this kind of research in these institutions.

Nonmission research is already well rewarded in universities. We should continue to reward it in the research universities. However, we should also reward mission-oriented research, on the basis of its likelihood to realize benefit. The criteria in assessing research in the research universities should include not only judgments concerning the contribution to the understanding of the basic mechanisms of movement, but also concern for whether the substrate of knowledge needed by the field is being strengthened. In other words, we should attempt to judge whether the work is important.

These issues are critically important to the field. Society's expectations for us and our technologies are increasing. We need to be able to deliver. A random approach to this will not be successful. We just do not have enough scholars to ensure success using that approach. It is time to guide our scholarship so that the professions that depend on it can thrive.

Summary

With the granting of academic freedom goes the expectation of responsibility. We should accept the necessity and desirability of directing the research of the field. Disciplinary departments of kinesiology in the major research universities have the greatest freedom and greatest responsibility. We should also accept responsibility to recognize that it is not in the field's best interest to permit those departments with professional identities to ape the research institutions, but that they serve best by studying mission-oriented and developmental questions.

References

CLARKE, D.H., & Eckert, H.M. (Eds.) (1985). *The Academy Papers. The Limits of Human Performance* (No. 18). Champaign, IL: Human Kinetics.

ELLIS, M.J. (1988). *The business of physical education: The future of the profession* (pp. 71-103). Champaign, IL: Human Kinetics.

ELLIS, M.J. (1990). Reactions to "The body of knowledge: A common core." In C.B. Corbin & H.M. Eckert (Eds.), *The Academy Papers. The Evolving Undergraduate Major* (No. 23, pp. 13-16). Champaign, IL: Human Kinetics.

ILLINOIS Institute of Technology. (1968). *Technology in retrospect and critical events in science* (Report to the National Science Foundation). Chicago: Author.

LAWSON, H.A. (1984). Problem-setting for physical education and sport. *Quest*, **36**, 48-60.

RICHMOND, J.B. (1979). *Healthy people: The Surgeon General's report on health promotion and disease prevention (DHEW* [*PHS*] *Publication No. 79-55071)*. Washington, DC: U.S. Government Printing Office.

RICHMOND, J.B. (1980). *Promoting health, preventing disease: Objectives for the nation*. Washington, DC: U.S. Government Printing Office.

SKINNER, J.S., Corbin, C.B., Landers, D.M., Martin, P.E., & Wells, C.E. (Eds.) (1989). *Future directions in exercise/sport research*. Champaign, IL: Human Kinetics.

U.S. Department of Health and Human Services. (1984). *Proceedings of Prospects for a Healthier America: Achieving the nation's health promotion objectives*. Washington, DC: U.S. Government Printing Office.

WILMORE, J.H. (1982). Objectives of the nation—physical fitness and exercise. *Journal of Physical Education, Recreation and Dance*, **53**, 41-43.

Thinking Along With Rorty About Disciplines as Cultural Traditions

William J. Morgan
University of Tennessee

As indicated by last year's Academy papers, there now appears to be consensus that physical education has an identifiable body of knowledge, that the content and makeup of that body of knowledge is centered about the biological and social sciences and the humanities, and that that body of knowledge is directed to a greater understanding of sport and exercise (Ellis, 1990; Thomas, 1990). What I intend to talk about today, however, and what I should like to get consensus about, is something different from, but not unrelated to, the consensus already achieved. And that is whether it makes sense to talk about such disciplines as physical education as more than formal areas of study. Is it implausible, in other words, to construe disciplines as cultural traditions that have discernible cultural and moral missions? Is it inconceivable to think of them as cultural forces that play, or ought to play, an important role in refashioning the social world in which we all live? Is it just wrong to suppose that disciplines have built into them cultural purposes, which, given their special characters, only they can discharge in the manners in which they do?

Now, some of you will think my above questions are simply wrongheaded and will dismiss them, and some of you will think my questions are on target and will supply an immediate, and what you regard as an obvious, answer to them. The first respondents are likely to be disciplinarians, who are apt to be offended by my intimation that disciplines might be more than technical repositories of knowledge. They might argue, and have argued, that being good disciplinarians is synonymous with being oblivious to such practical questions, that the pursuit of knowledge requires a studied indifference to the practical affairs of life. Indeed, they might charge that in posing these kinds of questions I have forsaken the mantle of the disciplinarian in favor of its practical-minded professional counterpart. But their argument is riddled with a contradiction. For saying that disciplines eschew practical questions is not tantamount to saying that they have no cultural value, but is merely an elliptical way of saying what that cultural value consists in: namely, in their being suitably scholarly in demeanor, suitably aloof, that is, to social and historical contingencies that might detract from the acquisition of new knowledge. What concerns me, however, is not the contradiction but the answer, which, I think, is flatly wrong.

The second respondents are likely to be professionals who find my questions more congenial to their view of academic disciplines. They might argue, and have argued, that the worth of a theory, of acquired knowledge, does not depend on its scientific grounding but on its implications for the daily and concrete details of life. And to ensure that disciplines don't degenerate into sterile and bankrupt formal subjects, they might argue, and have argued, that the professions should be their driving force, that professional imperatives should set the agenda for disciplinary inquiry. I find nothing contradictory in their answer, but I find nothing compelling in it, either. Simply put, it is not at all clear that the advance of humankind is best served by making professions the focal point of our disciplinary endeavors.

I thus find myself in the not altogether enviable position of opposing the two main, and as far as I can tell the only, antagonists in this debate. But I would be less than honest if I did not admit a certain delight in raising the ire of both disciplinarians and professionals, for I believe they have led us into a dead end, a conceptual cul de sac if you will, which we must find some way to get beyond. And that is what I hope to accomplish today. My argument will proceed as follows. I will first raise and try to refute the disciplinary argument that the cultural value of disciplines lies in their antipractical pretension of scientific rigor. I will next raise and try to refute the professional argument that the cultural value of disciplines lies in their servicing of the professions. And finally, I will present, with the help of Rorty and others, a third way, a view of disciplines as cultural traditions, that purports to get around the above impasse by opting for an open-ended disciplinary matrix that aspires to be neither scientific nor professional but simply relevant, in a very special and telling way, to the conduct of our lives.

The argument that physical education requires a scientific grounding dates back to the end of the 19th century. Though this call for scientific rigor did not go completely unheeded, neither did it take root. Indeed, it was not until the 1960s and 1970s, as Professor Park (1989, pp. 12-14) argues, that it was given a new lease on life. These, of course, were the heady days in which disciplinary types made their mark by treating physical education as an academic subject and by extolling the virtues of the scientific spirit. That spirit was not confined to the biological sciences but was extended to the social sciences as well, giving further credence to the methodological principles of science as *the* privileged access to truth. The notion that physical education was a technical subject defined by a set of identifiable and enduring problems, and a set of research programs that could deal with these problems in a scientifically precise way, thus gained currency here. And academicians began to tout the cultivation of a scientific cast of mind, a rigorous scholarly disposition, as a curative to the unscientific and excessively practical preoccupations of physical educators devoted to teaching and to the training of teachers.

Now what precisely is involved in this attempt to propagate a self-image of physical education as a rigorous, scientific discipline? It is first of all an attempt to pattern physical education after the model of natural science and mathematics, which requires it to withdraw from the cultural scene and to avail itself of scientific methods that are supposedly more rigorous and purer than those of nonscience. It seeks, therefore, "to escape the vocabulary and practices of its own time in order to find something ahistorical and necessary to cling to," (Rorty, 1982, p. 165). By basing itself on natural starting points that are unspoiled by human contingency, it tries to get hold of superconcepts and categories that are not the concepts and categories of any historical period or of any particular culture, but that can be used to analyze all other subordinate concepts and categories (Rorty, 1982, p. 222). In short, it strives to come up with a permanent, neutral, disciplinary matrix within which all thought, language, and experience can and must be fitted. Much then as Galileo claimed to have found in the language of mathematics the language of nature itself, physical educators qua scientists aspire after representations of reality that are not merely theirs, but those of nature and human nature "as it looks to itself and as it would describe itself if it could" (Rorty, 1982, p. 194).

I am not altogether unsympathetic to this effort to provide some scientific foundation for physical education, nor do I think it was a bad thing; on the contrary, I am persuaded that in many ways it was an effective corrective to the often mindless and capricious indulgences of practitioners. Nonetheless, it is deeply flawed in two senses. First, its appeal to the methods and manner of science to secure the immutable categories it sought to remedy the ills of physical education, cannot work, and only induces a falsified picture of science itself. The reason is that science is no more immune to contingency than is any other human endeavor. Its methods, that is, are not the privileged strictures disciplinarians made them out to be. As Kuhn (1970) observed of the puzzle solving that goes on in normal science, scientists use the same pedestrian methods that we all use in everyday life. They check off examples against criteria, they fudge counterexamples just enough to avoid new paradigms, and they try out various guesses, couched in the current jargon, looking for ways to cover the unfudgeable cases (Rorty, 1982, p. 193). Further, when science is forced by various anomalies to take up new paradigms, it often abandons its previous rules and methodological devices, no matter how well established. As MacIntyre and others have argued, there are numerous cases in science where the continued use of certain accepted methods would have led it astray. In such cases, scientific progress requires that it repudiate any fixed rules and rely instead on the judgment of those skilled in the practices that constitute the scientific tradition (MacIntyre, 1977, pp. 200-201).

The second, and most significant, flaw of the disciplinary appeal to scientific rigor as a way of putting off contingency, which prompted and still prompts scholars to ignore Kuhn's (1970) caveats, is the mistaken view that the success of science is due to its purity, to its operating free of human interests. On this interpretation, it is science's distance from the real world, from decisions about how people should live, from any hint of evaluative language, that accounts for its predictive power. Many established and aspiring disciplinarians have misread in just this way Franklin Henry's dictum that the acquisition of knowledge requires no demonstration of practical application (Henry, 1968, p. 282). The fallacy of this claim is that the farther removed our vocabulary is from issues of human life, the more socially and morally insignificant it is, the more scientific it is, and the more likely it is to be in touch with reality. Our ability to tap into and describe reality, in other words, to get it under our control and spell, is directly dependent on our purging of our social and moral sensibilities. There are actually, as Rorty argues, two mistakes here: that an explanatory category or term is more likely to refer to the real (a) if it is morally inconsequential and (b) if it can be put in the form of a predictively useful generalization (Rorty, 1982, p. 194).

It was in response to what was considered an overdose of "heartless" disciplinary efforts to scientifically ground physical education that the second argument, which championed the primacy of the profession, got off the ground. For on this account physical education is about the business not of simply knowing but of trying to engineer effects. This activist interest in producing concrete, palpable results was offered up as a counterpoise to the disciplinary emphasis on rigor. That balance could best be effected, it was argued, by making the discipline beholden to the profession, by gearing its research ventures to the interests, needs, and aspirations of the profession. The reason for doing so, it was further argued, was to honor the compact that had been struck between society and the profession. That is, resources were directed to departments of physical education with the expectation of some significant social payoff, some improvement in raising the stock of the nation's capital. It was this compact itself that warranted turning Henry's dictum on its head. Indeed, Ellis (1990), one of the main proponents of this argument, went so far as to suggest that all unrepentant disciplinarians be banished to the cognate disciplines and argued that physical education departments simply can't afford to keep on anyone who is not interested in underpinning the profession (p. 13). It is not clear that Ellis would tolerate their existence in the cognate disciplines either; for he observes correctly and not unsympathetically, even in these remaining bastions of basic research the push for results is apparent. And even if he were inclined to let them toil in their parent disciplines, it is not clear that he would let them teach their specialties, for fear that their subject-matter areas might be co-opted by academic departments desperate to find some avenue to utility (p. 15).

This argument could well be attacked as penny wise and pound foolish because it glosses over the unforeseen practical consequences of basic research. But to press this argument is to accept its central premise that it is the practical utility of disciplines for professions that should command our assent, and it is this very premise that I wish to contest. For it suffers from a deep and abiding equivocation. The equivocation goes to the heart of the supposed social compact that binds the profession, and by extension the discipline, to larger society. Just what sort of compact is this that inclines physical education to seek alliances with the health and leisure industries and to forsake a disinterested pursuit of knowledge in order to improve the stock of the nation's capital? Just who is benefited by these arrangements?

Though no straight answers are forthcoming from the professional camp, it is hard not to notice that the language it uses to describe this compact and its concomitant arrangements, its talk of transfer of resources and of services rendered, comes suspiciously close to the neoconservative language of economic accountability. It has, that is, less the look of a liberal, democratic covenant, which is based on a mutual recognition of the rights and autonomous standing of the consenting parties, than it does the look of an economic covenant, which is based on an imbalance of power that favors the resource-bearing party in such a way that it is not only able to exact a certain quantum of desired results from the recipient, but has a large say in defining what counts as a desired result. It is not at all clear that society is best served by arrangements in which results are molded to suit the interests of those who possess and transfer the requisite resources. Nor is it clear, without further argument or specification, that such arrangements have any more social or moral force than monied alumni contributing their capital to the athletic department with the expectation of producing a winning, though not necessarily an educated, team.

The most serious equivocation in the primacy-of-the-profession argument, however, regardless of what interpretation one gives to its founding social compact, is that it conflates the internal goods of the social practices of exercise and sport with the external goods of their supporting institutions. Because this distinction is central to my criticism of the professional argument, and because it sets up my own argument for reading disciplines as cultural traditions, I first want to develop it in a more general and careful way.

A practice is, as MacIntyre (1984) defines it, any coherent and complex form of social activity in which trying to achieve the standards of excellence that define that activity requires that its internal goods be realized (pp. 9, 187). Practices then are communal projects that extend our human powers to achieve excellence as well as our human conceptions of the ends and goods involved. So understood, tic-tac-toe, throwing a football with skill, and bricklaying are not practices, but chess, football, and architecture are (MacIntyre, 1984, p. 187).

There are two key features of practices. The first is the notion of internal goods, which are so named because they are specific to the practice itself, to the analytic skill, the creative intelligence, and the intensity required to participate in the activity. These goods are internal in two senses: They can only be specified in terms of what it takes to be excellent in the practice itself, and they can only be identified and recognized by the experience gained in participating in the practice (MacIntyre, 1984, pp. 188-189). So the internal goods of sport are those skills, values, and dispositions that come into play in trying to resolve its arbitrary obstacles, and the internal goods of, say, medicine, are those skills, values, and dispositions involved in treating and looking after the well-being of patients.

The second pivotal feature of a practice is the notion of virtue, which is an acquired human quality the possession and exercise of which enables one to achieve the internal goods of the practice and the absence of which prevents one from achieving such goods (MacIntyre, 1984, p. 191). All practices require the exercise of virtue, the exercise of judgment or practical reason that is not practical in any conventional sense. In fact, the exercise of this judgment is not to be confused with the expression of private feelings or aesthetic preferences and tastes, or with technical reason that seeks merely to arrive at a goal by the most efficient means, or with theoretical reason that aims for universal truths (Lasch, 1986, p. 68). Rather, virtue is a form of judgment that one learns in the course of training for a practice that chooses means with regard to standards of excellence and their associated internal goods.

Institutions, by contrast, are bureaucratic organizations that exist to serve extrinsic purposes. Though practices cannot survive without institutions to support them, they must not be confused with practices. Football, physics, and medicine are practices, whereas athletic departments, laboratories, universities, and hospitals are institutions. The central distinction between them is that institutions are necessarily concerned with external goods (MacIntyre, 1984, p. 195). That is, they are involved in the acquiring of capital, and they are structured in terms of power and status. Further, they distribute money, power, and status as rewards (MacIntyre, 1984, p. 194). And their survival depends on their being good at all of the above. The authority peculiar to institutions, therefore, has nothing to do with virtue, with a sensitivity for excellence and an appreciation of internal goods, but with the successful use of power to get others to comply with one's directives (MacIntyre, 1984, p. 194).

In saying then that the profession argument blurs this distinction, I am claiming that its talk of molding practices to accommodate the desires and expectations of resource bearers, that its pursuit of ties to health and leisure industries that have only an incidental interest in either health or leisure, that its interest in protecting its turf from piracy by cognate disciplines, bespeaks an orientation that is more bureaucratic than virtuous, more fitted to extrinsic ends than intrinsic ones. What makes this equivocation less than benign is that it is symptomatic of a general cultural malaise in our society that threatens to destroy the diverse social practices that give substance to our life. The problem is that practices have to be sustained by institutions that by their very design tend to corrupt them. It's not just that practitioners are tempted to engage in a practice for the wrong reasons, for money or status, but that the institutional structures in which practices are carried out underwrite and legitimize such reasons (Lasch, 1986, p. 69). We live in a society, then, that not only does not encourage an acquaintance with or appreciation of the nuances of practices, but one that encourages a contempt for them; how else do we explain the well-known aloofness and indifference of bureaucrats who oversee our practices: whether they be employees of the state who ignore the distress of the welfare client filling out complicated forms, or hospital administrators who treat patients as commodities rather than persons, or athletic officials who regard student-athletes as little more than fodder for their exorbitant budgets. In sum, as we've become inured to, and better versed in, the languages of institutions, we have become virtually oblivious to the languages of practices, so that "everything comes out looking like a system of external goods in which people are only moved by status, money, and the will to power" (Stout, 1986, p. 55).

In the little time remaining, I can only sketch out my alternative reading of disciplines as cultural traditions. What I am trying to convey by this reading is that disciplines are themselves best conceived as practices in which the exercise of specific technical and analytic skills, a sense of judgment and perspective, and the virtues of intellectual honesty, self-criticism, and disinterestedness are crucial, and in which those skills, judgments, and virtues are dedicated to the study and moral guardianship of select social practices—in the case of physical education, the practices of exercise and sport. There are two central features of this conception. The first is that it dispenses with any pretense of starting from something natural, immutable, or necessary. Simply put, it disavows any attempt to ground some element or other of our practices in something that is external to them. So understood, a discipline such as physical education is contingent in two senses:

1. Its own practice of rational inquiry can lay claim to no eternal verities, superconcepts, or pure methods, but must instead rely on the wits, skills,

ingenuity, creative imagination, and moral resolve of its academic community.

2. It is based on the study of practices (exercise and sport) that are themselves contingent social productions.

The recognition of this contingency requires one to forsake not scholarly rigor but only the false rhetoric of absolute rigor. What is required is not scientific precision but a disciplinary matrix that has the right mixture of rigor and openness. To be rational in this sense, therefore, is to be knowledgeable of, conversant with, and, when necessary, critical of the conventions of one's practice, to avoid fudging the data, and to keep one's hopes and fears from influencing one's conclusions unless conditions warrant otherwise (Rorty, 1982, pp. 194-5, 218). The only authority disciplines can claim, then, is one in which this kind of rationality flourishes, one that construes authority as a derivative not of weakness but of common participation in worthy, but fallible and transitory, communal endeavors (Hauerwas, 1986, p. 44).

The second feature of my reading of disciplines as cultural traditions is really a moral corollary of its first feature, but this time what has to be disavowed is not the vernacular of scientific rigor but that of institutions. And just as spurning the language of scientific rigor frees rational inquiry to set its own course rather than to seek its direction from some imagined outside force (some set of ahistorical supercategories), so spurning the language of institutions frees rational inquiry from all-too-real outside forces (bureaucratic organizations) that delight in expropriating its knowledge to serve their own narrow interests. The capacity of rational inquiry to stay the course, to withstand the corrupting allure of external goods, is steeped in what I take to be the central intellectual virtue of disciplines: their commitment to a dispassionate, disinterested study of, and regard for, the practices entrusted to them. "Disinterested" is understood here neither as the absence of any practical interest in, nor as a conventionally practical, utilitarian interest in, what is studied. Rather, it designates a disposition that combines a special, abiding interest in the standards of excellence and internal goods that define its practice and those that are the focus of its inquiry with a cultivated indifference to extrinsic effects and institutional structures. If it is plausible to render disinterestedness as just this sort of virtue, then it follows that disciplines have built into their souls not only a special theoretical mission but a decidedly moral one as well, whose point is to look after the good of the practices they are aligned with, to check their perversion by external goods, to see to it that they are accorded their due respect and that they are engaged in with dignity and integrity. Disciplinarians should insist, therefore, on controlling their own research agenda; should be leery of their colleagues who turn over physiological and sensitive psychological data to authoritarian types and to private interests; and should speak out against the bastardization of exercise and sport by bureaucratic organizations interested only in extending their own power.

Summary

What I have been trying to do is initiate a conversation about whether we can sensibly talk about disciplines as cultural traditions, and whether or not it makes any sense to reclaim for the Academy a position of moral and social leadership. These are not idle matters. For I fear that if we don't join in some such conversation, we, and I am speaking for both the discipline and the profession here, are likely to become what most everything else, whether it be labor unions or the AMA, has become in these trying times: a self-protective interest group concerned only with its own perpetuation. And if we succumb to this posturing as well, if we insist on extending our power over others by claiming to be something we are not—an absolute source of knowledge and expert service—we will have succeeded, I contend, only in becoming contemptible bureaucrats. Time is of the essence, however, for we are quickly reaching the point where we will no longer be able to bear either our vices or their cure (Stout, 1986, p. 32).

References

ELLIS, M.J. (1990). Reactions to "The body of knowledge: A common core." In C.B. Corbin & H.M. Eckert (Eds.), *The Academy Papers. The evolving undergraduate major.* (No. 23, pp. 13-16). Champaign, IL: Human Kinetics.

HAUERWAS, S. (1986). *Suffering presence*. Notre Dame, IN: University of Notre Dame Press.

HENRY, F. (1968). Physical education: An academic discipline. In H.S. Slusher & A.S. Lockhart (Eds.), *Anthology of contemporary readings* (pp. 281-286). Dubuque, IA: Brown.

KUHN, T.S. (1970). *The structure of scientific revolutions*. Chicago: University of Chicago Press.

LASCH, C. (1986). The communitarian critique of liberalism. *Soundings*, **69**, 60-76.

MACINTYRE, A. (1977). Patients as agents. In S.F. Spicker & H.T. Engelhardt (Eds.), *Philosophical medical ethics* (pp. 197-212). Dordrecht, Holland: Reidel.

MACINTYRE, A. (1984). *After virtue*. Notre Dame, IN: University of Notre Dame Press.

PARK, R.J. (1989). The second 100 years: Or, can physical education become the renaissance field of the 21st century? *Quest*, **41**, 2-27.

RORTY, R. (1982). *Consequences of pragmatism*. Minneapolis: University of Minnesota Press.

STOUT, J. (1986). Liberal society and the languages of morals. *Soundings*, **69**, 32-59.

THOMAS, J. (1990). The body of knowledge: A common core. In C.B. Corbin & H.M. Eckert (Eds.), *The Academy Papers. The Evolving Undergraduate Major.* (No. 23, pp. 5-12). Champaign, IL: Human Kinetics.

Mechanisms for Making an Interdisciplinary Doctoral Program in Exercise Science Work

Daniel M. Landers
Arizona State University

The program I am about to describe is formally interdisciplinary. Unlike most PhD programs in our field, the exercise science program at Arizona State University is not contained within a single department. The interdisciplinary nature of the program has led to some procedures that are atypical of most disciplinary PhD programs in our field. Before describing these policies and procedures, I will give some of the background factors that led to the development of this program.

Historical Background

Prior to 1981, two attempts had been made to establish a departmental PhD program similar to others in the College of Liberal Arts and Sciences. These attempts failed primarily because the higher administration did not believe the department possessed a critical mass of faculty who could effectively mentor doctoral students. In this case, the deans of the Graduate College and the College of Liberal Arts and Sciences wanted at least four or five faculty in each subspecialty or concentration (biomechanics, history, exercise physiology, etc.) in which the PhD degree was to be offered. They believed that a doctoral student would benefit more from exposure to a variety of faculty points of view within the given concentration. They also wanted to avoid a model of disciplines characterized as *soft* and *applied* (Krahenbuhl, this volume). In other words, the administration did not want to see one faculty member representing a specialization with 15 to 30 doctoral students under his or her direct supervision. Instead, the administration favored a mentor program where each faculty member approved for mentor status would work very closely in an apprenticeship relationship with no more than three or four students.

There also seemed to be a preference on the part of the higher administration that the physical education subdisciplines in which a critical mass should be developed first were those most related to the pure–hard approaches to knowledge, such as exercise physiology, and to a lesser extent biomechanics, motor learning/development, and sport psychology. Given the resources of the department at that time and the preference of the higher administration to develop a critical mass of faculty in a few areas of specialization, it seemed logical to propose an interdisciplinary model in order for a doctoral program to be realized in the short term.

So the evolution of the program was very much influenced by the context in which the department found itself in 1981. The program probably would not have evolved in this way in a university with a different mission or in a college with a greater emphasis on professional service (e.g., a college of education). There were also present many of the following factors, which have since been identified as elements critical to the success of programs attempting to develop interdisciplinary collaboration:

> administrative and institutional support, availability of adequate funding, open communication and collegiality, overlapping educational experience, availability of collaborators, and opportunities for practical application and technological transfer, [as well as a] strong leader or champion and collaborators willing to work for team recognition instead of individual recognition. (National Research Council, 1990, p. 7)

In 1981, Arizona State University was striving to become a top research university in the western United States. To ultimately achieve this status, the goal was to develop much like the University of California at Los Angeles had done earlier. This involved hiring faculty with good research training, providing them adequate start-up money so they had the potential of being productive right away, and encouraging them to apply for extramural grant funding so their research programs could grow and prosper. Given limited financial resources within the university and considering the administration's long-range goal, the reason that exercise physiology, biomechanics, and psychology of exercise and sport (including motor development, learning, and control) were initially encouraged becomes evident. These areas were considered to have greater potential of obtaining extramural funding and gaining the respect of faculty in other university departments who were likely to participate in this program.

Program Structure and Resources

With input from other faculty, Gary Krahenbuhl (former department chair and now interim dean) prepared the proposal for an interdisciplinary PhD program in exercise science during the fall semester of 1981. This interdisciplinary proposal was well received by the university administration. Following its approval by the board of regents in 1982, the dean of the Graduate College used this proposal as a model and encouraged people in other disciplines to use it in the design of interdisciplinary programs.

The proposed PhD in exercise science called for areas of concentration in biomechanics, exercise physiology, and psychology of exercise and sport. The faculty who desired to participate in this program were initially recruited from the Departments of Chemistry, Mechanical and Aerospace Engineering, Psychology, Zoology, and, of course, Exercise Science and Physical Education. More recently, faculty from the Departments of Bioengineering, Educational Psychology, and Family Resources and Human Development have also been added to the critical mass of faculty (now 21) that presently constitute this program.

One very important proviso in the initial program proposal was that the small budget for four half-time research assistants be housed in the Department of Exercise Science and Physical Education. In addition, the director of the program was to be appointed by the dean of the Graduate College from among the senior faculty in the Department of Exercise Science and Physical Education. The director of the exercise science program would be directly responsible to the dean of the Graduate College rather than to a department chair. Although this allowed some independence in the development of program policies, in practice the director's ties to the Department of Exercise Science and Physical Education meant that policies developed would be in the joint best interests of the department and the exercise science PhD program.

I was appointed as director and was charged with forming a five-member interdisciplinary executive committee. The director organized the work of the executive committee but was nonvoting. The current executive committee members, who serve 5-year terms, are from the Departments of Chemistry, Exercise Science and Physical Education (i.e., one biomechanist and one exercise physiologist), Psychology , and Zoology. This committee is critical to the program's function. They evaluate faculty recommendations about potential students, annually evaluate students currently enrolled in the program, approve faculty wishing to join the exercise science faculty, determine which faculty should have mentor status, and determine program policies.

The original proposal for the program called for four half-time research assistants, but there are now nine. Recently a budget for supplies, equipment, course buyouts, or travel has been added to the exercise science account in the Department of Exercise Science and Physical Education. A major resource is the 14,500 square feet of well-equipped research space called the Exercise and Sport Research Institute. This departmental research institute is where the PhD students in exercise science have their offices and conduct research in laboratories for biomechanics and exercise physiology (including biochemistry) as well as sport psychology, motor development, and learning/control.

Atypical Policies

Many policies established since the program began are not different from policies typically found in departmental PhD programs (e.g., having a supervisory committee, oral and written comprehensive examinations, and a dissertation committee). However, due to the interdisciplinary nature of the exercise science program, several policies are, I believe, atypical of policies in most departmental (disciplinary) PhD programs in our field. One of these policies is that students must pass a qualifying examination (master's-level knowledge) in the areas of biomechanics, exercise physiology, psychology of exercise and sport, and research methods/statistics. Although other programs require students to take a qualifying examination sometime in their 1st year, ASU requires them to take it during the orientation week before the start of their first semester. The reason for this examination being so early is that the executive committee members (particularly those in the natural sciences) wanted students to immediately begin their research programs rather than spend their first semester studying for an examination. Students fail this examination only if they do not perform adequately in their major areas; examination results in the other areas are diagnostic, serving to guide the supervisory committee in designing the student's program of study.

Whereas most PhD programs in physical education require a master's degree for entry into the doctoral program, outstanding undergraduates can enter the exercise science program. This policy is customary in the sciences but is not typical in physical education and other more applied programs. In our exercise science program, undergraduates must have completed a major research project, which usually consists of an undergraduate honors thesis or a publication in a refereed journal. They also must have very high grades, especially in the sciences and math, high Graduate Record Examination scores, excellent letters of recommendation, a letter of intent, and an interview that has convinced the proposed mentor of the student's potential. Given these considerations, it is understandable that in the 8 years since the program was begun, only two undergraduate students have been approved to directly enter into the PhD program in exercise science.

The only general requirement in the program of study is that students must take 12 credits of research and 12 credits of dissertation. The remainder of their course work is determined by

1. the student's performance on the qualifying examination, and
2. the mentor, in consultation with the student and one other exercise science faculty member who is in a department other than the mentor's department.

The 12 research credits taken in the first 2 years is to encourage students to develop a line of research that should conceivably lead to a dissertation topic. This line of research is necessarily related to the mentor's interests but usually independent of the mentor's funded research projects. This requirement serves two purposes: getting students involved in research early in the program and striving toward originality by developing some independence from the mentor's current research.

Before entering the program, students must identify a mentor with whom they want to work. In this way mentors (with agreement from the executive committee) control the number and quality of their students. Applicants also are required to know the mentor's research interests so that they can commit themselves to researching topics related to the mentor's expertise.

Once admitted, the student must be enrolled in the program continuously for the 3 to 4 years it typically takes to complete the program. Applicants who will be on leave and wish to spend only a year or two in residency and then return to their full-time jobs are not admitted. PhD students are discouraged from taking positions before completing the dissertation. The executive committee believes that if students leave before completing the dissertation, they will not learn as much; they will fail to complete their dissertations; and they will be at greater risk of producing a lower quality dissertation; or, given the fast pace of science, of someone else completing the research.

As students are expected to be full-time until completion of the program, acceptance into the program carries a half-time research or teaching assistantship for a 3- to 4-year period (including summers). The executive committee and mentor want the students involved as much as possible in research. Sources of support that take them away from research and teaching in their areas of concentration are avoided. For example, teaching in the area of concentration (e.g., assisting in an undergraduate biomechanics laboratory) is acceptable, but teaching activity or skill courses is typically discouraged. This requirement acts to moderate the number of students in the program—a faculty member who wishes to have more than one PhD student needs to acquire sources of funding. The program averages about 15 students, with anywhere from six to nine half-time research or teaching assistantships. Thus, over the years much of the student support has come from external funding. The executive committee believes that this policy encourages faculty to seek outside grant funding.

As a faculty member from a department different from the mentor's department provides input into the student's program of study, the student typically is required to take graduate course work in departments other than Exercise Science and Physical Education. For instance, independent of the 12 research credits, students in exercise science usually take 12 to 15 credits of formal course work in the department and another 9 to 12 credits in other departments. To be admitted to graduate courses in other departments, they must have taken various prerequisite courses. Therefore, prior to entering the biomechanics program, students must have had courses in biomechanics, calculus, statics, dynamics, and strength of materials; for exercise physiology, students must have had exercise physiology, mammalian physiology, and biochemistry; for psychology of exercise and sport, they must have had a course in the concentration area and two upper division courses in psychology. In all areas of concentration, students should have had some course work in research methods and statistics.

Cross-Disciplinary Research

The program has also been successful in fostering considerable cross-disciplinary (Henry, 1978) research—research combining areas of concentration (e.g., biomechanics and psychology of sport). One of the obvious reasons for the abundance of cross-disciplinary research is the physical proximity of students in the Exercise and Sport Research Institute. In the design of the institute, all of the laboratories for the three areas of concentration were placed in close proximity so that faculty and students could readily communicate. This communication is also enhanced by requiring students to attend a cross-disciplinary seminar that meets twice each month. They are also required to present their research in this seminar once each semester. This means, for example, that exercise physiology students must present their research so that it can be understood by students and faculty in biomechanics and psychology of exercise and sport. In their first semester, students usually report the results of their theses or proposals for research studies. By the second or third semesters they are usually reporting the results of research collected during the first or second semesters.

For students to better understand one another in the seminar or laboratory, most mentors require their students to take one graduate course at the master's level in the other areas of concentration. For instance, a biomechanics student would take at least one course in exercise physiology and one in psychology of exercise and sport (e.g., a motor development, learning, and control class).

In addition, students are expected to take written and oral comprehensive examinations in research methods/statistics, in their major areas of concentration, and one or more other areas of concentration that may relate to their programs of study. For example, students who have an interest in psychology of exercise will usually be tested in the area of exercise physiology and to a lesser extent biomechanics. With this in mind, the supervisory committee is composed of at least three faculty in the major area of concentration as well as one faculty member in each of the two remaining areas.

Enhancing Interdisciplinary Cooperation

In terms of program policies, the following formal requirements are designed to promote interdisciplinary involvement of faculty.

1. Most members of the executive committee must be from departments other than the Department of Exercise Science and Physical Education.
2. At least one committee member helping to develop the student's program of study must be from a department other than the mentor's department. This policy is important in keeping the mentor abreast of new courses or special topics offerings in other departments.
3. A balance of research experiences and formal courses is maintained, not only in the Department of Exercise Science and Physical Education, but from other disciplines as well. Having students take about one third of the course work in other departments not only helps to provide up-to-date knowledge from the parent disciplines, but helps promote our program by demonstrating the quality of our students to other academic units.
4. At the request of the students, the executive committee conducts an annual evaluation of the students. In addition to course grades, students must indicate the dates at which research projects were initiated and completed as well as the dates at which they submitted their work for presentation or publication. A student who is deemed not to be making sufficient progress is required to provide the executive committee with a timetable (typically over 3 months) and goals to be accomplished during this period. The executive committee along with the mentor then monitors the student's progress in reaching these shorter range goals.
5. As a result of a 5-year review of the exercise science PhD program, the dean of the College of Liberal Arts and Sciences has established a budget for the program. This operational money is designed to encourage the 10 exercise science faculty in departments other than Exercise Science and Physical Education to participate more in joint research projects. For example, travel money can be provided to present papers at exercise science meetings. Funds can also be used for equipment and supplies for exercise science projects and for course buyouts so that faculty from other departments can teach a specialized course of interest to exercise science students. During the current year this money is being used to provide equipment and

supplies for the dissertation of an exercise science student who is mentored by a faculty member from the Department of Chemistry.

Evolving Issues

Considering the results of the 5-year review as well as other indicators, the program has been successful over the past 8 years. Within the university, the program has been judged to be among the best in the College of Liberal Arts and Sciences. The Graduate College judged it as one of the few interdisciplinary programs that has actually worked. The program is recognized by the Western Interstate Commission for Higher Education (WICHE) as being among 125 distinguished graduate programs in 13 participating western states. A highlight in the evolution of this program occurred in 1987, when the interdisciplinary PhD program in exercise science was included (as a named program) in the university's 5-year mission and scope statement as one of five university programs that was nationally recognized to which the university would continue to give special support.

These developments have been very gratifying and have helped in the recruitment of better quality students. They have also led to greater prestige for our program among students and faculty in other fields who now desire to become more involved in the exercise science program, as either students or members of the exercise science faculty.

Despite this success, some evolving issues have been brought to the attention of the executive committee. One recurring issue is whether the program should be more decentralized, with greater autonomy among the individual mentors rather than decisions being made mainly by the members of the executive committee. This usually comes up when a mentor wants a student who does not uniformly meet admission standards. To equate standards across mentors from varied backgrounds and departments, the executive committee has opted for a more centralized role. This has led to uniformly high standards and greater selectivity of students. I believe that this centralized model has been one of the principal reasons this interdisciplinary program has succeeded. Without this, there would be little assurance that the kind of interdisciplinary program described above could continue to function effectively. The basic argument, that faculty should be trusted to make judgments about students in their areas, comes from a disciplinary model perspective. If students are to be successful in interdisciplinary and cross-disciplinary efforts, the common performance standards are important.

Another recent issue has been whether students should take a university position before completing all of the requirements for the degree. This is greatly discouraged in the hard sciences. In the course of the 5-year review of the program, a university vice president was very critical of our allowing students to take university positions before completing their dissertations. At present, several mentors are discouraging students from applying for academic positions or postdoctoral fellowships until they are well into data collection. Some mentors, for example, will not write letters of recommendation until most of the student's dissertation data has been collected.

Up to the present, the research grants that have supported most of the exercise science research as well as provided support for students have been procured by exercise science faculty in the Department of Exercise Science and Physical Education. Faculty in other departments have often obtained grant support, but their projects may not be closely related to exercise science, and instead of supporting exercise science students, these faculty support students from their own departments. Among some of the younger exercise science faculty from other departments this is beginning to change. Recently acquired operational funds are now being given to exercise science faculty in other departments with the hope that they will submit more grant proposals related to exercise science and request support for exercise science students.

There has been some discussion recently whether to expand to more than three areas of concentration. The Graduate College recently approved an interdisciplinary PhD degree in curriculum and instruction through the College of Education. Two of the areas of concentration that were approved for this degree program were in exercise and wellness education and in physical education pedagogy. Exercise and wellness education might be considered as an appropriate area to be within the exercise science program. However, the end result was that the faculty representing the exercise and wellness area decided that their research direction was more professionally and programmatically oriented (e.g., related to exercise programs) than the direction taken by exercise science, and that they should be associated with the curriculum and instruction degree. This distinction among programs has now become clearer; that is, students who desire to examine underlying mechanisms about exercise, sport, and movement belong in the exercise science program, and those who wish to do programmatic, outcome research as it relates to educational concerns belong in the curriculum and instruction program.

Finally, the addition in recent years of several new exercise science faculty to the Department of Exercise Science and Physical Education has led many faculty in this department to wonder if the critical mass might now justify a move toward a departmental PhD program. Discussions with the exercise science faculty and deans of the Graduate College and the College of Liberal Arts and Sciences have led to the conclusion that the study of human movement is interdisciplinary—the major advances in knowledge are occurring at the intersections of disciplines. Linking strong faculty from the various disciplines to attack research problems of mutual interest produces better quality research and ultimately attracts more grant support. This philosophy of the benefits of interdisciplinary research has been echoed by a committee of the National Research Council (1990). After pointing out numerous examples of the effectiveness of interdisciplinary research, this 16-member committee urged that foundations and the National Institutes of Health provide more mechanisms to foster interdisciplinary research.

References

HENRY, F.M. (1978). The academic discipline of physical education. *Quest*, **29**, 13-29.

NATIONAL Research Council (1990). *News Report*, **40**(3), 6-8.

Graduate Education in Kinesiology: A Cross-Disciplinary Approach

Glyn C. Roberts
University of Illinois

I agreed to contribute this paper when I discovered that it would constitute a counterpoint to the paper by Landers (this volume). The Department of Physical Education and Exercise Science at Arizona State has developed an interdisciplinary graduate program with several other units at Arizona State, and the program is jointly administered by the department and these other units. The units jointly oversee a graduate program that applies various disciplines to the study of physical education and sport issues. My argument is that this approach to graduate education is fraught with potential problems. (This is not to deny that the program at Arizona State is successful and to be admired, as Landers demonstrated.) My concern is with the perceptions generated in peer departments across campus when we adopt an interdisciplinary approach. These perceptions may be very positive about the graduate program per se, but the perceptions about the department are not always positive. Before developing this thesis further, let me set the stage by reminding ourselves of the political and economic realities that exist on our campuses. It is this backdrop that helps create the negative perceptions that too often reveal themselves.

In 1985, I wrote an article in *The Physical Educator* where I described the winds of change that were sweeping our campuses. The major changes were reflected in the shift of gravity away from the liberal arts, humanities, and social and behavioral sciences toward engineering and the hard sciences. This shift of gravity, and the reduction of the growth of funding for higher education, has meant a reallocation of resources within institutions, with our colleges and our departments having had to defend themselves as best they could from the reallocation-of-resources shakedown. Many of the professional debates we have today stem from our various reactions to this shakedown.

The Criteria of Demand, Centrality, and Excellence

Universities have criteria by which they decide how to reallocate resources. Generally, resources are allocated based on three criteria—demand, centrality, and excellence. All of our departments have developed strategies to meet these criteria at our respective campuses. But the strategies that some of us adopted to meet these criteria had the opposite effect to the one intended. In our quest to demonstrate demand, centrality, and excellence, we actually exposed our weaknesses, targeted ourselves for continued scrutiny, and reinforced negative perceptions.

Demand

Student demand is down, especially at the undergraduate level, but this has been true at the graduate level, too. There are many reasons for the decline in students, as has been debated in our professional literature. The numbers seem to have been increasing in the past 2 years at Illinois, but only time will tell whether this is a solid trend or a peculiar spike in our enrollment pattern. But for universities that have student-demand-driven fiscal formulas, this decrease in numbers has meant that our programs become targeted as a source for the reallocation of funds.

Each of our institutions has attempted to meet this decline in students, and there has been a trend to expand degree programs in physical education into nontraditional professional options. This is what has been called commercial physical educators. It is reasonable that some of these avenues be pursued, but these quasi-professional tracks further undermine resources at a time when resources to maintain quality graduate programs are stretched. But the real downside of developing alternative career options at the graduate level is that when these programs go through various approval committees on campus, they focus the attention of our peers and administrators on us. When universities are retrenching and focusing on established and traditional areas of study, we push new professional programs! At major research universities, it doesn't make political sense.

Centrality

In our respective departments, regardless of what we call ourselves, the perception in central administration is that we lack centrality. We don't offer programs or courses in demand by other students. When you look at it from the point of view of an administrator, it is easy to see why we lack centrality: We lack demand; we push quasi-professional tracks at a time when major universities are looking hard at professionally oriented programs; and we attract few students from outside the department. But in our quest to demonstrate excellence, we have, in my opinion, most exposed the lack of centrality of what we do.

Excellence

The path many of our respective departments have taken to demonstrate excellence is to ally with cognate disciplines. This is Arizona State's approach, as articulated by Landers (this volume). Faculty within such departments even seek joint appointments in the cognate discipline, and, in the quest to demonstrate excellence, faculty publish their articles in the parent-discipline journals. I have even heard some people boast that they send their best articles to the parent-discipline journals and save their other articles for our own journals in the field. The thinking is that we obtain our prestige and standing from the reflected legitimacy of the parent department. Others have written on how this avenue has led to specialization, which has sometimes led to a fragmenting of our graduate programs. This is what Greendorfer (1987) has decried as the vertical development of subdisciplines in our field. Our students take courses in the cognate disciplines, and we are justifiably proud that our students do well in these courses. In my institution in 1984, for example, PhD graduate students took more than half of their total number of courses in these cognate disciplines. Again, it doesn't make political sense: We recruit students into our graduate program, and then send them elsewhere for their education!

We expose our lack of centrality to university administrators when we behave this way. By strengthening what we do, we beg the question of why we are doing it. To any perceptive administrator, what we do can be done elsewhere on campus. Why can't exercise physiology be done in physiology? Why can't sport psychology be done in psychology? In an age of retrenchment and reallocation of resources, our tactics to enhance demand, centrality, and excellence have the potential to have the opposite effect. By seeking to enhance our own credibility by adopting the instant legitimacy of parent disciplines, we underscore our own vulnerability and weakness.

When we argue (or imply) that we wish to apply cognate disciplines to the study of exercise, physical education, or sport, rightly or wrongly, it fosters the perception that we have insufficient substance in our own field. Such arguments do make sense if one is prepared to narrow our field's focus to the study of issues pertinent to activity contexts. There is some merit to the argument that activity contexts dominate the academic interests of most of us. But I worry that such arguments are predicated on assumptions that weaken our program when perceived by our colleagues across campus. Let me cite an analogy: Newell (1990) argues that if the Department of Agronomy at Illinois called itself the Department of Corn and Soybeans (they certainly dominate the activities of agronomy at Illinois), or the Department of Religious Studies called itself the Department of Judaism and Christianity, they would be exposing themselves to scrutiny, too. The analogy to activity contexts is a good one. My argument is that the assumptions implicit in such labels have political and public perception costs in the eyes of our peers across campus. At research universities, we must demonstrate more than a focus on contexts.

An Alternative Strategy

There has to be an alternative strategy, one that does not create the impression that the field's conceptual substance is borrowed. We need a strategy that emphasizes the cross-disciplinary nature of our field and the unique and conceptually defensible discipline that drives our research and practice. The counterpoint to the interdisciplinary approach is the cross-disciplinary approach.

There have been many attempts to formulate coherent and integrated programs of study in physical education that are cross-disciplinary. In fact, I agree with Greendorfer (1987), who cites earlier studies to show that our current debates on this issue are, in reality, reinventions of the wheel. But there is a fundamental question we need to ask ourselves in these debates: What is the conceptual core of our field? What is the conceptual structure and body of knowledge of kinesiology? Or as Newell (1990) has asked recently, what is the central academic focus of the field? It is regrettable that because we do not have a consensus on this question as a field, we suffer in our arguments to our respective publics.

We cannot bring to bear the weight of a consensus and a national organization welded around our conceptual core. Our departments now have a whole series of different labels, which not only underscores our failure to reach consensus, but weakens our arguments at our own institutions because of our apparent inability as a group to articulate the field's center of gravity.

As many of us do when we engage in these debates, we can go back to Henry (1964) for the articulation of the issues that have spawned these points and counterpoints. It was Henry who argued that academic disciplines cannot be articulated by a curriculum comprised of courses selected from other departments, nor can they consist of the application of the cognate disciplines to the study of physical activity. We must move away from transplanting established disciplines and measurement techniques into physical education, and we must move away from courses that reflect the application of these disciplines (such as the psychology of sport!). Henry argued for a cross-disciplinary approach and stressed that the purely motor aspects of human behavior need far more attention than they currently receive.

The central focus of our field, we argue at Illinois, is human motor movement, or physical activity. (I know they are not synonymous, but I don't want us to get caught in the semantics of labels at this juncture.) It is not the context in which physical activity is manifested, whether it be exercise, work, sport, dance, or whatever, that is important! As a discipline, we need not exclusionary but inclusive models. We need to capture the many broad and diverse approaches to studying physical activity. In this way, we incorporate a broad range of disciplinary, professional, and performance thrusts in our rubric. And, as is obvious, we embrace sport, exercise, and a whole universe of other physical activity contexts. In other words, our departments become the centers for the study of physical activity.

We need to develop our own conceptual structure and body of knowledge around the study of physical activity rather than merely adopt the instant legitimacy of parent disciplines as applied to sport or exercise. We need to develop what Greendorfer (1987) has called a horizontal and integrated curriculum of the study of human movement. Many terms have been proffered to describe this conceptual basis. Whether we call it human movement, physical activity, kinesiology, human kinetics, movement science, or something else, we need to alter our perspective in physical education. Rather than taking an external focus, or the activity–cognate discipline approach (Newell, 1990), and expanding in a vertical manner into the cognate disciplines (Greendorfer, 1987), we need to take an internal focus, or a cross-disciplinary approach (Henry, 1964; Renson, 1989), and concentrate upon our conceptual core and the subject matter of motor activity as our conceptual core. As a point of debate, let us define our field as a consortium of academic subdisciplines focusing on the systematic study of physical activity. This means that we can investigate physical activity in such contexts as work, play, dance, exercise, games, and sport. In essence, we are functioning in departments that have as their unique and exclusive focus the systematic study of physical activity. It is then up to us to define that focus and articulate it to our various publics, both within the university and without.

I refer you to Newell (1990) for a more detailed articulation of this approach. The framework we are using at Illinois to attempt to bring coherence and convergence to the area is to utilize clusters of concepts where individuals identify with clusters rather than with cognate disciplines. Let me explain.

The faculty of the Department of Kinesiology at Illinois focus on the study of human movement in a range of physical activity settings that includes athletics, communication, dance, exercise, play, sport, and work. The departmental programs emphasize the study of humans as physically active organisms, with special reference to human performance and the development of motor skills, together with the impact that engagement in physical activities has on individuals throughout the life span. The undergraduate and graduate programs provide the scholarly basis for a variety of careers related to kinesiology and the application of physical activity in the arts, education, health, industry, the military, and exercise and sport.

The academic programs in kinesiology are organized around four clusters of core concepts related to the study of human movement. They are as follows.

1. Energy, work, and efficiency—the study of work output, energy, and efficiency of movement as they relate to exercise stress, and the mechanics of human movement and fitness throughout the human life span
2. Growth, development, and form—the study of the growth process, the influence of physical activity on body form and composition, and the complementary influence of body development and form on human behavior and personality
3. Coordination, control, and skill—the study of the mechanisms and processes involved in the acquisition and performance of human motor skills
4. Involvement, interdependence, and achievement—the study of the antecedents and consequences of involvement in physical activity in sport, the processes underlying achievement, as well as the impact physical activity and sport have on the individual, society, and culture

These clusters form the areas of specialization and encompass the areas of study traditionally found in departments of physical education. In addition, we have professional programs constructed around these clusters. We have therapeutic kinesiology—the study of movement as a therapeutic vehicle for health and wellness, particularly the prevention and rehabilitation of injury, disease, or movement dysfunction; and pedagogical kinesiology—the study of the organizational and instructional concepts essential for the efficient and effective conduct of physical activity programs, particularly those that relate to physical education and sport contexts.

Nested within these conceptual clusters are the traditional areas of graduate study. For example, sport psychology and sport sociology areas of graduate study are found in the involvement, interdependence, and achievement conceptual cluster, even though the course work in these areas can be found in the other clusters too. Exercise physiology is found in energy, work, and efficiency. Biomechanics has courses in this area, but it is found, along with motor learning and control, in the coordination, control, and skill area, primarily. In this way, we have tried to break down the traditional barriers to cross-disciplinary work generated by vertical curriculum planning into the cognate discipline that the interdisciplinary approach fosters.

I am not suggesting that every university should follow this model. Without question, missions at different institutions should vary. We do not have a national curriculum, nor should we. Local circumstances impose local constraints. But it is conceivable that we should agree on a common conceptual core of subject matter for the field of kinesiology. The translations of that common core may differ, but not the common understandings.

The Illinois Program

Just as Landers (this volume) used examples from Arizona State to punctuate his arguments in favor of the interdisciplinary approach, allow me to use some illustrations from our program at Illinois to punctuate some of my arguments above. A reasonable question to ask is whether our approach is working. It goes without saying that, for a program like this to work, we must have a faculty committed to making it work. We do have a nucleus of faculty committed to making this approach a viable one, but we also have some faculty who remain skeptical.

As you can appreciate, our revisions of the undergraduate and graduate programs to make them more consistent with our cross-disciplinary approach is still under way. But already there are some markers indicating that our approach is achieving success, at least within our own local constraints.

First, and consistent with the position taken here, there is some evidence that our approach has met the seal of approval of our central administrators. The previous acting dean and the current dean both have received information that the way the Department of Kinesiology has reconfigured itself is meeting with the approval of central administration. They believe that our mission statements and programmatic thrusts are consistent with the mission statements of the University of Illinois. Those perceptions are difficult to document, but we are getting consistent information from the units with whom we have collaborated in the past that they approve of our current approach. As an example, over the past 2 years, of the major research equipment requests we have submitted to the UIUC Research Board, more than 50% have been funded. Typically the Research Board grants less than 20% of requests. This is a small point, but it does illustrate an acceptance by our peers of our articulation of our research mission.

Second, the number of applications of graduate students is increasing. But more importantly, we now get many more requests from individuals from allied fields other than the traditional ones we have attracted in the past. We have always had a few requests from graduate students from other disciplines, but at Illinois the numbers are now increasing quite dramatically. For example, of the 40 or so applicants to the sport psychology program this year, approximately half were trained in psychology per se.

Third, we have always had faculty from our departments seeking joint appointments in other cognate disciplines and departments. We have achieved success in these quests (I have two such appointments myself). However, at Illinois, we now have a very strong reverse flow. We now have faculty members from other units requesting joint appointments with us in kinesiology. And these appointments are more than token, zero-time appointments. For example, a very distinguished psychopharmacologist requested and received a 100% appointment in our department. When he moved from the Institute for Research on Human Development, he could have moved to any one of several departments. But because his interests were in hyperkinesis and tardive dyskinesia, he chose our department. This is a significant appointment, as he is a world-renowned scholar in his area. Would that have happened with our old mission and nomenclature? We also had an aviation psychologist who requested a 40% alignment in kinesiology so that he could work with our motor learning and control individuals. In addition, the Aviation Institute has approached two individuals in our department to determine whether they wish to have joint appointments in aviation psychology, and we have had two requests for zero-time appointments in our department this year alone.

Fourth, we are now getting more graduate students from other departments in our courses. In fact, in one graduate course we offered in the fall of 1989, 90% of the 24 graduate students were from departments outside of the college. It is interesting to note that at Illinois our instructional units generated from the physical activity program are decreasing slowly over time. But our percentage of instructional units in the college is being maintained, through students seeking knowledges in our undergraduate and graduate courses. It is now rare for us to cancel courses at the graduate level for lack of student demand.

Fifth, with our reconfigured graduate program, more graduate students are staying home to do their courses in the Department of Kinesiology. In contrast to only 4 years ago, when more than 50% of courses were taken outside of the college, approximately 20% of courses are taken outside of the department currently. Our students feel that they can obtain the specialist knowledges within the department rather than obtaining these knowledges in the cognate disciplines. They still take some courses, but not nearly as many as they used to. This strategy, of course, presupposes an excellent faculty at the forefront of research in their areas of expertise within the department.

Concluding Remarks

The message I'm trying to convey is quite simple, and we all know it's certainly not new. We need to move away from an activity–cognate discipline approach and move more toward a cross-disciplinary approach, if we want to meet our campuses' criteria for demand, excellence, and centrality. We must identify the conceptual core of physical activity, and our activities and the curricula we adopt should reflect it. There are segments in the field that emphasize the differences and the uniqueness of specific activity–cognate approaches, rather than the potential benefits of the integration and coherence generated from a conceptual base welded around a physical activity concept. The elevation of physical activity as the essential focus of study for the field should help provide the organizing and unifying framework so that we can go to our various publics with a coherent and cohesive focus. A broad-based model of kinesiology makes political and public relations sense, as well as academic sense. But more importantly, for our various publics, we identify our unique and viable focus of interest—which will better allow us to be accepted as a viable entity in a major-league research university.

Point-counterpoint!

References

GREENDORFER, S.L. (1987). Specialization, fragmentation, integration, discipline, profession: What is the real issue? *Quest*, **39**, 56-64.

HENRY, F.M. (1964). Physical education: An academic discipline. *Journal of Health, Physical Education and Recreation*, **35**, 32-33.

LANDERS, D.M. (this volume).

NEWELL, K.M. (1990). Physical education in higher education: Chaos out of order. *Quest*, **42**, 227-242.

RENSON, R. (1989). From physical education to kinanthropology: A quest for academic and professional identity. *Quest*, **41**, 235-256.

ROBERTS, G.C. (1985). Graduate education in an age of change. *The Physical Educator*, **43**(3), 106-108, 160-161.

Paradigms, Paradoxes, and Progress: Reflections and Prophecy

George H. Sage
University of Northern Colorado

Early last fall when our president-elect, Robbie Park, invited me to make a presentation at these Academy meetings, she said she had chosen the theme "new possibilities, new paradigms?" because a number of events over the past 2 years suggest that important changes are occurring in our field. She specifically mentioned the 1988 Big Ten Leadership Conference and the 1989 Academy meetings as being significant. These recent professional meetings, and a number of other activities over the past 5 years, certainly do point to new directions and new potentials for the years ahead.

As I began to think about what I might say that would be relevant to the conference theme, I reflected again about the concept of a paradigm. Its usage over the past 20 years is derived largely from Thomas Kuhn's (1962) now-classic work *The Structure of Scientific Revolutions*. But Kuhn used this concept in a very narrow, very specific way that was primarily meaningful in describing the conduction of research in physical science, notably physics, chemistry, and perhaps astronomy. More recent scholars have broadened and expanded the meaning of this concept. They have suggested that a paradigm can mean a fundamental *image* of the subject matter within a discipline that involves methodological rules, values, and/or a distinctive way of operating within the domain of the discipline (Gutting, 1980; Ritzer, 1980). This is closer to the meaning I find helpful in thinking about our field.

I felt certain that one new paradigm Robbie had in mind is embodied in the efforts to identify a uniform and unifying name for the academic study of humans in movement and its various professional applications. Given that, I began to reflect on what our old paradigms have been and how we have evolved to the new, so I decided to devote part of this presentation to that issue. What about other new paradigm trends and issues? Well, it is abundantly clear that we are a cross-disciplinary field that is one of the few that are centrally concerned with the whole, integrated human being (Park, 1987). Thus, legitimate research interests vary from the biochemical level to the cultural level. Research is the sine qua non of academic disciplines, and recent trends in research paradigms have been an active topic of debate and controversy, so I thought I might address this as a "new paradigm" issue.

I would be remiss if I did not make some effort to discuss the other part of our theme, new possibilities. I shall do this in the last part of my presentation.

From Old to New Paradigms

Now to take up the first topic—that of our old paradigms and our movement to the new: What have been the images and distinctive ways of operating in physical education? What follows is one person's interpretation, one person's response to that question.

One of the preeminent leaders of physical education in the latter 19th and early 20th centuries was Luther Gulick. He declared that physical education was not only a "new profession" but also a "scientific field" that offered opportunities for the study of problems of great value for the human species (Gulick, 1890). Other leaders of the emerging field of physical education also referred to it as, or as needing to become, a scientific field. Now, of course, anyone can proclaim the creation of a new science, as Gulick and others did, but it is quite another thing to establish a new science that is solidly founded upon theoretical and empirical bases, and, equally important, that is recognized as a science by the scientific establishment. Was physical education of the latter 19th and early 20th centuries a new science, as its advocates claimed?

Apparently not. Last summer a research project on which I was working took me into the history-of-science literature. I did not find physical education even mentioned in the major publications. The various physical, biological, and social sciences are exhaustively described and discussed, but physical education is nowhere to be found. Why is that? It occurs to me that whereas the various sciences were formulating theories and testing them through empirical methods, thus advancing knowledge during the latter 19th century and throughout the entire 20th century, the major initiatives in physical education have been professional controversies—controversies about the "best" gymnastic system, education through the physical or education of the physical, a physical fitness curriculum, or a games and sport curriculum, and the appropriate name for the field.

In spite of rousing speeches by early physical educators about a science of physical education, they did very little in pursuit of science, little knowledge advancement. Instead, the professional discourse and record of achievements were actually more closely aligned with the health-promotion movement (Whorton, 1982). Park (1987) noted that "although numerous medical doctors were among the early leaders of the American Association for the Advancement of Physical Education, few had any experience with the type of experimental laboratory science that was needed" (p. 15) to advance physical education as a science. In 1905 Harvard's George Fitz noted that "because of the absence of a convincing mass of scientific literature . . . physical training has failed [to get] . . . full recognition [from] the medical and other professions" (Fitz, 1905, p. 16).

Thus, health promotion and development through exercise, gymnastics, and athletics became, in essence, the original paradigm of physical education. MDs were the first full-time practitioners to gradually acquire predominance over less committed amateurs. Indeed, the hegemony of medically trained people in physical education was nearly complete for most of its first 50 years. This was manifested in several ways: In the first 37 years of what is now AAHPERD, all but one of the presidents were MDs. In its first 18 years, from 1897 to the beginning of World War I, all but one of the presidents of the NCPEAM were MDs. The editors of the *American Physical Education Review*, the leading journal for physical educators, were MDs. For the first 10 years of the *Review* over half of the original articles were authored by MDs. What is disclosed in these articles is uneven and discontinuous research, some of great promise, but most quite modest in terms of scientific achievement.

By the 1930s, the situation had changed dramatically. The major thrust of the field had shifted from health promotion to education; teacher preparation, curriculum issues, testing and measurement, methodology, high school and college athletics, and administration of school and college programs were at the forefront. Physical educators' concerns centered around educational issues rather than the advancement of a science.

Teacher education had become the dominant paradigm, replacing health promotion and development. The last AAHPERD president with the MD was Jesse Feiring Williams; he was president in 1933. A similar pattern is found for leadership in other physical education associations. The first two volumes of the *Research Quarterly*, which began in 1930 (edited by a PhD, not by an MD), had over 60 original articles, only 3 of which were authored or coauthored by persons with an MD. There was little in the way of continuing research programs of high scientific standards.

The dominance of teacher education was a two-edged sword. It was a powerful impetus for promoting physical education for children and adolescents in the schools—certainly a valuable social function—but it was also a continual distraction from the task of building a cumulative body of knowledge about human movement.

But paradigmatic hegemony is never guaranteed. The structure of academic disciplines and professional programs of study and training are not static, and trends are not random processes. There are structured moments for intellectual enterprises in which alliances shift, older constellations are displaced, and new views arise. One of those structured moments began in college and university departments of physical education in the 1960s and gained momentum in the 70s with the creation and development of the so-called subdisciplines. This movement was spearheaded by young scholars wishing to promote and advance the disciplinary study of human movement. The distinctiveness and significance of the beginnings of this paradigmatic *perestroika* were products of the interplay of such diverse social circumstances as pressures to demonstrate a basic academic body of knowledge, the fragmantation of knowledge throughout higher education into numerous scientific specialties, the leveling off of secondary school enrollments, an enormous oversupply of physical educators, declining enrollments of physical education majors, new nonteaching careers in exercise and sport programs, and enormous growth in the scientization of high-performance sport, to name only a few. These events set in motion a paradigm shift in physical education that has been going on now for almost 3 decades.

Advocates of the paradigm shift have been dedicated to advancing knowledge, so their focus on analyses of movement activities, especially in exercise and sport, have been grounded in disciplinary concepts, theories, and methods of empirical research. The upshot of all of this is that scholars, wishing to promote and advance the serious study of human movement, have adopted goals of legitimacy and professionalization that can be attained only by the development of recognized scholarship along academic disciplinary lines. From the day scholars committed themselves to the disciplinary growth of the study of humans in movement—dedicated themselves to other than physical activity courses and teacher preparation—the days of the term *physical education* have been numbered as an appropriate designation for such a field of study. This, of course, is not to suggest that the term might not be quite appropriate for one aspect of the study of human movement as well as a description for a professional field.

What has happened in physical education is not all that unique in the annals of science and applied fields of study. It is not the first time a new academic discipline got its start, or at least a strong boost, from the sponsorship of an applied setting, and then pushed beyond the confines of that setting. Government sponsorship of national geological surveys and land explorations enabled geography to dominate American sciences in the first 7 decades of the 19th century. Astronomy, taxonomic botany, geology, and meterology were all part of geography. In time all these disciplines outgrew this cocoon of sponsorship and struck out on their own.

The growth of chemistry owes much to the agricultural experiment stations between 1870 and World War I; the agricultural experiment stations also played an instrumental role in sheltering and supporting the formative period of several biological sciences, particularly bacteriology, biochemistry, and genetics, before these disciplines grew to justify their own separate identities. From these examples, and others that could be given, the restructuring that has occupied our own efforts for over 2 decades can be seen to have antecedents in the larger scientific and academic world; it can be seen as an example of the constantly shifting patterns of American academic disciplines.

Actions taken at the 1988 Big Ten Leadership Conference and the 1989 Academy meetings, where a unified term for our field of study—*kinesiology*—was agreed upon, were actually the culmination of 25 years of paradigm shifting. This restructuring has been very personal at times, and it has left scars on some of us who have been in the trenches of this battle. But in the context of science and the academic disciplines over the past 100 years, it is not that unusual. During this period, science and the academic disciplines have been dynamic, changing phenomena, buffeted by the winds of many social forces. If we honestly look at the historical record, we will discover that academic disciplines have always been created by the conflicts and compromises that are themselves products of wider social movements and pressures that extend well beyond the academic world. Political, economic, and social considerations have been integral parts of the making of both science and academic disciplines. Because of this complex articulation, some disciplines have grown and expanded, consuming and incorporating others; others have regrouped around a different set of disciplines. Some disciplines and professions have served as custodians for new ones while they were struggling for identity, and then—like parents—let go as the offspring matured and struck out on their own.

Trends in Research Paradigms

Now I want to switch my focus to a broad trend in research paradigms. New paradigm issues beyond kinesiology have implications for all of us and demand our attention and deliberations. The dominance of the positive-science paradigm has been subjected to intense criticism during the past decade, especially in the human sciences where research is expected to lay a scientific basis for professional applications—and most research in kinesiology is expected to ultimately have such applications. The criticism began in the social sciences and humanities, but it has gradually crept into intellectual discussions in the natural sciences as well.

A variety of antinaturalist, interpretivist, and critical research paradigms, often employing qualitative rather than quantitative methods, now challenge the hegemony of the positive-science orientation as an appropriately grounded way to understand and improve our ways of knowing and especially as a basis for professional and clinical practices. I'll call them collectively *alternative paradigms* as a shorthand characterization.

One tenet of the alternative paradigms is that positive-science methods used to study the natural world are simply inadequate for studying many of the most important questions about human affairs, because human actions are intricately involved with a variety of intentions, purposes, and goals that give them meaning. With respect to research on human movement activities, especially in sport and exercise contexts, one implication is that these activities cannot be regarded as neutral practices devoid of wider social significance and free of specific cultural values. This suggests that any adequate account of kinesiology—past, present, and future—must be rooted in an understanding that human movement activities are cultural practices embedded in the social, economic, political, and cultural contexts in which they are situated. Even some natural scientists are beginning to realize that the scientific process is socially constructed and embedded in the sociocultural milieu.

The alternative paradigms also suggest that in our research we need to address the problematics of knowledge production and dissemination in kinesiology. That is, knowledge for whom and for what ends? Who benefits and whose interests are served? Such questions might be organized around research focused upon understanding how to foster personal growth and socially liberating human movement activities rather than only the pursuit of techniques of peak performance and the promotion of commercialized exercise and sport forms. We must not let our penchant for technical sophistication be at the expense of "those who are subordinate in the capital/labor relation and/or who cannot pay consultants' fees" (Ingham & Donnelly, 1990, p. 60). In short, we need to be aware of and incorporate a sensitivity to the social, economic, and public-policy aspects of exercise, sport, and physical activities in the research questions we ask.

Of course, there is no single true research paradigm. Positive science and the alternative paradigms need not be seen as being mutually exclusive and antagonistic. What is needed is research conducted from multiple perspectives.

So What Are the "New Possibilities"?

A strong case could be made for using the program of these meetings as an illustration of "new possibilities." By extrapolating from what we have heard and seen in the past day and a half, we see at least some of the short-term potentials for research and professional practices.

Because of our shared interest in human movement, kinesiology researchers and professionals working in applied areas have a unique opportunity to collaborate across disciplinary and professional boundaries. Within the past year, I have served on three departmental review committees at major universities. As part of the process of examining and appraising these departments, I have seen exciting cross-disciplinary and interdisciplinary work going on. Such increased intellectual power through the creative use of diversity and thoughtful interaction is something that all of us can get excited about. With much scholarly action moving toward a blurring of traditional disciplinary boundaries and increased multidisciplinary pursuits, it is evident that kinesiologists wishing to be contributors to this action will have to become more eclectic and creative in their deliberations.

It is becoming clear that although there is a diversity of interests and expertise within kinesiology, there are enough similarities in terms of common themes, values, and purposes that are leading to important questions by those advancing the body of knowledge, those interpreting the knowledge, and those working directly with people to lead the way out of the contentiousness that has afflicted our mood for over 2 decades. These are signs of harmony and friendly relations within a more mature and understanding intellectual enterprise, and it bodes well for the field of kinesiology.

The boundaries of academic disciplines are extending and reconfiguring. Serious scholars and professionals are thinking beyond narrow specializations, visualizing and conceptualizing larger pictures, and this is leading to more general, unifying intellectual themes. Indeed, much visionary theoretical thinking involves eclipsing traditional disciplinary boundaries and increased interdisciplinary cooperative work. R. Tait McKenzie lecturer Marian Diamond's research is a good example of what some scientists are doing.

Student Preparation

Broader scientific perspectives and increased cross-disciplinary and interdisciplinary scholarship will have important implications for curriculum design for our undergraduate and graduate students. We will have to address the issue of whether we are preparing our students with sufficient common understandings and technical proficiencies beyond their own specialties for them to be able to join with others in formulating significant questions and hypotheses. Tendencies toward specialized learning must be balanced by opportunities that give broader scope and meaning to discoveries both in scientific and in clinical and other applied domains. A major challenge will be how to balance depth and specialized preparation with the broader forms of which specialization is a part. Other academic disciplines and the professional training programs—medicine, law, engineering, education—are wrestling with the same issue. They all agree that there must be a learning core that integrates various types of knowledge and ways of knowing. A report on the general professional education for physicians speaks of a common foundation of knowledge, skills, values, and attitudes (Muller, 1984; also see Levy, 1988). The reform movements in education all emphasize the need for a broad understanding in the social sciences and humanities as well as the natural sciences.

Concluding Remarks

I realize that I may have not said anything that has not been said in other ways by some of you as well as by others in our profession. I confess I am not blessed with any special insights or prophetic wisdom. I do, however, have full confidence that the field of kinesiology is on the threshold of an exciting era. However, perhaps we should take guidance from what one economist had to say recently about the federal deficit. A reporter interviewing the economist asked: "Do you think it's really possible to eliminate this terrible situation that we are confronted with by this enormous national debt?" The economist answered, "Yes I think it is. As a matter of fact, there are two ways to do it. There's a natural way, and there's a miraculous way." The reporter asked, "Well, all right, what's the natural way?" "The natural way," said the economist, "would be for a band of angels to descend from heaven and pay off all government debts." "If that's the natural way," the reporter asked, "what's the miraculous way?" To which the economist responded, "The miraculous way would be if Congress and the President worked out a way among themselves." We in kinesiology have no band of angels to solve our problems. We'll have to make our miracle happen ourselves.

References

FITZ, G. (1905). Editorial note and comment. *American Physical Education Review*, **10**, 61-64.

GULICK, L.H. (1890). Physical education: A new profession. *Proceedings of the 5th annual meeting of the American Association for the Advancement of Physical Education*,

GUTTING, G. (1980). Introduction. In G. Gutting (Ed.), *Paradigms and revolutions* (pp. 1-21). Notre Dame, IN: University of Notre Dame Press.

INGHAM, A.G., & Donnelly, P. (1990). Whose knowledge counts? The production of knowledge and issues of application in the sociology of sport. *Sociology of Sport Journal*, **7**, 58-65.

KUHN, T. (1962). *The structure of scientific revolutions*. Chicago: University of Chicago Press.

LEVY, R. (1988). The impact of science on medicine. In P.T. Marsh (Ed.), *Contesting the boundaries of liberal and professional education: The Syracuse experiment* (pp. 130-139). Syracuse, NY: Syracuse University Press.

MULLER, S. (1984). Physicians for the twenty-first century. *Journal of Medical Education*, **59**(Part 2), 1-27.

PARK, R. (1987, April). *Formation of paradigms: Some considerations*. Paper presented at the National Association for Sport & Physical Education Symposium on Science, Inquiry, and Progress: The Future of Physical Education, Las Vegas, NV.

RITZER, G. (1980). *Sociology: A multiple paradigm science* (rev. ed.). Boston: Allyn & Bacon.

WHORTON, J.C. (1982). *Crusaders for fitness: The history of American health reformers*. Princeton, NJ: Princeton University Press.

Of Dreams and Dinosaurs: The President's Address

Charles B. Corbin
Arizona State University

Thirty years ago, when I started my career as a teacher of elementary school physical education, it was not my dream to be standing here in front of this august body delivering an address such as this. I was not even aware of the existence of the American Academy of Physical Education. But dreams have a way of changing. Though this opportunity is far from any of my original dreams, it is a part of a dream come true.

Changing Dreams

My early dream of becoming a major league baseball player was revised after I first faced a top-quality college pitcher who appeared to throw golf balls rather than baseballs. I had been a physical education major from the day I entered college, and my dreams now shifted to becoming a successful basketball or baseball coach. If I couldn't play, maybe I could find the same feelings as a coach. However, student teaching in an inner-city high school convinced me to modify my dreams once again. I decided a first job as an elementary school physical education teacher might be a more realistic goal. The love of physical activity was intact, but the dream had changed.

The Dream: Our Common Goal

Years of involvement in sports as an athlete, a coach, and a teacher helped me revise my dreams. But I was still convinced that regular physical activity was necessary to a healthy and enriched life. I embraced the goal of using physical activity to help all people become fully functioning, healthy individuals. This goal has been the focus of my writings and research since that time. My dream: to help every person meet this goal.

Obstacles to the Goal

Now 30 years later the dream is alive! I have, and we all have, done much to make this dream come true. But the dream has not been fully realized. Any grandiose dream is a series of small dreams. As one small dream comes true, others are envisioned. Not all of the dreams come true, because there are many obstacles. I believe that our inferiority complex and the nature of our schizophrenic higher education system are obstacles to the dream I have for physical education.

Since I began my studies as a physical education major in the 1950s I have been aware of the need to defend my major or my choice of careers. I was taught that I was not a second-class citizen, but the constant protestations by professors and colleagues told me that we had a collective inferiority complex. To this day I believe that we still have it and that it clouds many of our decisions. For example, we seem to value publications in journals outside our field more than those in our own, and we model our curricula after those in other fields even though we know that we are different from them in many ways. The point: Our inferiority complex makes us do things to improve our image rather than do the things that would make our collective dreams come true.

Our schizophrenic system of higher education has also, I believe, been an obstacle to fulfilling our collective dreams. Universities exalt broad, liberal education but advertise their "nationally ranked professional schools" during nationally televised athletic events. The point: The schizophrenia of higher education establishes a model that we try to follow even though it may not be appropriate for us.

What Are We?

We do not have to apologize for who we are or what we do, but we must come to grips with what we are—a group of professions that draw principally, but not exclusively, from the discipline of kinesiology. I believe the following.

1. We are more than one discipline. Though kinesiology (AAPE, 1990) is the single discipline most common to what we do, it is not the only discipline that provides the basis for our many professions.
2. We are more than one profession. Though teaching physical education in schools is our historical profession, it is not our only profession.
3. Both professionals and disciplinarians must be experts. Regardless of the role served within our field, we must be experts. Excellence is a reasonable expectation in both areas. However, expertise in one area does not constitute expertise in the other.
4. Professionals and disciplinarians must understand and appreciate each other. Professionals need disciplinarians to provide a knowledge base. Disciplinarians need professionals to transmit the knowledge base.

5. We need experts in many areas.
6. Our disciplinarians and professionals share a common thread.
7. Our common thread is our common dream.

Sharing a Common Dream

Earlier I shared my dream for our field:[1] full functioning and good health for all people through physical activity. I believe that it is a dream that we can all share. I believe that there is enough dream for all of us. For the moment I would like to assume that you share this dream and make some recommendations for the Academy.

1. We must not change the name of the Academy.[2] It is part of our heritage. As Larry Locke suggested last year, "This organization is not ours. We hold it only in trust for others" (Locke, 1990, p. 40). The flame that represents a collective dream is for a field that is much broader than any one discipline.
2. We must induct more new fellows to the Academy. We set a limit of 125 fellows, and it has not changed in these past years of explosive expansion of our field. Surely we can find more than four or five people each year who are capable of contributing and "passing on" what we hold in trust.
3. We must select the best fellows from all areas in our field. Realizing a collective dream takes the best of us. We should not select less than the best. But there are many excellent people who help us in pursuit of our common dream who are not selected because they are different. They are different because they do not meet standards that we accept from our schizophrenic universities. We must be free enough from our inferiority complex to allow admission of those who will help us in the quest of our collective dream, both disciplinary and professional. Supertenure as a criterion for membership is not the answer. In academia we have developed the concept of protected classes to encourage appointments of minorities, women, and other groups deserving of the classification. I propose that we use a similar scheme to assure induction for those in the humanities, the professions, and other areas underrepresented in the Academy.
4. We should have more "associate fellows." Those people who have demonstrated excellence in areas related or similar to ours should be inducted as associate fellows if they do not share our collective dream or if they have

[1]*Field* is used as a comprehensive term to include the discipline of kinesiology, the professions of physical education, and any other disciplines that are basic to these professions. It is the field of physical education to which I refer in my discussions in this paper.

[2]At my request, historian John Lucas researched the history of the Academy concerning purpose. It is clear that the founders intended the organization to be both professional and disciplinary. Last year we defined the body of knowledge (one discipline) as kinesiology. We also clearly pointed out that *kinesiology* is not a descriptor of the professions. The name of the Academy must be inclusive, not exclusive.

only a peripheral interest in passing it on. These people can be honored without the burden of having to attend our meetings if they are not interested.

5. We should continue to meet with AAHPERD. Though we are not a part of AAHPERD, it is the only organization that draws together those of us with different roles who pursue our common goal.
6. We should be proactive on issues. We are the scholars and leaders in our field. We can do much to influence the future and to make the collective dream come true. Being proactive on issues, including issuing statements on current issues, is the best way to pass it on.

Dreams and Dinosaurs

Now that you have indulged me, you might say it is time to come back to reality. Maybe your description of what we are does not match mine. Maybe my dream is not your dream. Maybe my concepts of a collective inferiority complex and schizophrenic universities are figments of my imagination. In fact, I have been told that my ideas are those of a dinosaur, soon to become extinct. There is no common goal! There is no common ground!

I do not believe it! I cling to the dream, because it is not a figment of my imagination but a dream that comes from a collective wisdom acquired through the years. The sparks of a dream I had when I first began my studies of physical education became the flames of a torch I still carry as Academy president. Fuel was added to the flame by Williams and Nash, whose works I studied early on. Armond Seidler challenged me to think about their ideas. Cureton and Jackson challenged in graduate education where I worked alongside Skinner, Pollock, Barney, and Haskell, all now Academy fellows. Contact with Burt, Johnson, Updyke, Montoye, and Van Huss early in my career taught me more than graduate classes. Contacts with colleagues including Lindsey, Laurie, Pangrazi, Krahenbuhl, Thomas, Wells, Landers and many others[3] have impressed on me the importance of our dream. Early teaching from the books of Bucher, DeVries, Eckert, Espenschade, and Esslinger all made their mark. Discussions with Holbrook, Abernathy, Lockhart, and Steinhaus all made me think. Being accepted into the Academy by the likes of Ulrich, Clarke, and Zeigler, and working as an officer with many of you in the Academy, made the pursuit of my dream that much richer. The torch burns hot! I continue to carry that torch. I got it from you!

Passing It On

Later this evening I will have the honor of passing the gavel of the office of president of the American Academy of Physical Education to Roberta Park. The

[3]There is a danger in listing names as I have done here. The intent was to illustrate the importance of others to the development of a dream. I offer apologies to the many others not listed here who have made important contributions.

Academy medallion designed by R. Tait McKenzie illustrates the traditional pass-it-on ceremony, symbolizing the passing of tradition from one generation of physical educators to the next. But what does the cherished flame represent? Is it the core of knowledge (kinesiology) that we pass from one to another? Is it the professional skills that we give to those who follow? I do not think so! It is the passing of dreams. The soul, the heart, of physical education as represented by the flame is what makes our field unique. It sets us apart from all others.

What we received from those who preceded us are ideas, wisdom, and dreams. I characterized the flame as the unifying force that binds us together. I have told you of my dream for us. But is my dream your dream? Or is my dream a dinosaur?

Over the years I have revised my dreams. I have tried to keep them up to date. But if they are not realistic for the Academy in the 1990s, then what are our dreams? What are we? We must decide!

What do we pass on? If the dream of the Academy and its members is only to pass on knowledge, then I must confess to being a dinosaur. We are all intelligent people. We will gain new knowledge without the American Academy of Physical Education. Surely knowledge gained at Academy meetings will be of value to us all. But such new knowledge is a drop in the bucket compared to what we can do if we pool our talents to keep a collective dream alive. If we have a dream, let us pass it on. If not, it is the American Academy of Physical Education that will join me among the dinosaurs.

References

AAPE. (1990). Resolution. In C.B. Corbin & H.M. Eckert (Eds.), *The Academy Papers. The Evolving Undergraduate Major* (No. 23, p. 104). Champaign, IL: Human Kinetics.

LOCKE, L.F. (1990). The new game: Power and turf at the 61st meeting. In C.B. Corbin & H.M. Eckert (Eds.), *The Academy Papers. The Evolving Undergraduate Major* (No. 23, pp. 35-41). Champaign, IL: Human Kinetics.

PRESIDENTS

American Academy of Physical Education

*1926-30 Clark W. Hetherington
*1930-38 Robert Tait McKenzie
*1938-39 Robert Tait McKenzie
Mabel Lee
*1939-41 John Brown, Jr.
*1941-43 Mabel Lee
*1943-45 Arthur H. Steinhaus
*1945-47 Jay B. Nash
*1947-49 Charles H. McCloy
*1949-50 Frederick W. Cozens
*1950-51 Rosalind Cassidy
1951-52 Seward C. Staley
*1952-53 David K. Brace
*1953-54 Neils P. Neilson
*1954-55 Elmer D. Mitchell
1955-56 Anna S. Espenschade
*1956-57 Harry A. Scott
*1957-58 Charles C. Cowell
*1958-59 Delbert Oberteuffer
*1959-60 Helen Manley
1960-61 Thomas E. McDonough, Sr.
1961-62 M. Gladys Scott
1962-63 Fred V. Hein
*1963-64 Carl L. Nordly
*1964-65 Eleanor Metheny
1965-66 Leonard A. Larson
*1966-67 Arthur A. Esslinger
1967-68 Margaret G. Fox
*1968-69 Laura J. Heulster
1969-70 H. Harrison Clarke
1970-71 Ruth M. Wilson
1971-72 Ben W. Miller
1972-73 Raymond A. Weiss
1973-74 Ann E. Jewett
1974-75 King J. McCristal
*1975-76 Leona Holbrook
1976-77 Marvin H. Eyler
1977-78 Louis E. Alley
1978-79 Marguerite A. Clifton
1979-80 Harold M. Barrow
1980-81 Aileene S. Lockhart
1981-82 Earle F. Zeigler
1982-83 Edward J. Shea
1983-84 Henry J. Montoye
1984-85 David H. Clarke
1985-86 G. Alan Stull
1986-87 Margaret J. Safrit
1987-88 Robert J. Malina
1988-89 Waneen W. Spirduso
1989-90 Charles B. Corbin (current)
1989-90 Roberta J. Park (elect)

*Deceased